ANIMAL HEALING

with AUSTRALIAN BUSH FLOWER ESSENCES

For a complete list of suppliers of Australian Bush Flower Essences
in your country, go to:
www.ausflowers.com.au

Also available from Findhorn Press:

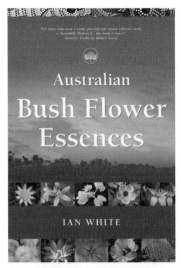

Australian Bush Flower Essences

IAN WHITE

HOLISTIC Aromatherapy for Animals

A Comprehensive Guide to the Use of Essential Oils & Hydrosols with Animals

Kristen Leigh Bell

Bach FLOWER REMEDIES FOR ANIMALS

Helen Graham and Gregory Vlamis

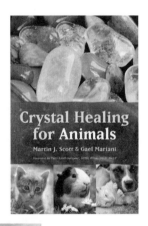

Crystal Healing for Animals

Martin J. Scott & Gael Mariani

Bach FLOWER REMEDIES FOR CATS

Martin J. Scott & Gael Mariani

Bach FLOWER REMEDIES FOR DOGS

Martin J. Scott & Gael Mariani

*Please visit www.findhornpress.com for a complete list of titles,
with secure online order facility*

ANIMAL HEALING

with AUSTRALIAN BUSH FLOWER ESSENCES

Marie Matthews

FINDHORN PRESS

ANIMAL HEALING
with Australian Bush Flower Essences

Published in 2013 by Findhorn Press Ltd
117-121 High Street, Forres IV36 1AB, Scotland, UK
Email: info@findhornpress.com Website: www.findhornpress.com

under licence from
Bush Biotherapies Pty Ltd
45 Booralie Road, Terrey Hills NSW 2084, Australia
Email: info@ausflowers.com.au Website: www.ausflowers.com.au

First published in Australia (paperback) in 2007. Revised 2011. This new edition 2013

Editor: Anne Cullinan
Design, typesetting, print management: Reno Design R25067
Art director: Graham Rendoth
Cover photograph: Lisa Kruss / www.petphotos.com
Back cover photographs: Ian White, Denis Matthews, Helen Megginson
Illustrations: Vicki Swift
Printed and bound in the EU

Contents

Foreword *by Peta Clarke*   7

Acknowledgments   9

Introduction *by Ian White*   11

1   ANIMALS *and* THEIR HUMANS   13

2   AUSTRALIAN BUSH FLOWER ESSENCES   23

3   A NEW ANIMAL ARRIVES   34

4   COMMUNICATION *and* TRAINING   44

5   OVERCOMING FEAR *and* RELATED PROBLEMS   53

6   STRESS, DEPRESSION *and* OTHER PROBLEMS   60

7   RESOLVING BEHAVIOURAL PROBLEMS   68

8   GRIEVING *and* LOVE   81

9   BREEDING *and* FERTILITY   88

10   AGEING, SLOWING DOWN *and* DYING   101

11   ANIMAL SPIRITUALITY   109

12   LIVING IN ZOOS, FARMS *or* THE WILD   118

13   PHYSICAL AILMENTS   135

Repertory of Symptoms ... Physical and Emotional   149

Information about Individual Essences and Combinations   173

Bibliography   184

Index   187

Foreword

Often when I look into the eyes of my dogs, I am reminded that there is much I have forgotten. Far from convincing me of the superiority of human beings, a life of living and working with animals finds me greatly humbled.

I first ventured into the world of alternative veterinary medicine over ten years ago when the newest love of my life, a Boxer called Russell, was diagnosed with ulcerative colitis at the tender age of 12 weeks. After exhausting what was on offer traditionally, I began to explore, with a mind forced open, any other options available. Thanks in part to what I found, Russell lived a long life filled to the brim with the love only an animal can bring.

Animal Healing is a wonderful introduction to the animal worlds with which we share this planet and the energetic healing properties of Australian Bush Flower Essences that unites us all. As a professional animal trainer I have often used alternative supports such as our beautiful Essences to assist animals in various journeys during their life-time. Behavioural modification programs for problems such as separation anxiety and fear aggression in our domestic animals – to whom I am sure our world seems nothing less than alien at times – can be supported and enhanced so readily by the addition of well chosen Essences, as pointed out in chapters five through to seven. In fact, as we are reminded throughout the book the Essences are there as a support for us and our friends in both times of great joy and great sadness, as from birth to death there is an Essence appropriate for every step, assisting us and our animals to re-centre and align with the energies of nature.

The animals you share your life with will benefit greatly from the addition of *Animal Healing* to your bookshelf. I think it also must be said, however, that the benefit will not be theirs alone. Our evolution as a species has granted us some wonderful blessings, but the journey has not been a free ride, for loss as well as gain has been our path. Perhaps now we are retreading our path, picking up some of the gifts we left by the wayside during our initial passage. The book you hold in your hands may help you remember some long forgotten truths, truths that our animal friends live with every day.

Peta Clarke
International animal trainer
Animal Training Solutions Australia

Acknowledgments

To me this book is a prime example of how something can manifest once there is a willingness to be open to whatever eventuates. My original task was to write an Animal Correspondence Course. It was only after the outline of the course was drafted and work started on the first module that it became clear that there was no suitable text book available to support the course. It was then that Ian White suggested that I had better write a book about animals and the Australian Bush Flower Essences.

This at first seemed a Herculean task. However, it quickly became an exciting and wonderful adventure through the energy of the flowers and the world of animals and animal consciousness. I was continually amazed at how easily the information came to me. There were wonderful moments of synchronicity when a subject which had me temporarily stumped would unexpectedly be discussed in detail on a TV documentary or radio interview. Books which were non-existent one week in the library were suddenly available; not just one or two, but a whole shelf-full, giving me lots of useful and usable information. Web searches provided me with solid information almost every time I logged in. People unexpectedly turned up with animal stories that fitted in with what I was writing. It was wonderful. But probably most fascinating of all was the way that understanding and knowledge just came as I wrote. Working with material like the Bush Essences and the spirituality of animals, I found myself in magical places on many, many days. It has been a soul-growing experience and I am very grateful to the Spirit Beings who have supported me in this project.

I want to thank many people who helped in pulling this book together. Firstly Ian White for giving me the opportunity to write this book and for his continuing support, input and very useful comments along the way. As I read and wrote I came to appreciate the huge amount of work that Ian put into gathering and recording the original information about the Essences and I have drawn freely from his three books in this publication. I thank Shaz Wray, Chris Andreas and Paul Loveday of Australian Bush Flower Essences who were always very supportive when at times I was not quite sure where I was heading with this work. And Sallianne and Karen who patiently looked up the office files for case studies which I knew I had read but was unable to locate in my records.

I want to thank Dr Clare Middle, Veterinary Surgeon and Flower Essence Practitioner who lives and works near Fremantle, Western Australia. She read the text and provided me with technical and practical information when I needed it.

She was always ready to help and I very much appreciate her great pool of knowledge and experience, and respect the professional and sensitive manner with which she works with animals.

I thank Caroline Pope and Billie Dean, both animal communicators, who helped to make animal communication become real for me. Also Jan Fowles and Jill Franks who gave me the benefit of their years of experience using the Essences with animals.

I thank Lainie Jones, good friend, animal lover and Bush Essence true believer who gave me very useful positive criticism about the content and style of the book. And a variety of other people who willingly read through the text and gave their opinions.

I thank all the Bush Essence practitioners who provided the stories about the use of the Essences with animals, which have appeared in the book. Also the hundreds more who emailed, posted in or dictated their own animal Essence experiences and provided us with the material from which a large portion of the text for this publication was drawn.

I thank the authors of other publications about animals and related subjects from which I learned so much. They opened new worlds for me. Details of their publications are listed in the Bibliography.

I thank my husband Denis who came to believe that I was glued to my computer for life, but still stayed around and cooked meals even though it wasn't always his turn!

I particularly want to thank my editor, Anne Cullinan, whose constructive and positive criticism, suggestions and encouragement helped to pull all this material into a cohesive whole. Her enthusiasm for the project was contagious and very energising.

And to Vicki Swift, who has beautifully illustrated the book, and was so adaptable to what we wanted, I give my thanks.

Finally, I would like to dedicate this work to Millie, our first milking cow, who we bought as a very young calf and lived with for 14 years. She produced many beautiful calves and was very patient with our early inexpert care. We loved her.

With love
Marie Matthews

Introduction

I have shared a very close working relationship with Marie for well over a decade. Marie has tremendous passion, commitment, expertise and knowledge of the Bush Essences, qualities she has brought to her roles as Tutor of our Correspondence Course as well as having been Editor of the Bush Essence Newsletter for the last eight years. Marie was also the catalyst for my second book, becoming so frustrated with hearing me talk about it for many years, without ever having started to write it, that she eventually offered to travel the thousand kilometres from her house to Sydney and have me dictate the book to her while she typed. One month later the manuscript was completed, (though goodness knows how much longer it would have been without her help, discipline and role as a sounding board to discuss many ideas about the book). Marie loves researching and writing and was the perfect choice to ask to write this book. I was actively involved with her on this book and as ever I was deeply impressed by the labour of love she brought to this project and her great excitement for sharing this information, knowing the great benefit it will bring to so many individuals and animals.

I would as well like to thank Anne Cullinan for her wonderful contribution in not only editing the book but also for her extensive contribution in writing the text and providing many astute suggestions and input generally.

This book is in direct response to the growing need and frequent requests we have from people wishing to enhance the wellbeing and healing of their pets and animals. The Australian Bush Flower Essences are totally safe and work incredibly quickly with animals (as they have far less emotional imbalance/baggage than humans).

I highly commend this book and the Australian Bush Flower Essences to you and the animals in your life.

Ian White BSc, ND, DBM
Founder and CEO of Australian Bush Flower Essences

For a complete list of suppliers of Australian Bush Flower Essences
in your country, go to:
www.ausflowers.com.au

Chapter 1

ANIMALS and THEIR HUMANS

If all the beasts were gone, men would die from a great loneliness of spirit, for whatever happens to the beasts also happens to the man. All things are connected. Whatever befalls the Earth befalls the sons of the Earth.

CHIEF SEATTLE OF THE SUWAMISH TRIBE,
LETTER TO PRESIDENT FRANKLIN PIERCE, 1854

The history of animal/human inter-action is a long one. Animals had inhabited this Earth for hundreds of millions of years before the appearance of the first humanoids at an unknown date more than four million years ago. The interaction between people and animals in those very early years can only be speculated upon, but small animals were probably hunted for food, with the opportunistic harvesting of animals that had died from natural causes occurring from very early times.

The hunting of big game began with *Homo erectus*, approximately 600,000 years ago. Pitting their wits against the strength, natural cunning and survival instincts of these big animals was an important factor in the evolution of human beings. It encouraged the development of language and group cooperation, as well as the making and skilful use of tools. At Balladonia homestead in South Australia, the bones of humans and giant marsupials have been discovered alongside stone tools, in the same layer of conglomerate. This is an indication that Australian Aboriginal people were interacting at some level with these animals over 31,000 years ago, around the time when these animals became extinct.

Stories from the Aboriginal Dreamtime indicate that these huge beasts were remembered by succeeding generations with awe and fear. Cave paintings in Lascaux in France, dated at around 15,000 BC, depict large, beautiful animals that lived in the region at that time. The fact that the images are located in difficult-to-access caves, a long way from the main entrance, suggests that these animals were associated with sacred ritual or ceremony. Archaeological digs in later periods have discovered ritualistic animal burials in many ancient cultures. The earliest burials of dogs, dated at around 5,000 BC, were found at a Mesolithic site at Skateholm in Sweden. A Neolithic site in China in the Henan Province has also uncovered dog burials. Cat and bird burials have been found in Iron Age Britain after 700 BC while horse internments were common in China at the time of the Han Dynasty, around 200 BC. Mummies of cats and birds have been found in many ancient Egyptian tombs. The care that was taken preparing these animals for burial suggests they were highly valued by humans both before and after death.

Animals, it seems, have been part of our life experience since long before recorded history and living in association with them is deeply embedded in our psyches. We are far outnumbered by animals on Earth. In Australia alone, farm and wild animals are counted in hundreds of millions, and pets are to be found in the majority of Australian households. Barring a catastrophic event, animals are here to stay. They are our co-inhabitants of this planet. It is up to us to learn to live with them in a way that is of the greatest benefit to us all – both animals and humans.

In order to co-exist in harmony with animals it is important to understand them, and to know the normal instinctive behaviour of the particular species or breed. It is also necessary to see beyond the presenting symptoms or behaviour patterns and to discover what is going on at a deeper level. Some of the most effective animal carers are those who study their animals for long periods of time and learn to read them, identify their emotions, understand their communications, and respond to them with sensitivity.

INSTINCT

Instinct is very strong in animals and usually determines their first reaction to any situation. Human beings can override instinct and choose how to behave in many circumstances, but other species have only a limited ability to do this. For example, a horse will respond to its natural instinct and run from what it perceives as a dangerous situation unless its confidence in its owner or trainer is very strong. Similarly, a mother cat will defend her kittens unless she completely trusts the person wanting to handle them.

Some instincts rise to the surface even after long periods of domestication. The endangered Mexican Gray Wolf (*Canis lupus baileyi*) has been released in Arizona in the USA over the last several years and studies show that these animals quickly regain their instinctive behaviour even though raised in captivity for many generations. They learn to form packs, hunt together, mate, dig dens and successfully raise their young without the influence of older, experienced animals. Recently, endangered Orange-bellied Parrots (*Neophema chrysogaster*), which had been bred in captivity in south-east Australia, were released into the wild. Within weeks, some were found on the island state of Tasmania, their natural home, after travelling several hundred kilometres, most of which was over water.

However, many animals do in fact lose some of their survival instincts after living in captivity or domestication for long periods. Zoo animals are rarely suitable for release, particularly if they have been in captivity since they were very young, and if they have lived alone or with limited numbers of their species. In these situations they become dependent on human support and have no social skills to interact with their own kind. Nevertheless, instinct does dominate an animal's behaviour and by working with that instinct, and with the nature of the individual animals, carers can learn to live amicably with them.

To romanticise animals and place them on a pedestal as the 'noble beast' ignores the fact that survival in the wild can be rough, savage and merciless. Tasmanian Devils (*Sarcophilus harrisii*) screeching and fighting over a road kill doesn't fit our romantic view of how a wild animal ought to behave, but the powerful instinctive drive to survive, grow to adulthood, and reproduce to keep the species going can override all other behaviours. Male lions may kill cubs sired by another male. A killer whale will sometimes toy with a baby seal before killing and eating it. Male walruses will fight each other to exhaustion, sometimes resulting in serious injury, in order to achieve dominance in a herd. Some adult birds push unwanted young from the nest to assist the survival of the strongest of the brood. The action of a butcher bird taking a baby wren to feed its own young, often hanging the dead chick in a tree 'larder,' might seem barbaric particularly if you have been observing the mother wren raise her babies. Most animals will destroy, abandon or simply neglect a less-than-perfect offspring and as a result help to maintain a healthy and vigorous family line. But such patterns of behaviour have evolved over thousands of years and serve to maintain an ever-adjusting balance in various species in the wild. In the animal kingdom, survival of the species takes precedence over the survival of the individual.

While the natural world can be cruel, it can also be gentle, joyful and awe inspiring, and some instinctive behaviour of animals is quite beautiful. The ability of a troop of chimpanzees to live within invisible limits, move with the seasons and the fruiting trees, and adapt to the prevailing conditions, illustrates nature in action and in balance. Flocks of migrating geese flying in formation to warmer climes as winter approaches are spectacular. A mother leopard carrying her young to a safe den will stir the heart. A pack of wolves hunting together with obvious interaction and mutual support is quite amazing.

There are also stories of animals indulging in what we would see as compassionate behaviour towards a weaker animal. Broadcaster and naturalist David Attenborough tells the story of a baby elephant born with its front legs bent at the knees as a result of its awkward position in the uterus. The young calf was unable to stand and reach its mother's teats. The whole herd stayed with it and gradually the little animal was able to straighten its legs. By day three it was able to feed from its mother and walk with the herd, and they all moved on. Another story on an ABC (Australia) TV news programme showed the report of a wildlife documentary team which had been following another herd of elephants for some weeks. One day they came across a very young orphaned elephant, stuck in mud in a river bed. This young animal was not one of the herd that was being documented, but several of the elephants helped it out of the mud, thereby saving its life. Even though it belonged to a different herd, it seems that their compassion for the young animal overrode their natural instincts to drive away an animal belonging to a different family. Whales too, have evolved social mechanisms to support injured or sick family members, surrounding them and physically supporting them until they are able to move on, or until they die. Peter Tyack, a senior scientist in the Biology Department at the Woods Hole Oceanographic Institution, believes that this social support is one of the causes of mass strandings of whales.

No doubt there are many ways of explaining both individual and group animal behaviours that have not yet been considered. Are there undetected communications or energetic patterns that may yet provide new insights into our understanding of the animal world? Maybe animals draw on a deeper intuition or soul connection that takes priority over the basic instinct of individual herd survival. Only time and further research will give definitive answers.

In general, members of each species behave in particular ways that characterise that type of animal. A dog behaves like a dog. But every animal is also an individual with its own particular personality, intelligence, life experience and behaviour patterns. Not all Labradors will make good guide dogs, although there is a general tendency for that breed to be good at that job, and some individual Labradors are extraordinarily capable at this type of work. In the *Smarter than Jack* collection of animal stories there is an account of a working dog who could apparently count. Once shown the number of sheep to go into the first compartment of a transport vehicle, without further instruction, it was able to load the rest of the sheep, putting the same number in the rest of the trailer compartments. Do all dogs have this ability or was this dog exceptional? Surely animals can be as individual as humans. Domestication allows us to see these differences at close quarters and people who have studied wild animals have found quite distinct personalities amongst these creatures as well. Joy Adamson, while studying a pride of lions in Kenya for many years, found very real individuality in the members of the group as did Dian Fossey when studying gorillas in Zaire. Camera men working on the BBC TV series *Life in the Undergrowth* discovered unique behaviour amongst the insects in any one group that they were studying and found themselves giving names to many of the 'key players'.

LIVING IN PRESENT TIME

Animals tend to live more fully in present time than most humans do. This focus on the present affects how they see the world around them and it is this acceptance of what is, rather than what might be, that is a contributing factor in making animals particularly responsive to any vibrational medicine. Although an animal will fear the repeat of a past hurt it does not appear, from current knowledge, to think ahead to what tomorrow might bring. A fox caught in a trap might gnaw off part of its paw to escape but it will not think of the consequences of living permanently with that damaged paw. However, it will certainly experience shock, and feel pain and fear.

People who work regularly with animals have found that an animal can often adjust to living with chronic pain because that is its present state. That doesn't mean that pain isn't causing suffering in the animal, just that there is a slight difference in the way that pain is experienced because of the lack of fear of future consequences. Another issue involved here is that an animal will hide pain as a survival strategy. Because an obviously wounded animal in the wild is in greater danger of being attacked by another animal, it will at times ignore the pain of a serious wound and keep moving from a source of danger. Similarly, an excited or eager-to-please dog will run with an injured knee, and birds damaged by crashing into windows will sometimes fly away only to die later from injuries not obvious to a casual observer. Sometimes it takes careful examination by the carer to discover if something is wrong with an animal.

ANIMALS AND EMOTIONS

Much has been written about animals and emotions. Pre-scientific peoples had no problems in attributing emotions and intelligence to animals. Aboriginal raconteur Bill Neidjie records that we all experience feeling, humans and animals, *'no matter what sort of animal, bird, snake… all that animal same, like us'*. In North American Indian mythology, animals are associated with individual emotions. The moose, for example, is seen as being connected with self-esteem and the recognition of our own wisdom while the bear is seen as being introspective and a seeker of truth. By calling on the power of an animal it was believed that you could draw on the strength of that creature's essence, particularly in emotional areas.

Early Western philosopher, Aristotle, believed that both humans and animals learned, remembered, solved problems and benefited from experience, but he felt that humans performed these tasks better. The early Christian Church brought in the idea that an animal did not have a soul and went on to reject the possibility that animals had intelligence, emotions, consciousness and other developed qualities of mind and spirit. During the eighteenth century, as science evolved into investigating physical phenomena rather than philosophical ideas, many scientists supported the idea that animals were devoid of emotions and did not feel pain. This led to horrific cruelty to animals over many years in the Western world.

By the late 1800s thinking was beginning to change. Charles Darwin, for example, expressed the belief that animals experienced a whole range of emotional states. But even today the idea persists among some people that animals are lesser beings, and the resulting cruelty needs to be taken into account as a possible cause of behavioural, emotional and physical problems in an animal.

Anyone who has lived with or observed animals interacting with other animals or with their human companions, for even a short period, soon recognises that mammals and birds do indeed experience emotions similar to our own. Our own feelings of joy, excitement, grief, desolation, contentment, sadness and compassion all have their counterparts in the animal world. The ecstatic exuberance of animal reunions, whether they be elephants, chimps or family dogs, is undeniable. A cat welcoming you home with tail raised and its special miaowing purr leaves little doubt about its pleasure at seeing you. The grieving of an animal over the loss of a mate, companion or owner is obvious. Such animals are really hurting. People recount various stories of honey bees swarming to the funeral of their keeper and of cats spraying in the house or behaving aggressively after a family member moves away from home. The expression of sadness on a dog's face, and the accompanying body language, can be heart wrenching. Reptiles are reported to respond emotionally to their owners. There is the story of a turtle who used to regularly climb on its owner's back and sit there happily as she lay on the floor reading. If we are to positively interact with animals and really understand them, it is important to learn how animals express their emotions. Working with animals is about caring with awareness and sensitivity, consistency and knowledge. It is also about unconditional love and respect for the animal's biological makeup.

ANIMALS AND HUMANS

The bond between animals and humans is an interesting one. Certainly, for humans, it can be a very satisfying and rewarding experience. Recent research indicates that people who have pets are healthier and happier than those without them. The American Heart Association has reported that when hospitalised heart patients received 12 minute visits from therapy dogs there was a reduction in blood pressure, decrease in the release of harmful hormones and a reduction in anxiety. This compared very favourably with the readings taken when a patient had a visit from a human or was left alone. In a pilot study conducted by the HeartMath research team of California, four horses were observed as they interacted with Dr Ellen Gehrke, of the Alliant International University in San Diego. As she worked with them the heart energy of horses and doctor was observed, using a heart rhythm monitor, and it was found that the horses responded directly, at heart level, to her emotional and energetic states. Bonnie Treece, the founder of Horse's Way Equestrian Arts, suggests that humans respond in a similar manner to the heart energy of the horses and that horses can help humans to heal.

But do animals generally benefit from their interaction with humans? A domesticated or zoo animal often lives in isolation from its own kind and although animals respond to their carers, they do not always receive the same level of understanding and communication in return. They often mirror our emotions and attitudes and, if the animals are used as emotional props by their human owners, then they may suffer their own behavioural and health problems as a result. Many people are happy with their animals as long as they behave like well-mannered humans, but become distressed if they behave like the animals that they are. However, animals are not human and projecting human attributes onto them, although it may suit us, does not do them justice. As one un-named animal psychologist is quoted as saying, *'The hardest thing to convince an owner to do is to treat a dog like a dog.'* Still, there is much evidence that well-cared-for animals live comfortable, healthy and enjoyable lives. Most domesticated animals live much longer than their peers in the wild. Eastern Grey Kangaroos (*Macropus giganteus*), for example, live 10–15 years in the wild but can live for up to 20 years in a sanctuary. A feral cat will rarely live longer than eight years while pet cats regularly live into their late teens with reports of some cats living up to 40 years.

DOGS

In general, dogs are pack animals and are very sociable. They enjoy the company of other dogs and of their human companions. Their human family takes on the role of the pack but for this arrangement to be successful, the dog needs to know that its owner is the leader of the pack. In early history, dogs probably chose to live with humans because they enjoyed, first of all, the scraps of food, and then the company. The relationship was mutually beneficial. Dogs are eager to please their owners and are very loyal and protective of their human family. These characteristics can give great pleasure to the owner and can also be wonderful tools to use in learning to handle a dog with ease and enjoyment.

Dogs have a hierarchical order within the pack, with a dominant or alpha animal as the pack leader. So, if there is more than one dog in the household, the owner and human family must come first and then the dominant or alpha dog and so on down the line. The alpha dog should always be fed after the humans but before any other dogs. It should also be greeted first and have the bed nearest to the bed or bedroom of the owner. The alpha dog sometimes expresses dominance by pushing down on lower-ranked dogs at the base of the neck. This is another method the owner can copy to establish their position as top 'dog'.

CATS

Cats are very independent by nature and in the wild would normally live alone, although mother animals will stay with their young offspring for up to two years. Lions are the feline exception, living in prides of up to 30 individuals. Unless they have been raised with other animals, domestic cats tend to spend time alone. They are very territorial and can have trouble adjusting to other animals in the family. Cats are very sensitive creatures and have little of a dog's great desire to please or a natural inclination to follow a leader.

Cats probably joined human settlements because it was to their advantage. Mice, rats and food scraps would have been abundant in the early villages and that meant easy pickings for the felines. And for humans, it would have been advantageous to have cats controlling the rodent populations, as furry waste disposal units and, if tamed, as responsive pets and foot warmers in winter. Some would believe that cats have never been genuinely domesticated. But these days many cats are indoor animals and have become completely dependent on their owners for their food, exercise, contact with nature and general well-being. Their owners have taken on the role of surrogate mother and provider. A recent survey in the UK indicated that one in four households had at least one cat and that the total number of pet cats exceeds 10 million, making cats the most popular pet in that country.

HORSES

Horses and other grazing animals live in herds in the wild, where they are prey for carnivores. Their natural inclination is to flee when frightened or threatened. Horses have a structured hierarchy within the herd. A horse will not accept being bossed around by another horse or person who is rightfully 'below' him in the hierarchy. Horses are very curious animals and will follow if they feel safe, but can be upset by direct eye contact. They also feel more comfortable if you approach their shoulder rather than their head directly. A horse's herd instinct is so strong that a horse can bond for life with other members of its herd. If conditions are good, it will also bond willingly with its human carer. It can, however, take time to establish such a bond. Horses base their behaviour patterns on their need to find safety, comfort and food. Anything that interferes with this causes anxiety. It is important to prove to your horse that you are its ally – not a threat to its safety.

BIRDS

Most birds are flock animals and do not normally thrive in captivity without the company of their own kind. Parrots, in particular, become very stressed if living alone, often becoming withdrawn, cranky and irritable. Although some of the big parrots can live successfully as lone birds, they are intelligent animals and need plenty of attention from their owners. Five minutes company once a day and a weekly clean out of the cage is not nearly enough. A Sulphur-Crested Cockatoo (*Cacatua galerita*) can live for over 80 years and which of us can make a commitment to care constantly for a bird for that length of time? Another point to consider is that parrots and some other birds mate for life. Without a parrot mate around, they will bond with one of their human carers and may become very aggressive towards any person or other animal interfering with that relationship. The arrival of a new baby, partner or animal into a household can be quite traumatic for all concerned.

ABOUT ANIMAL HEALING

Like all living things, animals have unique energetic vibrations and keeping that energy in balance is essential for their well-being. Australian Bush Flower Essences, a form of vibrational medicine, help to process the effects of negative experiences and address behaviour patterns that can undermine the well-being of any living creature. There is a significant connection between the emotions and the physical body and by dealing with the emotions the Bush Essences can help the body to heal itself. Humans can sometimes block vibrational healing but animals rarely do, so it can be particularly powerful for them. When we domesticate animals we remove them from their natural environment and so from many of the natural foods and remedies which, in the wild, they would seek out for themselves. The Bush Essences are an effective way to help an animal restore its natural balance and promote emotional and spiritual healing. They help animals to connect back to the healing energies of nature.

Using this book

In the following chapters of *Animal Healing* we will look at ways of understanding animal behaviour and of maintaining an animal's well-being by working with these natural remedies. We will explore many different case studies and suggest Australian Bush Flower Essences that will support sound management, balanced diet, exercise and good veterinary care in maintaining an animal's prime physical and emotional well-being. While the focus of this book is mainly on dogs, cats, horses and to a lesser extent birds, other animals feature throughout the text and also in the Repertory of Symptoms at the end of the book.

Testimonials in this book

Every effort has been made to contact the practitioners whose testimonials have been quoted in this book, however up-to-date contact details were not available for some and we apologise to any practitioners with whom we were unable to make contact. Most of the cases are from Australian Bush Essences practitioners. However, where a case comes from someone in another country, that has been noted.

Finding the most suitable Essence

Note that throughout this book the Essences suggested for any symptom or problem are in alphabetical order, not in order of most appropriate Essence for the particular problem. For example there are many Bush Essences that are useful to support a frightened or timid animal.

Bauhinia is for fear of new technology, new ways of doing things, new equipment, a new car, a new cat door or a swinging gate.

Boab will help break a pattern of behaviour that has been taken on from family.

Boronia could be useful for an animal that becomes fixated about something. It helps to break the pattern of repetitive thoughts and actions.

Confid Essence or **Five Corners** will boost self confidence.

Crowea helps the animal that worries. It helps to keep it emotionally and physically balanced.

Dog Rose is for niggling fears, for anxiety, for ongoing low grade fear, shyness, timidity and phobias.

Dog Rose of the Wild Forces is for the fear of things going out of control and also for helping to prevent an animal panicking in a frightening situation.

Emergency Essence is always beneficial to help an animal through a frightening situation. It is good for the owner or handler as well. It will also help wild, stray or very timid animals to overcome the initial shock of regular human contact, and can be used as either a mist or as drops.

Flannel Flower or **Relationship Essence** will help the animal to adjust to being touched and to interacting with others.

Fringed Violet is for any trauma and shock which happened either recently or long ago, or happened in a previous life and comes up in dreams. If an animal wakes terrified but with no obvious cause then this Essence could be the one to consider – for example fear in a puppy that has had no obvious bad experience to cause this.

Grey Spider Flower is for terror, deep paralysing fear and panic. It also can help where an animal has nightmares.

However, the first Essences to think of for fear would be **Dog Rose**, **Dog Rose of the Wild Forces**, **Grey Spider Flower** and **Emergency Essence**. But some or all of the other Essences will also help, depending on the animal, its particular personality and the presenting problem.

Chapter 2

AUSTRALIAN BUSH FLOWER ESSENCES

What is love? Is it only ours?
Or does love whisper in the flowers?

J. DONALD WALTERS

THE HISTORY OF FLOWER ESSENCES

Flower Essences are made by extracting the healing vibrational qualities from specially selected flowers. The Australian Bush Flower Essences are continuing a very long tradition of healing with flowers. Ancient records show that over 3,000 years ago the Egyptians collected the dew from flowers to treat emotional imbalances. Australian Aborigines have used flowers to heal the emotions. They would eat the flower or sit next to a flowering tree to obtain the vibration of the plant. In fact, flowers have been used for healing in virtually all countries and cultures.

The earliest European records date back to Abbess Hildegard von Bingen in the twelfth century. She was an amazing woman who, from an early age, experienced visions instructing her in many areas of theology, medicine and music. In her major writings, *Physica* and *Causae et Curae*, Hildegard showed great insights into the Doctrine of Signatures, understanding the healing properties of a plant from its appearance,

colour, size, texture and growth habits. Of the rose she wrote, *'The rose is cold, and this coldness contains a useful mixture. During the early morning or when the day has already begun, take a petal of a rose and place it upon your eyes. It extracts the moisture, that is the seeping, and makes them clear.'* Of an evening, Hildegard had her nuns place muslin cloth over flowers or other plants so that they would absorb the dew that formed on the plants overnight. Next morning she would wring out the cloth, collecting the water and using it to treat emotional and physical problems in her patients.

Hildegard became a great healer and monastic leader but also an outstanding musician, writer, theologian, prophet and advisor to kings, emperors and popes. Although she was never formally canonized she has been long venerated as a saint and is listed in the Roman Martyrology. Of her visions she wrote, *'These visions which I saw, I beheld neither in sleep nor dreaming nor in madness nor with my bodily eyes or ears, nor in hidden places; but I saw them in full view and according to God's will, when I was wakeful and alert, with the eyes of the spirit and the inward ears.'* Her books are still consulted to this day and much of her music is now recorded and played worldwide.

Paracelsus, a famous Swiss alchemist and healer in the sixteenth century, is also credited with the use of flowers in healing, collecting the early-morning dew on flowers and using it to treat emotional problems and physical ailments. Paracelsus gave medical advice to the Dutch scholar Erasmus and came into contact with some of the more prominent scholars of the religious Reformation. He was appointed city physician and Professor of Medicine in the city of Basel. When describing his beliefs about healing he wrote, *'The art of healing comes from nature, not from the physician. Therefore the physician must start from nature, with an open mind.'*

More recently Dr Edward Bach (1886–1936), an English doctor, became the modern pioneer of Flower Essences and brought them back into popular use. He had studied medicine at the University College Hospital, London, and was a house surgeon there. He worked as a bacteriologist and later a pathologist. Even though he was a success in his work with allopathic medicine he was not happy with the traditional focus on diseases rather than on the person being treated. He gave up his lucrative practice and devoted the rest of his life to a new system of medicine that could be found in nature. Over time he found the remedies he wanted in the fields and lanes of England. He discovered that when he treated the personalities and feelings of his patients their unhappiness and physical distress would be alleviated. Dr Bach wrote that the function of Flower Essences is …

'… to raise our vibrations and open up our channels for the reception of our spiritual self, to flood our natures with the particular virtues and to wash out from us the faults which were causing them. They are able, like beautiful music or any gloriously uplifting thing which gives us inspiration, to raise our very natures and bring us nearer to ourselves and by that very act to bring us peace and relieve our suffering. They cure not by attacking disease but by flooding our bodies with beautiful vibrations of our higher nature in the presence of which disease melts as snow in the sunshine.'

Since the early 1980s there has been an explosion in the use of Flower Essences right around the world. One of the pioneers in this area is Sydney naturopath and homoeopath Ian White who developed the Australian Bush Flower Essences.

Ian White comes from a family of herbal healers and is in fact a fifth generation Australian herbalist. As a small boy he used to spend much time in the bushland around Sydney with his grandmother, who like her mother before her had a passionate interest in the healing powers of Australian native plants. They were some of the first white people to work with the local flora. Ian started off his tertiary education in mainstream science but after a trip to India, where he became very ill with dysentery, he returned to Australia with his physical and emotional health in tatters. Attempts by his family to build up his strength with three good hot meals a day didn't work. So he turned to alternative medicine and decided that was where he really wanted to go with his life. He enrolled at the New South Wales College of Natural Therapies and graduated as a naturopath and homoeopath. His interest in Australian plants continued but his initial training was with the Bach Flower Remedies. It was about this time that a dear friend of his was dying from bowel cancer. Ian started a meditation circle which met once a week to direct healing to his friend. The friend in time died but through his dying the Australian Bush Flower Essences were born. While meditating in the healing group one day, Ian was shown a picture of a plant and the best place in which to make up its Essence. As time went on these visions continued with a different flower being shown on each occasion. In his book *Australian Bush Flower Essences* he wrote, *'If I was unfamiliar with a flower its name would appear beneath it. I was also given an understanding of its healing properties.'* Following these instructions he gradually made up 50 remedies.

Through observation of the effects of the Essences he was able to verify the channelled information. He also tested the remedies with kinesiology, Kirlian photography and medical electronic diagnostic equipment. Today there are 69 Essences which have all proved to have extremely powerful healing properties. These Essences are very safe – it is impossible to overdose – and they can be taken alone or in conjunction with allopathic treatment or other alternative healing modalities. The Bush Essences are now used right around the world. Ian travels in Australia and overseas presenting seminars to the public and to healthcare professionals. He has published three books about the Bush Essences and is a regular contributor to healthcare magazines, radio and television programmes.

HOW FLOWER ESSENCES ARE MADE

The Australian Bush Flower Essences are made by floating specially selected flowers in good quality purified, spring or mineral water in a clear glass bowl and leaving them in sunlight for approximately two hours in Australian conditions, longer in cooler climates. During this time an energy exchange occurs whereby healing qualities are released from the flowers into the water. The flowers are then removed and the newly charged water is added to an equal quantity of brandy, which is used as a preservative. This makes the ***Mother Tincture***.

Seven drops of Mother Tincture are added to a 15–30 ml bottle containing two parts brandy to one part purified good quality water. This is the **Stock Strength**. Then seven drops of the Stock Strength are added to a 15–30 ml bottle filled with a mix of one part brandy to three parts water and this is the **Dose Strength**. The Dose Strength is the one recommended to be given to any animal (or human). Specific dosage is described later in this chapter.

HOW THEY WORK

In the wild, animals seek out plants that will improve their health or just make them feel good. A dog eating grass is a common example. The response of some cats to catnip is extraordinary as they go into paroxysms of pleasure rolling in the leaves of the plant. I remember one cat I had as a child who would regularly jump onto the top of the piano, select a fresh pink rose from a vase of mixed flowers and delicately pull off the petals one by one and eat them with obvious enjoyment. I have no idea what her attraction was to the rose petals but they appeared to bring her great pleasure. In the *Hidden Powers of Animals*, Dr Karl Shuker relates many stories of animals actively seeking their own therapeutic treatment from the plants around them. The leaves of the paradise flowers in India are a good source of quinine which sparrows have been observed eating and lining their nests with during an outbreak of malaria. Menstruating baboons in Africa chew the leaves of the candelabra tree which have analgesic properties and are believed to bring relief from pain and cramps. Chimpanzees in Tanzania have been seen to regularly eat the leaf of the aspilia plant, a relative of the sunflower. These leaves have been found to contain a powerful antibiotic which is effective in killing harmful bacteria and fungi. Certain African monkeys are accomplished herbalists, eating the fruit of the balanite tree to cure parasitic infections and the leaves of the sodom apple to halt bouts of diarrhoea.

Flower Essences go a step beyond herbalism. This special healing energy of the flower vibrates at a very high frequency which enables the Essences to work, not just within the physical body as the herbs do, but right out to the very edges of the energy fields which surround the body.

ENERGY ANATOMY

These energy fields or energy bodies are similar in all animal species, including humans. Different writers, healers and clairvoyants describe these fields in various ways. Chiron healing, for example, describes 26 energy bodies, but the most general description is of five main classifications. These start from the physical, through the etheric, astral and mental bodies, out to the causal or spiritual bodies. We usually describe a rainbow as having seven colours whereas in fact it is the break-up of pure white light into an infinite number of colours ranging from white to the darkest of purples. Similarly, perhaps, the energy around a living being is like a graduating field starting with the dense energies close to the body and ending with the very fine vibration at its outer perimeter. Whatever way this energy is described, its condition greatly influences the state of well-being of all living things.

Ayurvedic and Yogic traditions describe the chakras, which are special energy centres in the etheric field of the body. In humans there are seven main chakras along the line of the spinal column. Animals also have these energy centres though the number of main chakras varies with the type of animal and, according to some writers, the heart and throat chakras are often not well developed in many animals. However, the chakras do have the capacity to develop, and in some individual animals they can be very well-defined. Dogs appear to have an active heart chakra but often there is an excess of love. They sometimes give too much and may develop heart conditions. Cats, on the other hand, rarely have heart problems. Is this because they tend to give out love in carefully measured doses? Dr Carl Shuker describes some interesting research conducted at the Veterans' Administration Hospital in Long Beach California. This indicates that cats can detect X-ray radiation, not with their eyes, but with receptors in an area behind the upper part of the nose. This could well be the position of a chakra. An article by Calidad on the circle-of-light website describes an animal chakra in this area. '[There is a chakra in animals] located at the bridge of the nose between the eyes. It is pale silver blue and governs sensory intake and the transmission of sensory input to the brain. This is not the third eye which is located a bit higher than the bridge of the nose.'

Mammals also have a chakra, similar to another solar plexus, between their shoulder blades. This is called the brachial chakra. From currently available information it is not clear what the purpose of this chakra is, but in four-legged creatures this area is much more exposed to the world than the same area in humans, so it could relate to the way they respond to the energies in their environment. Whatever its function, it would be wise to take this into account when an animal is being micro-chipped or receiving an injection, as this is the area that is often used for such procedures.

The chakras have been found to connect with each other and to portions of the physical cellular structure by subtle energetic channels known as 'nadis'. These fine threads of energetic matter parallel the physical nervous system. Each chakra is associated with a major nerve plexus or ganglia and also with major endocrine glands. Light energy, which heals and energises the whole system, flows into the etheric body through the chakras which are all connected, either directly or indirectly, with the meridians (the energy lines in the body). The chakras transmute the energy to a level that is usable by the physical body, and it then moves via the meridians into the physical system. In embryos, the meridian ducts are formed well before any of the organs or vascular systems. It seems that the meridian system is the first physical link established between the energy fields around the body and the developing physical body, and it forms an interface between them. Different emotions and their associated physical problems are linked to individual chakras. When a Flower Essence is taken internally, the energy of the Essence goes into the physical body via the mucous membranes, the digestive and nervous systems, to the meridians, out to the outer energy layers and then back to the physical body via the chakras and meridians. Gurudas' book *Flower Essences* and Richard Gerber's book *Vibrational Medicine* describe this process in detail.

Although the energy fields around animals are invisible to most people, some healers have the ability to see them and can tune into them just by looking at the animal they are dealing with. It is possible to train your eyes to see these etheric bodies. Certainly, most people can feel the energies by holding their hands well out to either side of the physical body and, with eyes closed, gradually moving the hands closer in. Rubbing the hands together first, to help sensitise them, can facilitate this process. As the hands come in towards the body the different textures, temperatures, strengths and weaknesses of the various energy fields can be sensed.

An animal's main chakras can be picked up in a similar manner by running the hand along, though not touching, the main line of the body. By picking up varying textures, temperatures and intensity of energy in the chakras or the energy fields, and recognising what is normal for a particular animal, it is possible to gather information about its well-being. With practice this process can be a useful diagnostic tool.

An important aspect of healing with Flower Essences is the premise that behind virtually all physical disease is emotional imbalance. Each emotion affects a different body part. Recent research by biological scientist Candace Pert indicates that hormones are released by the body when emotions are stimulated. These are taken up by the appropriate receptor cells and, if the emotion is recognised and expressed in some way, then the hormones dissipate. However, if an emotion is blocked, suppressed or ignored, or if a physical action such as fight or flight is not manifested, then the 'hormones of emotion' become stuck in the receptor cells. In time, if the process is often repeated, this can lead to disease in a particular area of the body. The Essences play an important role in unblocking these unprocessed emotions and so help prevent the body from developing disease.

In animals, the most frequently used Australian Bush Flower Essence is **Emergency Essence**. This is a combination of seven Essences and is used to deal with trauma, shock, pain and stress. However there are currenly also 69 individual Flower Essences in the Australian Bush Flower Essence range, as well as special creams, mists and combination drops which cover a huge spectrum of emotional, mental and spiritual conditions. These products can all be very effective in treating animals, their owners and handlers in a multitude of situations.

HOW TO USE AUSTRALIAN BUSH FLOWER ESSENCES

The Bush Essences can be used with animals in a similar way to how they are used with humans. First, interview the animal's owner to find out all the information you can about the animal and about the family situation in which it lives. With a feral or stray animal, try to find out where it was found and how any presenting injury was sustained. Examine the animal and identify the problem. Then look for the emotional imbalances behind it and select the appropriate Essences. There are many ways of selecting Essences for animals. You can look up the symptoms in the Repertory of Symptoms at the end of this book and then select from the suggested Essences.

You can use the Australian Bush Flower Essence Insight Cards which are a set of beautifully coloured photographic images of each of the Bush Essence flowers. You could select a card yourself or ask the animal's owner to choose on behalf of the animal. Or you can allow the animal to choose for itself. Jan Fowles and Jill Franks, animal carers who work on Queensland's Sunshine Coast, have a special room in which they lay out the Insight Cards and then allow an animal to select its own Essence either by sitting on it or repeatedly sniffing or showing other interest in a particular card.

There are other methods to select for an animal, which bypass the conscious mind and allow access to the Higher Self of both practitioner and animal. You can use a dowsing tool to select an Essence from a list or from the actual Essence bottles. To do this you need a pendulum, usually a crystal attached to a string – though you can use a gemstone, metal, wood, shell, ring or even a key. Energetically cleanse the tool by soaking it in salted water or leaving it in the sun for a couple of hours. Then you need to test your pendulum. With your arm bent to 90 degrees at the elbow and the string held by thumb and forefinger make a statement or ask a question that will illicit a yes/no response and for which you know the answer, such as your name. 'My name is Marie.' Note how the pendulum swings. It will vary with individuals. Repeat the process with a 'no' statement. It will usually swing one way for a 'yes' and the other way for a 'no', or perhaps you will get a sideways movement. Test it a few times until you are confident of reading the responses. The pendulum has no power of its own, it is merely a tool to pick up on electrical energy within yourself. You can then select an Essence, using learned knowledge or intuition, and place the bottle of Essence on the animal and ask if this Essence is the correct one at this time. You can put one hand on your animal and ask the animal, or your Higher Self, if a specific Essence is good for that animal now. Alternatively, you can go to the boxes of Essences and ask if the Essence for this animal is in this box, in this row etc. until you find the Essence that is needed. Always ensure that your questions require only yes/no answers and phrase your question carefully so as to get the most accurate response you can. A question could be, 'Is this Essence the best Essence to benefit this animal at this time?'

You can also surrogate muscle test to select your Essences. Anyone can learn to perform accurate muscle testing, but it is a skill and it takes practice to master as a selection tool. As with dowsing, muscle testing uses the electrical energy of the person testing and of the animal being tested to access the Higher Self. Muscle testing can be done using several different muscles. The most commonly used are the deltoid muscle at the shoulder, or the muscles of the thumb and/or forefinger. When a question is put and the resisting pressure is weak – where the arm or finger will yield to the pressure – a negative response is indicated, but where the muscle holds against pressure you have a positive reply.

To use the forefinger as the muscle indicator hold it out straight and firm. Then use the middle finger of the same hand to apply pressure just below the nail of the forefinger. Your other hand can be on the animal or you could hold a bottle of Essence and focus on the animal. When you ask your question the forefinger will either hold straight for a positive, or curl down for a negative response.

Using two hands, you can put the thumb and little finger of your left hand (if you are right handed) just touching, palm up, forming a circle, a circuit. To test, place thumb and forefinger of the right hand into the circle formed by the two fingers of the left hand. The right hand thumb and finger should be parallel, pads touching. Ask your yes/no question and then press your two left circuit fingers together, while using a similar amount of pressure to try to pull them apart with your right hand thumb and forefinger. If the answer is positive the fingers will stay together. If negative, they should easily come apart. Test several times to get the feel of this system. It is important that your focus be on the animal. You can make physical contact with the animal by resting your left hand or fingers on the animal. To test for specific Essences you can place the Essence somewhere on your body as you ask the question.

A third method is to use a second person who touches the animal while holding out her other arm to the side at shoulder height, palm down. Again, you ask the question then ask the person to keep the outstretched arm up while you gently push it down, applying pressure on the back of the wrist. If the arm holds the answer is 'yes'; if it yields you have a negative response.

With all these methods it is important that the focus is on the animal being tested and that your intention is made clear before you start. By careful wording of your testing questions and making use of information you have learned from your interview and from your examination of the animal you can quickly uncover what is behind the presenting symptoms. Look for any troubling emotion and also for the object of that emotion such as another animal, a previous owner, a child in the family, etc. Take note of any recent trauma – change of home, death of a family member – human or animal, or any emotional upset within the family. For instance you could ask, 'Does next door's dog frighten you' or 'Do you miss grandfather (who has just died)?' etc. In this way it is possible to work out the animal's issue and then prescribe the appropriate Essence.

If you have the ability to hear the answer, you can ask the animal directly what the problem is and what Essence it would like to have. The answer may come as clearly heard spoken words but for most people it is more likely that the answer will come as an image or words which come to mind or a sense of what is needed. This will be discussed further in Chapter 4.

DOSAGE

Treatment is usually seven drops of dose strength Essence given twice daily, squirted directly into the mouth or patted onto the head and body of the animal. However, Essences can be added to drinking water or food, though water is preferable. The Essences can also be used in an atomiser and sprayed on an animal, into its energy fields or around its immediate environment. The Bush Essences easily lend themselves to being combined with massage oils and creams and can be combined with essential oils and homoeopathic tinctures. They are very gentle, safe and self-adjusting. Some animal workers have found that many animals only need one dose of an Essence to deal with a problem, though two weeks' treatment is the recommended regime, and no harm will come to the animal if the Essence is given over a longer period than needed. All animals are different and it is important to listen and look for indications from your animals of what their particular dosage should be. If you are separated from your animal you can hold the bottle of Essence and ask that the healing energy of the Essence be sent to the animal, though taking the drops is stronger and is the preferred method.

To make up a dosage bottle with more than one Essence you add seven drops of each selected Essence to a mixture of one part brandy and three parts purified, spring or mineral water in a 15-30 ml bottle. It is recommended that the number of Essences included in any one bottle be limited to four or five (though there will always be exceptions) and that the Essences all address the same broad area. It is best to deal with only one problem at a time.

USING FLOWER ESSENCE MISTS AND CREAMS

These beautiful products are made from the highest quality ingredients and have a broad range of healing properties. Each contains Bush Essences which are appropriate to the particular theme being focused on. The base creams and oils include shea and cocoa butter, sweet almond, rose hip, avocado and wheatgerm oil, as well as Vitamin A, emulsifying wax, arnica, chamomile, calendula and aloe, in various combinations. They also contain exquisite essential oils which vary from product to product. There is some discussion about using essential oils with animals. Some aromatherapists believe that animals do not like them and prefer to seek out their own scented plants in the wild, which is good if the animal has access to those plants. Others find that their animals love them and respond to them very well. All the essential oil experts who were approached about this subject agreed that the level of essential oils present in each of these Bush Essence products is not so high as to cause any problems if used with animals. As with any skin product, it is best to try a small amount on your animal and see how it responds. If there is any negative reaction then obviously stop usage. However, if the response is good then use it confidently. Each of the products is clearly labelled with its ingredient contents.

The creams should be applied sparingly to the skin to ease emotional and physical conditions. The mists can be used to help create environments free from negative energies and each mist is conducive to a particular scenario. Mists are sprayed into the room or other area or into the animal's energy fields. The mists can also be used on the skin to freshen or to relieve distress, being careful to avoid the eyes.

Calm & Clear Essence Mist and Cream. The mist creates a calm environment. It can help an animal to relax and focus. The cream can ease stiffness and tension in muscles and joints, particularly the head and neck, and can relieve head pain if applied to forehead and base of skull.

Emergency Essence Mist and Cream. The mist will defuse an agitated or emotional situation, and if sprayed on the skin can relieve the pain of insect bites and stings. The cream can soothe painful joints and ease bruising, rashes and other skin problems.

Face, Hand & Body Essence Cream is a good general skin cream and, as it was formulated to use on the delicate facial skin, is particularly gentle and soothing on irritated skin.

Sensuality Essence Mist is helpful for the animal that is not comfortable with being touched.

Space Clearing Essence Mist clears negative energies from rooms and other areas, or from an animal's energy fields. It is good when moving to a new house, etc.

Travel Essence Mist can be sprayed in animal transport vehicles or family cars to improve conditions for travel.

Woman Essence Mist and **Cream** can be used for any 'female' problems – rubbed or sprayed on the skin of the abdomen.

Woman; **Face, Hand & Body**; and **Travel Essence Creams** all contain **Mulla Mulla** which can help deal with sun damage and radiation. So they could be considered for problems with sun-damaged ears and faces, particularly in pale-skinned animals. The **She Oak** Essence in these creams would also help with dryness of skin.

These creams and mists are luxurious to use and can bring about wonderful changes on many levels. Other possible uses for these products with animals are suggested in the following chapters and the individual Essence and Combination Drops will be discussed in depth throughout the book.

Some animals may go through a healing crisis early in their treatment with Flower Essences and other remedies. This shows as a temporary worsening of symptoms and has several causes. One, the animal is processing emotions or physical toxins and so the body and emotions are temporarily in overload. Two, the animal may be resisting the change that the remedies are bringing about in its body, though this is less common in animals than in humans. Three, some animals are super sensitive and need a smaller dose of the Essences. There are several ways to deal with this situation. You can stop the current Essences for a couple of days and maybe give the animal **Emergency Essence** if that feels appropriate. Or you can reduce the dosage by giving fewer drops per dose, or reduce the number of doses per day from two to one. Also you could try adding the Essences to water so that they are going into the body and energy fields in a more diluted form. If symptoms do not clear within a couple of days, or if they are severe, consult a health professional. The presenting symptoms could be an indication of something serious that is quite unrelated to the Essence treatment. It would be very rare to get a severe reaction to a Flower Essence.

OBTAINING BUSH ESSENCES

Individual dose strength Essences can be obtained directly from Australian Bush Flower Essences headquarters at Terrey Hills, Sydney, ordered from their web-site or purchased from many leading health food shops and Flower Essence practitioners. Pre-prepared dose strength Combination Essences are available from many health foods shops, natural therapists and local and international distributors. Stock strength bottles, from which you can make your own dose bottles, are available from Australian Bush Flower Essences or your local distributor. Contact details are at the back of the book.

Flower Essences are very hardy: however there are some precautions that should be taken to keep them at their best. Never store the Essences near electronic equipment. Don't store in full sun for long periods or in other places where they will get excessively hot, such as in the boot of a car. Occasional exposure to such conditions will not harm the Essences but long term it could reduce their efficacy. Always close the bottle immediately after use and don't allow the dropper to touch the mouth or other parts of the body or anywhere else that it could contaminate the Essences when it is returned to the bottle.

Using Australian Bush Flower Essences is a good way to bring the healing power of plants to animals that have no regular access to them.

For a complete list of suppliers of Australian Bush Flower Essences in your country, go to:
www.ausflowers.com.au

Chapter 3

A NEW ANIMAL ARRIVES

If you have men who will exclude any of God's creatures from the shelter of compassion and pity, you will have men who deal likewise with their fellow men. Not to hurt our humble brethren is our first duty to them, but to stop there is not enough. We have a higher mission – to be of service to them wherever they require it.

ST. FRANCIS OF ASSISI, 1181–1226

The arrival of a new animal marks the beginning of a whole new relationship. It offers the potential for a new set of experiences which can be wonderful for both human and animal. Some experts believe that acquiring a pet calls for a similar amount of planning to buying a car or having a child. A potential animal owner needs to be well informed about the task they are taking on and do their best to ensure the well-being and happiness of all concerned – animals and humans.

In the wild, interaction with other animals is a normal part of life for young animals and may remain important for many adult animals. Wolves, primates and many other mammals form family or community groups where members support each other in the acquisition of food, the care of the young and protection from danger. Even with traditional loners such as leopards and polar bears, the mother will stay with the young for up to two years. Grazing animals mostly live in herds, finding safety, companionship and leadership there. Elephants travel as a group and the way they protect their young and stay with a sick or injured family member is legendary. With many animals this closeness, social interaction, discipline, education and protection are crucial, not just for physical survival, but for their psychological and emotional well-being.

Many domesticated animals, certainly most pets, lack regular contact with their own kind and with the natural environment. Even those in open runs or paddocks are limited in the area in which they can hunt, graze or forage. They can rarely find all the food they need, or the medicinal plants or naturally occurring minerals that help to keep them healthy. So the carer of any domestic animal has a responsibility to act as substitute for the animal's natural family group and to supply what the animal can no longer obtain for itself from the wild.

Our pet's instincts often lead it to behave in a way that might seem completely illogical to us, so an understanding of what is normal for any particular animal is essential. We need to recognise the way that our animal thinks. Normal instinctive behaviour in one animal may be quite different from another, even of the same species. A short-nosed and short-sighted pug would have no interest in the rabbit running in a distant field, an activity which would attract the immediate attention and pursuit of a greyhound. Most animal carers are guilty at some time of treating animals in their charge as though they are humans in furry coats. But animals are animals and are happiest if treated that way. Because of their instinctive natures and tendency to live in the present, they often respond quite differently from us to what is happening in their environment.

SELECTING A NEW ANIMAL

It is easy to romanticise the concept of pet ownership. The reality can be very different from the dream, so it is important to understand your real motives for wanting an animal and ensure that they are strong enough to persist once the initial novelty and excitement have passed. Wanting a German Shepherd because you enjoy watching Inspector Rex on TV will not be enough, especially if you live in a small apartment in the city and work all day. Taking the time to face the realities of what animal ownership really involves will reap benefits in the long run. There are some basic areas to be considered.

Why do you want an animal?
Because it is cute? Because most of your friend have pets? To give an abandoned pet a good home? As a fashion accessory? Does your life feel empty without one? Do you think it will help you overcome your sadness over a personal loss? Maybe you want a watch dog to make you feel safe. Perhaps you think it would be good for your children. Or perhaps you want a reason for exercising. There are no right or wrong answers, but it is important to be honest with yourself and acknowledge exactly why you are taking on this new responsibility in your life.

What will it cost?
The expense of animal ownership is not just the initial cost of buying an animal. You also need to consider the costs of adapting your home to cater for it plus all the ongoing costs of feeding, health care, equipment, veterinary treatment,

damage to furnishings or garden, obedience training and pet motels when you go away. If your chosen animal happens to be a pony, then add the costs of a farrier, riding gear, riding boots and clothes, riding lessons and maybe stabling.

Time for cleaning up?

This is ongoing – regularly cleaning the enclosure, cage or kennel; hairs off lounges; food bowls and litter boxes; puddles, poo and spew messes; chewed up everything; big holes in back lawns that need refilling. The list is endless and the work can be particularly onerous when the animal is young.

Time for caring?

You need time to do all the above cleaning plus grooming, washing, walking, playing, and just spending time with your animal. Will the animal have to spend long hours alone? Loneliness is a serious problem for pets particularly a very young animal or a newly-adopted older animal.

What is your present situation?

Do you have the space? Will a new animal in your yard affect your neighbours and will they be tolerant of that? A continually barking dog or a yowling tom cat can seriously strain good-neighbourly relationships. If there are other animals in the house, will a new animal upset the status quo? A young dog joining a house-hold where elderly cats are already in residence could cause chaos. Are there possible hazards from traffic, other animals or other people? Are there dangerous structures or poisonous substances in your house or yard? Many young cats and dogs die needlessly because they have eaten snail or rat baits.

What are your needs and temperament?

These should closely match the needs and temperament of the animal that you are planning to acquire. A very active animal that wants constant play and roughhousing might not be good if you really like to veg out of an evening and watch TV. Read about the animal you want and talk to people who have owned one. Find an animal that suits you and your family.

Consider the possibility of allergies within the family. Some people just cannot live with cats no matter how much they love them. Take note that Bush Essences such as **Fringed Violet, Dagger Hakea** and **Crowea** can help relieve symptoms of a person with an allergy to cat or other animal hairs.

Accept the fact that even though a child wants a pet, the job of looking after it will eventually be yours. And very importantly, realise that the cute little baby animal you bring into your home or yard will grow up and become a large, or at least larger adult. A baby python could be a delightfully novel pet but having a three metre carpet snake crawling about your place several years later might not be quite so enjoyable! A fluffy yellow baby gosling is lovely on the back verandah for a few days but a full grown gander is a different matter.

Most of all you must be sure that you want this animal more than anything;

that you have the capacity to give it the love that it will need, and that you can deal with the practicalities, and are willing to embrace the responsibilities, involved.

There are some Essences that potential animal owners can take to help them come to a good decision about acquiring their animal.

Green Spider Orchid is good for non-verbal communication.

Jacaranda will help if you are indecisive and afraid of making the wrong decision.

Meditation Essence will help you access inner wisdom and knowledge. It will help you find a quiet space within where you can really ask yourself the relevant questions and hear the answers. Consider the idea of trying to communicate with your prospective pet at a spiritual level.

Paw Paw will improve access to your Higher Self and help you integrate information and come to a decision easily.

Sundew can ensure that you are well grounded, focused and are being realistic about the decisions you are about to make.

ARRIVAL OF THE NEW ANIMAL

When a new animal arrives you need to provide warm, dry housing, a constant supply of fresh water and regular nutritious feeding. You need to protect the animal from other animals and small children, and also from road traffic. It is essential to follow the advice of a good vet or alternative animal health professional with regard to worming and protection against serious infectious disease. And it is important to set and implement rules for animals in your care right from day one. Training and communication will be discussed in more detail in Chapter 4.

Very young animals need to feel loved, secure and wanted and shouldn't be left alone or confined for long periods. This is the time in an animal's life when it will imprint with humans and with other animals. Imprinting is a learning process whereby a young animal identifies with another animal, usually its mother or other animals of the same species, but imprinting also occurs between a young animal and a human, or an animal of another species if the natural mother or others of its own species are not around. This identification is permanent and greatly affects how an animal sees itself in relation to others. The age at which an animal imprints varies with species. With most birds it is soon after hatching, but with mammals it can be much later.

It is during these first several months that the young animal also learns basic socialisation skills. The length of this socialisation period varies according to the species. With dogs it is up to 16 weeks. Some wild animals have a very short period. If domesticated animals do not have frequent positive contact with humans and other animals during that period, and if their emotional needs are not met at this stage of their lives, there can be subsequent unwelcome behaviour which can be difficult to change.

When a new animal arrives at your home, farm or zoo it usually comes with some fears or uncertainty from the change of routine. It is important to recognise this and to find out as quickly as possible just what the fears are. Obtain as much of its history as you can from the previous owners and observe how it is reacting to the new environment and the new community. Spend time with the animal, observing quietly and unobtrusively, not anxiously hanging on its every move, which will only increase its anxiety. Allow it to get used to you and know that it has nothing to fear. If the animal is very young, it is important to recognise that it may be going through anxiety resulting from the separation from its mother and litter siblings. Touch is important, but be guided by the animal as to how much and how soon.

Bringing an animal into your life is a multi-faceted experience. If you are well-informed, consistent, caring and generous with your time, emotions and energy in your interaction with your chosen animal(s) your human/animal experience will be a very rewarding one. There are various Bush Essences which can help.

Bottlebrush will assist the animal in letting go and adapting to change. It will also help bonding with the person in the family who carries out the main role of physically caring and mothering, whether that person is male or female.

Emergency Essence is the principal remedy to help any animal adjust to a new situation. It can be given directly by mouth, added to drinking water, patted onto the fur or feathers or made into a spray and misted in the area around the new animal. It can be used quite frequently during the initial settling in period. Add **Freshwater Mangrove** or **Bauhinia** to help the animal accept new things such as wearing a collar or head stall and for coping with veterinary procedures such as micro-chipping and worming.

Red Helmet Orchid helps an animal (and a human) deal with authority and improves the bonding in a father/child type relationship. In this sense **Red Helmet Orchid** will help with bonding whether the 'real owner' is a male or female. There will be situations when one person plays the role of both 'owner' and 'mother' and in that case **Red Helmet Orchid** and **Bottlebrush**, taken by owner and animal, could help in the bonding process.

Other Essences, for owners and carers, help them deal with the responsibilities and joys of animal ownership.

Bush Gardenia will support the inclusion of the animal as part of the family.

Confid Essence or **Five Corners** helps the carer take on the role of leader with confidence and supports the shy, fearful animal.

Flannel Flower engenders comfortable physical touch between animal and human.

Freshwater Mangrove helps a person to be open to new ways of thinking and doing in relation to the animal.

Green Spider Orchid will encourage non-verbal communication between human and animal and could usefully be taken by animal and carer.

Little Flannel Flower could be considered to enhance enjoyment, and encourage play with new animals. After all, they can be such great fun.

Peach-flowered Tea-tree can help if enthusiasm for pet caring wanes once the novelty has worn off.

Sturt Desert Rose and/or **Flannel Flower** could be useful for setting up healthy boundaries, and can be taken by both the animal and carer.

Wedding Bush will support commitment.

ADOPTING AN ANIMAL

Adopting an animal from an agency, refuge or another person saves many animals from unnecessary euthanasia and it can be a wonderful way to acquire a new pet. Animals from good homes will often pine for their previous owner and this needs to be acknowledged and dealt with. If the animal has been badly handled, suffered cruelty or been largely ignored in its previous home it may be very timid, erratic or unresponsive. Older animals can arrive with bad habits that may prove difficult to break and earlier poor treatment can result in aggressive or over-submissive behaviour. All animals need to recognise very quickly that the owner is boss and that there are limits to how they behave and where they are allowed to go. Loving, firm and consistent handling, in conjunction with the use of appropriate Bush Essences, will help the animal to settle in.

Adol Essence, which is a combination of Essences developed for use with adolescent humans, could be very good with an animal whose behaviour is inappropriate or destructive.

Bluebell given to the new animal will encourage the wonderful realisation that it is OK to give love to everyone.

Boronia could be considered if the animal appears to be pining for its previous owner.

Bottlebrush will help an animal adapt to change and enable it let go of the past.

Dog Rose is good if the animal is generally fearful, shy or timid.

Emergency Essence is the first Essence to think of for newly adopted animals. It will help them to process any old trauma as well as assisting them to cope with the fear and confusion that a change of ownership will bring. It can also be good where the animal is inclined to panic. **Red Suva Frangipani** could be added for an older animal experiencing grief after separation from an earlier owner.

Five Corners or **Confid Essence** will build up confidence.

Flannel Flower is about enjoyment of touch and touching and also helps to set healthy boundaries.

Illawarra Flame Tree could be used if the animal has a sense of being rejected.

Little Flannel Flower will help a sad or overly serious animal to become more playful.

Mountain Devil can be used if there is aggressive behaviour.

Red Helmet Orchid could be used if the animal has trouble accepting the authority of the new owner.

Relationship Essence will help an animal bond with the new family.

Tall Yellow Top can help if there seems to be a sense of 'not belonging'.

Also consider that the animal's past negative experiences might be influencing its current behaviour. There are several Essences to be considered here.

Boab will help an animal break down patterns of behaviour taken on from its previous family, both human and animal, or down its genetic line.

Grey Spider Flower is for terror.

Pink Mulla Mulla is for fear of a past hurt being repeated.

Sturt Desert Pea helps the animal to deal with old grief and pain.

Sunshine Wattle allows the animal to realise that, although things may have been grim in the past, they can improve.

There are many ways of using the Essences to help new animals settle. Here is a story sent to us by an Essence practitioner – about a Staffie who didn't know how to play.

'Jake, my Staffordshire bull terrier, came to me when he was three months old. He had basically been ignored by his previous owners and his nutrition and health were poor. Through lots of food, hugs and kisses I was able to bring him to good health. But the thing I found most sad about Jake was that he didn't play! I decided it was time to bring out his positive qualities and give him a confidence boost. Every morning I put seven drops of **Confid Essence** *in his water and again in the evening. Within seven days I noticed an incredible difference. Jake was chasing the ball and had learned to sit and no longer feared going for walks. I know Jake will grow into a beautiful and loving dog.'*

A story from Josephine Weir of Bristol, England tells about the arrival of Flynn, a very young Jack Russell terrier.

'Flynn was only five weeks old and came directly to me after his mother was killed in a car accident. The pups had been left unattended and unfed for 12 hours. When I collected him he was very still and very quiet and his little eyes stared at me all the way home. He looked to be in shock and was obviously traumatised by the event of losing his mother and by being removed from his siblings and security. I gave him **Sturt Desert Pea** *and after two weeks he was a playful and adventurous little puppy. When I later saw his litter mates I was amazed how much better Flynn was, both physically and emotionally, and so much more confident than they were.'*

Emergency Essence would also have been good for this animal.

Elaine Challenger, from North Narrabeen in Sydney, has a lovely story about her little cat who was abandoned when it was only three weeks old.

'Splotch was left on the doorstep at a vet practice. While there she went home with one of the nurses each evening until we bought her when she was about five weeks old. She is not an affectionate cat and doesn't like to be touched much. She can be very bad tempered, biting my fingers or toes when hungry and sometimes she attacks and scratches me for no obvious reason. If I say "no" to her she reacts instantly by biting and scratching. However, she is a very patient cat, quiet, but very active. And she does allow me to pick her up and put her on the kitchen bench to be checked for ticks; possibly she got used to this as a tiny kitten at the vet's. When we first got her we gave her a small wombat soft toy to play with, assuming she would treat it as prey. Instead it became her friend. She often had nightmares, waking up crying, and at such times she would carry Wombat around the way a mother cat carries a kitten and would wash it and chatter to it and sleep with it. Obviously Wombat was a substitute for her mother and littermates. The vet estimated that Splotch was born around 23 February 2002, giving her at least four 2s in her birth date. Ian White suggests **Sturt Desert Pea**, **Crowea** and **Illawarra Flame Tree** for people who have more than two 2s in their birth date. After testing with a pendulum I gave Splotch a mixture of **Sturt Desert Pea** to deal with the sadness she must have felt at being separated from her mother and littermates and **Illawarra Flame Tree** to deal with any sense of rejection – not just being abandoned but also being separated from all the different people and animals she stayed with while living at the vets. I gave her the Essence once a day for eight weeks. The changes have been very noticeable. She has stopped having nightmares and stopped talking to Wombat. In fact, we don't know where Wombat is. She now asks for food by licking my hand or toes instead of biting. Now, if I say 'no' she hesitates before deciding whether to bite me or not – which gives me time to move away. I doubt that she will ever be a demonstratively affectionate cat but she has ceased to be as bad tempered and wilful as in the past. My partner referred to the Essence drops as 'Ritalin for cats'. Since then I have given her **Flannel Flower**, **Dagger Hakea** and **Tall Yellow Top**. She now comes up to me every now and then and wants to be patted. I am amazed at the positive results'.

MULTIPLE-PET HOUSEHOLDS

Multiple-pet households often strike problems when a new animal arrives. Dogs and horses have to sort out amongst themselves where the new animal fits in the hierarchy and there can be displays of aggression until this is settled. Cats have strong territorial boundaries and if these are continually breached by a new animal it can result in frequent spraying and spatting. As much as possible, give the new animal the space it needs. If possible, give it an area where it is separate from the resident animals but from where it is able to see and communicate with them until they all adjust. Before releasing a new horse into its paddock, lead it around the perimeter fence, so that if it panics and tries to gallop away it knows the boundaries and is less likely to get injured.

Bauhinia could be given to the animals already resident in the house to help them to be open to change.

Calm & Clear Essence Mist sprayed around where the animals congregate will help create a peaceful atmosphere.

Dagger Hakea helps to deal with angry reactions between animals and to resolve jealous behaviour.

Flannel Flower and/or **Sturt Desert Rose** can help the animals sort out healthy boundaries.

Mountain Devil, for aggressive behaviour, is another Essence to consider.

Relationship Essence can help the animals to relate well to each other.

Slender Rice Flower will be useful for all the animals and people, to help them get along together as a group.

Raelene Markham from Geilston Bay in Tasmania adopted Chance, a Border Collie, from the pound.

'He was a beautiful looking dog but when I first met him he was very timid and had no confidence at all. The workers at the pound told me that his previous owners had mistreated him and basically dumped him at the pound. I had another dog, Penny, a young female Blue Heeler who was very confident and sure of herself. I was concerned about how the two dogs would get on and at first Penny took on the role of leader and Chance just kept out of everyone's way. He remained aloof and his confidence remained low. I decided to try him on Australian Bush Flower Essences. I chose **Five Corners** *for his low self-esteem and* **Grey Spider Flower** *because he was very frightened and always cowered when anyone approached him. And also because he had nightmares (which this Essence can help resolve) and when sleeping was very restless and would make groaning noises. I put in* **Pink Mulla Mulla** *to help with trusting and opening up to his new home and also to release deep wounds in his psyche.* **Tall Yellow Top** *was another choice because of his anti-social behaviour and isolation from us all. I wanted him to feel at home with us. Finally,* **Bluebell** *for opening up his heart and trusting in us because he didn't trust anyone at all and was sometimes defensive. I gave Chance seven drops of this combination morning and evening. He was quite easy to work with but would only let me give him the Essences. After one week there seemed little change but about the tenth day we noticed a difference. Chance let my husband give him the drops. We kept him on the same Essence for another two weeks and that is when dramatic changes started to happen. Instead of sleeping under the dining room table every night Chance jumped up onto the couch with my husband and myself and actually stayed there with us. His nightmares stopped and he was not restless in his sleep at all. It was a nice change from the anti-social dog he had been up to that time. But the biggest change of them all was his behaviour with my other dog. They actually began to have disagreements whereas previously Penny would dominate everything including his food. Now Chance would snap back at her for touching his food and bones. The changes were slow but Chance has become a very different dog from the frightened, timid animal we had picked up just a few weeks earlier.'*

Another story came from Pam Foster from The Channon in New South Wales.

'We had two cats, an elderly cat called Pussy-la and a younger cat. They got on well together. However, recently we acquired a new kitten. Pussy-la was very upset and gave the kitten a really

*hard time, hissing at her and cuffing her at every opportunity. The little kitten was terrified and tried to stay out of the way of the older cat; it was a very upsetting situation for all of us. I gave Pussy-la a mix of **Bottlebrush**, **Bauhinia**, **Pink Flannel Flower**, **Dagger Hakea** and **Slender Rice Flower**. I also used **Emergency Essence** when needed if things got too tense with the animals. The Essences have worked wonders. Pussy-la has really calmed down and is accepting the new kitten and peace reigns once more in the household.'*

CHILDREN AND ANIMALS

Children and animals usually get on well together. Even so, there are some matters to consider when bringing an animal into a family with young children. The children must learn to follow the rules of the household in relation to the animal to ensure consistency in treatment. The children should be encouraged to be gentle with the animal, and to avoid teasing or hurting it. They have to learn that there are times when a cat or dog does not want to be picked up or patted. They need to give the animal space and learn to read the signs as to when it has had enough of play and roughhousing. Adults should ensure that the animal has a place to escape to, particularly if it is an older animal.

The animal should never be allowed to steal food from a child, jump up, knock a child down or bare its teeth, bite or kick when playing with the child. It is really useful if you can get a child to feed a new dog, make it wait before a command to eat and ideally be able to take the bowl away from the dog while it is eating. With a horse, allow it to get to know the child, and the child the horse, before there is any close interaction. Teach the child basic rules such as never walking behind a horse in case it kicks, and offering food with flattened hand so the animal doesn't bite the fingers by mistake. This means constant supervision when child and animal are together until the rules have been learned and imple-mented by all concerned. Never leave a young child in charge of a new animal.

There are health matters to be considered with children and animals. Discourage children from kissing chickens and ducklings which have come from poultry farms as they can carry salmonella and other diseases. Salmonella can also be carried by other animals such as pet tortoises, snakes, dogs and cats. Parrot fever (*psittacosis*) is common in Australia with symptoms much the same as the flu. Children have less resistance to these diseases than adults and so need to be careful when handling birds from the parrot family, including budgerigars. It is wise to insist that hands are washed with soap and water after the handling of any animals.

Essences to consider for children and animals include the following.

Dog Rose or **Grey Spider Flower** will help the child who is afraid of an animal.

Flannel Flower for both child and animal can help to encourage gentle touch and establish healthy boundaries between them.

Freshwater Mangrove can help to enable the child to see things differently and realise that an animal is not a toy.

Chapter 4

COMMUNICATION and TRAINING

If we could talk to the animals, learn their languages, what a wonderful world this would be.

FROM THE SONG 'TALK TO THE ANIMALS'
BY LESLIE BRICUSSE, 'DR DOLITTLE' MOVIE

COMMUNICATION

One of the most important factors in animal/human relationships is communication. Imagine the difficulty of communicating in a foreign country where you do not understand the local language, where no-one around understands yours and you do not have a clue about the local customs. This gives you some concept of the difficulty of an animal trying to communicate with us.

Animals have a different evolutionary history from our own. When they come into domesticity they are living in an alien environment. It is as though they have arrived from another star system and it is easy to judge them as being of lesser intelligence because they are so different from us. But, as has been written, *'Intelligence is that which can be measured by intelligence tests'*. It all depends on the questions being asked. Animals have evolved with the skills and instincts for survival in their natural environment. Their native 'intelligence' for survival in the wild is far in excess of ours. Book learning has no relevance for them.

Measuring an animal's intelligence on the limited human IQ scale is totally pointless. Some physicists wonder if humans are hard wired in such a way that they will never be able to completely understand the physics of the Universe. They feel that perhaps we do not have the concepts or the language. In a similar way the brains of animals are hard wired in a form that is unique to their own species. Some humans might be able to understand the theory of pure mathematics but it is unlikely that a canine ever would. A dog, however, can pick up the faint odour of the clothes of a missing child, interpret what that means and do something about it. A turtle can find its way back to the beach of its birth across thousands of kilometres of ocean after many years, without any obvious navigational aids. Coastal birds know when the salt lakes of Central Australia fill with water and fly there in their tens of thousands to breed near the food-rich waters, even though they normally live thousands of kilometres away. We animals are all different from each other in many ways. But it is not necessarily intelligence that is missing in the animal/human relationship; it is often simply the ability to communicate with understanding. Learning to communicate better with animals could totally change our relationship with them.

The sensory perceptions of animals are different from our own in many ways. They are often more acute, and the way they communicate is also different. They use a lot of non-verbal communication amongst themselves, but most mammals and birds also communicate with sound. Even giraffes, long considered silent animals, do in fact have a voice. Research by von Muggenthaler and others, presented in 2001, indicates that giraffes communicate in infrasound, a low frequency sound that is inaudible to humans. Thanks to a number of remarkable breakthroughs in inter-species communication, some researchers have been able to converse with non-human individuals, including dolphins, apes and parrots, on a scale that once would have been thought impossible. By using cards, printed with words and other symbols, they have been able to communicate to a limited degree, sometimes in complex sentences, about actions, physical items and feelings. In the 1960s and later, scientist John Lilly experimented with dolphins in separate tanks that could not see or hear each other and could only communicate with each other via underwater telephone. He found that these animals 'talked' to each other in a variety of ways using clicks and other sounds. Their talk was not repetitive and had some of the hallmarks of genuine conversation.

There is much more to the communication of animals than we can physically hear or see. There have been amazing tales of pet animals knowing what is going on with family members even when the people involved are long distances away. Dogs have howled when an owner has died in war time, even though the war was on the other side of the world. Stories abound of animals travelling great distances to their homes without knowledge or experience of how to get there. Author and scientist Rupert Sheldrake has written about animals who 'know when their owners are coming home' and has given a lot of thought to this phenomenon. He relates many stories of dogs that, even when the owners deliberately altered their time of arrival home, would go to the door or window and bark or otherwise indicate when the owners were on their way. Sheldrake felt that between the animal and owner there was a flexible energy connection of which the animal was aware and which only death could break. He tells of a much loved cat of Winston Churchill. When the old statesman was dying the cat sat with him virtually all the time. However, about 20 minutes before he breathed his last, the cat moved away. It is believed that the cat sensed the life force leaving Churchill's body, well before the old man's breathing and heartbeat stopped. Anne Cullinan of Sydney tells a similar story of when her mother was dying. Her mother's cat sat under her bed for three days, but just before she died the cat disappeared and was not seen again for 24 hours.

Animals communicate with one another on many levels using sounds, signals, smells, behaviour and that elusive 'sixth sense'. Cats have scent gland under their chin, and when they are rubbing against you they are marking you as their property. Unlike most humans, animals have not lost their ability to communicate telepathically with one another. They would communicate in this way with humans, if only we would listen. Some people, however, do have the ability to communicate directly with animals and this is a wonderful gift. Animal communicator Billie Dean says, *'The voices of the animals can come in the form of subtle niggling, or thoughts of that animal constantly in your mind. Other times it's as clear as human conversation'*. Sandra Helton, another animal communicator, describes her way of communicating psychically with a new animal. *'After your pet has eaten and is ready to settle down, sit with him and relax. It helps to have a hand on him for closer contact. Mentally visualise a blank movie screen. Ask to be shown on the screen what your pet's life was like before you met him and what he is feeling now. The most important thing is to be open to whatever you mentally see.'* A different approach comes from Michael Bray, author of *Angels Are Real*. He believes that all animals have angels around them, as humans do. By asking our angels to communicate with the angels of our animals we can communicate with them more easily than by other means.

Animal communicator Sandy Lee believes that if you want to communicate with an animal you need to be calm and focused, with the clear intention of wanting to connect with the animal. You need to be well grounded and in your body, quiet and still. *'Ask the animal if it wants to connect with you and then introduce yourself and tell it what you want to do. It is important to show respect and treat the animal as an equal. Then listen. Stop and listen. The answer might come as a flash, as pictures, as emotions, words, mind thought or physical feelings. And then trust what you get. Everybody can talk to animals.'*

Green Spider Orchid to increase your telepathic ability could help here. One Flower Essence practitioner was amazed at the effect this Essence had on her.

> *'I was not as much in tune with my dogs, my spirit and the wildlife around my home as I wanted to be. Since taking the **Green Spider Orchid** I have developed a deeper understanding of my dogs and the messages they relate to me; a deeper understanding of myself and a closer connection to the teeming wild birds around my house. The strongest connection I have had is with the flower and insect kingdoms; just noticing the tiniest life around me has made my spirit flow even stronger.'*

Other Australian Bush Flower Essences that could boost animal to human communications include the following.

Bush Fuchsia increases access to and trust in your own intuition and helps with all communications.

Confid Essence or **Five Corners** will boost confidence in your ability to acquire this new skill.

Freshwater Mangrove would enable you to believe in completely new paradigms of doing and thinking, and so render you more open to this form of communication.

Kapok Bush is another one that could help here. This Flower Essence links the awareness from the higher chakras with the practicality of the base chakra, so it could heighten perception and help an animal carer pick up information at that higher level and put it into practical action.

All of these Essences could also be given to your animal. It too has to overcome its previous experience that humans cannot understand its attempts to communicate.

For those of us who do not succeed in direct communication with our animals, there is still much we can do to increase our ability to communicate and understand them. There are many ways we can use our five physical senses more acutely to pick up on what an animal is thinking and feeling. Laid-back flattened ears can indicate that an animal feels threatened, or is likely to attack, and this is true whether the animal is a cat, dog or horse. But a wagging tail can mean an angry cat, a happy dog and a horse flicking flies off its rump. There are many body postures, facial expressions and vocalisations specific to an individual species or animal. The best way to learn about these is to find a good book on the subject, so you will know what particular actions, sounds and postures generally indicate.

Then you need to go one step further. You need to understand the specific behavioural characteristics of your particular animal. You can learn to read an animal's emotions by spending time with it and becoming more and more aware of how it expresses itself emotionally. You need to be able to think and feel like the animal you are working with if you are going to be able to understand what it is communicating to you.

Just as we can learn to read our animals, so an animal can learn to read us. In fact, animals often understand us much better than we can understand them. They pick up not just conscious communications but also our unconscious moves, gestures and emotional states. Although an animal might not comprehend our every word, it will recognise the tone of our voice and the sense of what we are saying. Your dog will understand an angry or disapproving tone when it has done something wrong, whatever words you might use. A cat knows when you feel miserable and will often come to give you comfort. But an animal will also pick up on the vibrations of love and empathy. Greeting an animal each morning and communicating what is going on is important. This will make it feel part of your life, your day and your activities. If you are going out, ensure that you tell your animal, not with any guilt or anxiety on your part. Just state your plans aloud and let it know that you will return soon.

Flannel Flower is beneficial to both the carer and animal for expressing emotions and for enjoyment of touch and closeness. This is another Essence to consider for improving communication generally

Illawarra Flame Tree, which deals with rejection, real or imagined, could be considered if your pet appears to feel rejected by your going. And if the pet is very upset or traumatised by your absence then use **Emergency Essence** as well.

TRAINING AN ANIMAL

All animals need some basic training to fit comfortably into the company of humans. Pack and herd animals need to know that you are a kind and loving leader, but definitely the leader. All animals living with humans have to learn, and respond to, basic commands and develop acceptable habits of social behaviour. It is important that every animal learns to trust and respect his carer. To develop a good relationship with an animal, the human needs to demonstrate sensitivity and understanding, firmness and gentleness, and most of all consistency. The whole family, not just the 'head of the pack', must be consistent in the way the animal is treated. If an animal is getting mixed or contradictory messages from different carers it will become confused and will probably behave inappropriately.

Watch your animal unobtrusively and anticipate its next move. If you can see that it is going to eat the prize roses or run onto the road, call it back before it does, and reward with praise or a food titbit. The connection between perform-ance and reward has to be instantaneous. There is no easy way of telling an animal that something it did two hours, or even two minutes, ago was not acceptable. You just have to wear the damage and be better prepared next time.

There is a simple belief about training animals, no matter what their species, that whenever any animal doesn't do what you want it to do or misbehaves, you should ask yourself what *you* have done wrong. All actions have a cause, and if you look for the cause and deal with it then usually the 'bad behaviour' will disappear. If you come home to find your favourite dog has chewed up your best shoes or ripped the curtains to shreds, screaming won't remedy the situation. Far better to say little and next time you leave the animal alone make sure that it is confined to a safe area and that nothing of value is left in its reach. Also, arrange things so that it is not left alone for over-long periods and leave something to chew on or otherwise play with when it is alone. Even a radio or TV playing while the humans are at work will help a lone animal feel less deserted and bored. Having a second animal for company is another solution, though this can sometimes double the trouble!

DOGS

Much has been written about the training of dogs. The one principle that comes through regularly is that dogs are pack animals, and that the owner must be the leader of the pack. This reflects the natural behaviour of pack animals in the wild. Even when a puppy is quite small it must learn who is boss. Training should be done by rewarding the animal and making use of its natural desire to please, not by punishing or even acknowledging wrong doing. Consistency is essential if the dog is to learn what it is or is not allowed to do. If the owner does not move into the role of leader then the dog will try to take over the role and a dog does not have the ability to manage a human/animal household with any sort of success, so relations between people and dog will deteriorate.

In his book *Dog Stories*, Scottish vet and author James Herriot tells the story of two white West Highland Terriers who ruled the roost in their household. They were never disciplined and their owners treated them like spoilt children, laughing at their anti-social behaviour and continually giving them special treats even when they were jumping up and snapping at visitors and growling at anyone in or near the house. When these two dogs eventually died of old age they were replaced with another pair of Westies. At first these two dogs were delightful, playful, enjoyable puppies but within months they too fell into the same pattern, baring their teeth and growling menacingly, even biting anyone who tried to handle them, including their owners. The owners of these dogs had allowed them to take on the role of leader and they were not doing a very good job of it. Had the owners been firmer with their dogs and taken Essences such as **Five Corners** to boost their confidence and given **Red Helmet Orchid** to the dogs to help them accept authority, they could have avoided this situation.

It is wise to take any dog to training school, but this becomes particularly important if the dog belongs to a big breed. A big dog that is out of control can be a dangerous animal.

Cognis Essence, which helps with learning, could help when a dog is learning either basic or more sophisticated skills. The Essences included in this combination mix are:

Bush Fuchsia for coordination and learning

Isopogon for boosting memory

Jacaranda for dealing with scattered attention

Paw Paw for integrating information, and

Sundew for focus.

CATS

Cats are carnivorous hunters, like dogs, but very different in temperament. They are by nature more likely to be loners, are generally more nervous, less adaptable to change, and very conscious of defending their territory. Because they don't have a dog's strong need to please their owner, cats are not as easily trained as dogs, but they will respond to rewards and discipline and react positively to verbal commands. There are many Essences which can support this training.

Flower Essence practitioner Jenny Bradford of Pomona in Queensland told us about a seven year old female cat, Saree, which she had acquired when its owner was moving overseas.

'Although I had been assured she did not hunt I soon discovered that she was in fact a very adept hunter. So I mixed up a combination of **Rough Bluebell** *(for manipulate behaviour),* **Dog Rose of the Wild Forces** *(where things are going out of control),* **Gymea Lily** *(for dominating, overriding personality) and* **Boab** *(to break old negative patterns). The* **Rough Bluebell** *and* **Dog Rose of the Wild Forces** *were especially indicated because Saree had developed a very aggressive tendency, which I hoped was only a reaction to her new and strange environment and to her feelings of insecurity. She took this mixture for four weeks and finally settled down. But now she has totally changed to the point that the magpies, which I have raised, have her bluffed and she is hardly game to poke her nose out the door if they are around, let lone try to catch them!'*

Maybe, in this case, confusion and the trauma of the change of ownership had unmasked this animal's aggression and natural hunting instincts. The Flower Essences brought things back into balance and allowed her training as a domesticated cat to re-emerge.

It is important to instigate rules for your cat and stick to them. Is it allowed to jump on the table at meal times? Do you mind a nip at your ankles when you are preparing its food? Decide what you find acceptable and gently but firmly stop your cat doing what you don't want it to do, and praise and reward it when it does your bidding. You could try using a water pistol to catch your animal when it is in the middle of climbing the curtains. It shocks the animal out of the current action and acts as a warning for the future but doesn't hurt in any way.

Cats become very attached to their owners and when left alone for long periods suffer real loneliness. This is especially so for indoor cats who become completely reliant on their owners.

HORSES

Horses in the wild live in a herd with a dominant mare or stallion as boss. Similarly, in captivity they need to know, trust and respect their leader. Being prey animals they tend to be timid, cautious and ready to run to protect themselves from danger. Horses think differently from humans. While we use logic in our thought processes, horses base their thinking on patterns of comfort – basically they want to feel safe and comfortable at all times.

Much has been written in recent times about the principle of 'horse whispering' as a training method. This method is not about actually whispering to the horse but rather about making use of the horse's natural instincts and body language and communicating with it in such a way that the animal willingly does what is required of it. The trainer can show seeming indifference to the horse, looking away and walking away from him within the training ring. The horse's natural curiosity and reaction to follow a leader will soon kick in and in a very short time it will follow the trainer without anything else being done. The horse is also presented with situations in which it makes a choice. If it does the 'right' thing, pressure on its side or bit or whatever is relieved. By doing the 'wrong' thing the pressure becomes firmer and the horse knows not to persist in that behaviour. This is very different from literally breaking the spirit of the animal with force and punishment, which, for a long time, was the accepted way for horses to be trained.

When a horse recognises you, at first as something interesting and then, if you handle it correctly, as its leader it will follow you and allow you to handle it. Horses don't generally talk aloud to each other – they do most of their communicating within the herd by pushing each other around. Imitating that when working with your animal will generally give good results. A horse will become 'gentle' once it realises that it has nothing to fear from those around it.

Using Bush Essences to support this learning process is illustrated in the following story from a Flower Essence practitioner.

*'Carioca is an Andalusian mare who was very nervous with human contact due to mistreatment when being broken in. It made her unpleasant to ride though she was never spiteful, mean or dangerous. Her main problem was being impatient, rushing, hard to catch, fearful and lacking in trust. I gave her **Flannel Flower** for trust in human contact when being touched, and therefore being caught more easily. **Dog Rose** was given to release her fears of being separated from the herd, to give her confidence and courage with human contact, for trust in her rider and to give her the ability to relax and open her heart and listen to her rider; **Black-eyed Susan** was to slow her down, to help her relax and find calmness and peace when she rushed and pranced because she was nervous. I also gave her **Wedding Bush** to bond the relationship between horse and rider and **Silver Princess** to support enjoyment of the journey in the partnership between horse and rider. I gave her seven drops on bread or syringed into mouth, twice daily for two weeks. By the end of that period Carioca could be caught easily in a large paddock. She stood quietly and calmly when being saddled and mounted. She was not as fearful at being parted from the herd in her home paddock. When she was ridden her rushing decreased and she responded to her rider. She was more relaxed and could be ridden on a loose rein. I also gave these Essences to her owner because the rider can transfer a lot of fear and nervousness to the horse. The Essences can help horse and rider to be a team and have the partnership they should have, working together as one.'*

There are many Bush Essences which can help an animal that is being trained and also the trainer.

Angelsword could help an animal contact its natural instincts and help it see itself as the animal that it is. This is important if it lives only with humans. This Essence could also help it draw on skills and wisdom learnt in previous life times.

Boab helps to break negative family behaviour patterns. If an animal seems to have unacceptable behavioural characteristics which are typical of its breed, or just like those of one of its parents, then it would be worth trying this Essence.

Bottlebrush and **Boronia** can help to break bad habits your animal has learned either from a previous owner or from lack of early training.

Bush Fuchsia could also help an animal access its intuitive self and on another level assist with coordination, left and right brain balance and learning generally.

Cognis Essence will support an animal's concentration, reduce hyperactivity and so facilitate training.

Emergency Essence will always be useful with an animal in any unfamiliar situation or routine and will help overcome initial fears.

Five Corners or **Confid Essence** can be of great help in building up an animal's confidence and will boost the confidence of an owner who is not completely sure about their role as carer and trainer.

Green Spider Orchid will support non-verbal communication and could be taken by both owner and animal.

Kangaroo Paw could help with immature and inappropriate behaviour.

Red Helmet Orchid, in the case of a dogs and horses, will help the animal to acknowledge the position of the owner and respect the owner as leader of the pack or herd. And if taken by the carer, it will help bonding with the animal and make it easier to accept the role of leader.

Relationship Essence, or **Bush Gardenia** and **Flannel Flower** will encourage positive communications and enhance relationships between the animal and the rest of the household.

Other Essences to help deal with some specific behaviour problems will be covered in following chapters in this book.

Chapter 5

OVERCOMING FEAR and RELATED PROBLEMS

God made all the creatures and gave them our love and our fear,
To give sign, we and they are His children, one family here.

ROBERT BROWNING, 1812–89

Fear, as a response to a frightening situation, is normal and healthy. It is a defensive reaction, present in all animals, and is essential for their survival in the wild, and to a lesser extent for survival in domestication. Most animals' fears relate to their evolutionary history and many problems in this area come from the environment in which they find themselves today. A dog's fear of thunder can be a well-primed startle reflex and a horse's fear of going into a float can be related to its deep instinct that, in terms of survival, it is safer in open spaces. A big factor here is the animal's inability to remove themselves from

frightening situations as they would in the wild. They cannot easily react to their fight or flight hormones and so often feel trapped.

Fear releases hormones which trigger short term changes in the body. These changes enable an animal to spring into action and defend itself or its group members from attack, or to escape from danger by running or climbing. Whenever an animal experiences fear, a memory of that event will be stored and the next time it is exposed to a similar situation that memory will be triggered. This process helps an animal to avoid situations that could cause harm. However, if the memory results in the animal being fearful of situations that are not harmful and that are part of its day-to-day life, then fear becomes a problem. A frightened animal is an unhappy animal and it can, in some circumstances, become aggressive and dangerous.

Corinne Durmuller, of Kenmore, Queensland, has been involved with horses since she was a child and has worked with them most of her adult life.

'These days I treat other people's horse using mostly homoeopathics and Flower Essences. I use **Emergency Essence** *to settle frightened horses but I have found that* **Dog Rose of the Wild Forces** *is particularly helpful for horses that become dangerous because they are frightened. To handle a horse, the handler needs to be seen by the horse as the leading mare or stallion, and the horses should listen to what the leader says. When horses are very scared they won't listen any more and so become dangerous. If children are around them they could be hurt or even killed. I suggest that the horses take the Essence two or three times a day for a week and then report back to me. I work out the dose on a proportional weight basis, and the Essence is given straight into the mouth – pull the lip down and squirt it in. Usually within the week they have calmed down considerably and are then able to listen, to take commands etc. The fear might not have gone completely but it is back to a level with which the handler can work. Sometimes one or two doses are enough – with other horses it may need to be taken for up to two weeks.'*

There are many causes of fear in an animal. It could be timid by nature, either because it is just that sort of personality or because it has come from a family of timid animals. Many people when choosing a puppy will be attracted to the most timid one in the litter because it stimulates a protective feeling with any dog lover. However, they do not always make good pets, particularly in family situations.

An animal that is continually harassed by its bigger and stronger litter mates or other members of their animal or human family often becomes timid. Its way of coping is to give up and withdraw into itself. Such an animal loses its natural social skills. It finds it easier to stay in the background than risk the possible conflict with its peers and with its human family. This situation is only found in domesticated animals because in the wild a young animal living on its own would rarely survive. If an animal has had little contact with humans during that critical socialising period when it is very young, it can be frightened of any human contact and not receptive to human touch or interaction. An animal that has been treated cruelly or that has experienced any physical or emotional trauma can also become very fearful. One Bush Essence practitioner tells the story of a farm dog who was frightened badly one night while its owner was away from home.

'The owner felt that it had probably been terrorised by foxes or wild dogs. Next morning the dog would not come out of its run. It was given **Emergency Essence** *to help it get over the trauma of the experience and get it out of the run, with* **Confid Essence** *to be given to the dog twice a*

day for two weeks to help build up its confidence in its ability to cope. The owner phoned back later and said that he had done as suggested and that now the dog was back to its normal self, bouncing around the place and enjoying life.'

There are many other possibilities for an animal being fearful. It might be grieving for its litter or stable mates, its mother or its previous owner. It could be suffering from chronic pain or minor injury, or just old and tired. Over-expectation from owners with competition animals can be a cause, especially if they have been reprimanded for failing. Owners who lack confidence, or who are timid with their animals, for example a frisky horse or a very big dog, are in danger of creating a timid animal lacking in self confidence. (Such owners can also produce bossy out of control animals!) Disease can be another reason – chemical imbalance, brain tumour or other physical problem. So always check with a health professional if an animal's fearful behaviour is ongoing and is preventing it from enjoying life. Try to find out all you can about the animal's past history to give you an idea of possible reasons behind the behaviour.

The most natural thing for a human to do with a timid animal is to give it lots of petting and encouragement. But too much attention will only increase the animal's sense that there is something to be afraid of. Instead give it space but plenty of opportunity to be around you and, as it gains confidence, to come to you. As leader of the 'pack' you should not approach a dog or a horse – it should come to you! In fact any animal will feel safer if you just sit by it, but not in its space, until it feels ready to approach you. Some bribing with food titbits can encourage a very timid animal to move out of its safe place in the corner. Gradually it will begin to see you as a benevolent leader and companion and start to trust and interact with you.

There are many Bush Essences that are useful to support the frightened or timid animal.

Bauhinia is for fear of new technology, new ways of doing things, new equipment, new car, a new cat door or a swinging gate.

Boab will help break a pattern of behaviour that has been taken on from family.

Boronia could be useful for an animal that becomes fixated about something. It helps to break the pattern of repetitive thoughts and actions.

Confid Essence or **Five Corners** will boost self confidence.

Crowea helps the animal that worries. It helps to keep it emotionally and physically balanced.

Dagger Hakea and **Bottlebrush** would help an animal to let go of a hurt, forgive past aggressors and move on in life.

Dog Rose is for niggling fears, for anxiety, for ongoing low-grade fear, shyness, timidity and phobias.

Dog Rose of the Wild Forces is for the fear of things going out of control and also for helping to prevent an animal panicking in a frightening situation.

Emergency Essence is always good to try to help an animal through a frightening situation. It is good for the owner or handler as well. It will also help wild, stray or very timid animals to get over the initial shock of regular human contact, and can be used as either a mist or as drops.

Flannel Flower or **Relationship Essence** will help the animal to adjust to being touched and to interacting with others.

Fringed Violet is for any trauma and shock which happened either recently or long ago.

Green Spider Orchid is useful where there is a great fear of something that happened in a previous life, which comes up in dreams. If an animal wakes obviously terrified but with no obvious cause then this Essence could be the one to consider – for example for fear in a puppy that has had no obvious bad experience to cause this.

Grey Spider Flower is for terror, deep paralysing fear and panic. It also can help where an animal has nightmares.

Grey Spider Flower with **Flannel Flower** can help if there is fear of open spaces.

Illawarra Flame Tree is good for an animal that has been previously rejected and is expecting further rejection.

Kapok Bush will assist animals who have given up and crawled away.

Little Flannel Flower will help the animal to be more playful, joyful and bouncy.

Pink Mulla Mulla will support the animal that appears to be frightened of something being repeated which caused severe emotional or physical hurt or pain at a previous time, even a previous life time.

Southern Cross helps to rid the animal of the sense of being a victim.

Tall Mulla Mulla can help if there is fear of social interaction.

Tall Yellow Top is for the sense of not fitting in.

Waratah will give the animal courage.

One very successful case of treating a timid animal with Bush Essences was that of Wilbur, a beautiful cross Border Collie. He was brought home from the dog pound by a very loving family when he was nearly three months old. He had been found in the street at six weeks old. When he first went to live in his new home he was very unsociable. He wouldn't come inside or allow anyone to touch him. When someone tried to pat him his body would go stiff, as in rigor mortis. He shunned affection. His eyes were full of fear. He would hide in the backyard until everyone went to sleep and then come alive. Open spaces and loud noises terrified him. He would walk around all day with his tail between his legs and any fast movement would send him running. There was no joy in his life, his tail never wagged and he was devoid of puppy energy. To take him for a walk the family would have to take him through the house and most often he would lose control of his bowels and bladder inside. This would also happen if he was reprimanded or surrounded by too many unfamiliar people. It was very difficult to train him as these symptoms would get worse with scolding.

*'I made up an Essence of **Dagger Hakea** for his held-in anger and bitterness. I also added **Macrocarpa** to give him inner strength, **Pink Mulla Mulla** for his prickly persona and **Tall Mulla Mulla** to help him feel secure with people. Positive changes started appearing immediately but there was still a long way to go. One month later, I gave him **Dog Rose** for his shyness and fear, **Flannel Flower** to help him overcome his dislike of being touched, **Fringed Violet** to help in the removal of past distressing events and **Tall Mulla Mulla** once again to encourage social interaction. More improvement was noticed. His next mix was **Sunshine Wattle** to help in accepting the beauty and joy in the present, **Freshwater Mangrove** to help open the heart to new experiences, **Grey Spider Flower** to help restore faith and trust, **Mountain Devil** to help overcome the grudges and suspiciousness, and **Tall Yellow Top** to help him realise he was safe and at home. Wilbur now bounces around like a puppy, wags his tail and will let his family pat him. He loves being inside and follows them everywhere. He is being trained by his owners and is responding well. There is still room for improvement and follow up Essences will be given.'*

PANIC

Fear can result in panicking, particularly noticeable in cats and horses, and also in wild animals that are trapped, cornered, or under threat. But it can happen to any animal in a frightening situation. A terrified animal will generally not respond to verbal commands and its behaviour can be alarming, even dangerous to itself and to its carer. After an especially stressful episode, which may be life-threatening, but could be just a trip to the vet, an animal might lash out in fear, even at its owner. The owner needs to remain calm and speak quietly to ease the panic. With a small animal, holding it firmly can help. With a horse or other large animal, releasing it into a safe paddock or enclosure where the animal cannot hurt itself or others, is the safest action. With a wild animal, placing it in a warm, quiet, darkened area works best. **Emergency Essence** should always be on hand for such occasions. For an animal that panics easily and often, add **Dog Rose** to the **Emergency Essence** and give this to the animal twice daily for up to two months, with extra doses in times of panic.

FEAR OF PLACES OR SITUATIONS

Buildings and other areas can retain the energies of people who have lived there and events that have happened in the past. Humans and animals can be very sensitive to such energies. An Irish Bush Essence practitioner, Yvonne Murphy, tells a story about returning to her father's old house in Ireland after she had spent 23 years in America. She stayed with her father until he died and, although she cleared the house from top to bottom and used all the cleaning aids and air fresheners she could find, she was unable to rid it of a strange smell that permeated the building. She asked devas to help and put up protection and white light, and did more cleaning and burned incense but still the smell persisted.

*'The house looked scrubbed and clean and fresh, but it was not, even with weeks of fresh sea air blowing through the rafters. All the protection and psychic guards around the house were useless against "the smell". I could taste "the smell" – it was actually a presence, which built up when the windows were closed. I had gone beyond being embarrassed and was planning to sell up and move away from this entity "the smell". My salvation came when I attended a seminar run by Ian White, aided by those magical Oz genies in a bottle. **Space Clearing Essence Mist** sprayed around the house removed the smell in no time.'*

Some animals can be particularly sensitive to the energies around them, picking up on the lingering vibrations of horrific events or sensing the presence of the energies of other people or animals from earlier times or even the energy of the Earth itself.

Space Clearing Essence Mist sprayed around stables, kennels or a new home can help clear old negative energies from an area and help an animal settle better.

If you feel that the energy of the Earth in your area is out of kilter, Ian White suggests a process of applying **Emergency Essence** topically to the Earth in the form of an encircled Celtic Cross over which you ask to be used as an instrument for God or the Light, and then direct healing energy towards the Earth through your hands.

Flower Essence practitioner Dianne Gillepsie treated a dog whose behaviour changed radically when the family moved house.

*'Kova was an eight year old female Malamoot. She was afraid, as though someone was hurting her when her owners were at work. She was throwing up and disgracing herself on the carpet in their new home. This had never been a problem in their previous home. Normally Kova was extremely well-behaved but now she was cringing and aggressive towards small children, which was totally out of character, as she usually loved to be with people. It seemed that there was an energy present in the new home which Kova did not like and was afraid of. The Essences prescribed for her were **Fringed Violet, Angelsword** and **Paw Paw**. The symptoms ceased after she had the Essences – no more mess on the carpet, no fear and hiding behind the bar. No watching, with fear and wide eyes, as "something" moved around the house. Her usual lovely nature returned, and with it her liking for children.'*

We have many stories about the Bush Essences being used to help frightened animals. Here are a few more.

'Jack was a two year old Jack Russell who was adopted when he was approximately 18 months old. He had required surgery for the removal of 'rat shot' from his legs and hips. He was generally a well-behaved dog but he was very fearful of any raised male voice. He cringed whenever his owner spoke to him loudly or if anyone else raised their voice around him. He kept

leaving home and wandering around the streets. He often became very fearful for no obvious reason. The Essences prescribed for Jack were **Emergency Essence** *to settle and calm him (and deal with old trauma). This Essence was applied directly to the back of his neck. Other Essences were added to his food twice daily for two weeks. They were* **Tall Yellow Top** *to deal with his sense of alienation,* **Red Helmet Orchid** *to deal with rebellion (and improve the bond with his new owner) and* **Grey Spider Flower** *to deal with terror. The owner saw a big improvement to Jack's behaviour. He was not as fearful and much more settled in himself. Definitely a big improvement.* – Elizabeth Smith, Taylor's Beach, Queensland

'My little dog was given to me – but before this he had experienced much trauma. I gave him one bottle of **Mountain Devil**, *and he changed from being suspicious, snappy and changeable to being loving, gentle, trusting, and even tempered. He is a different dog.'*
– Margaret Baker, Brisbane, Queensland

'I treated a horse that had not been ridden for around seven years. When anyone tried to ride her she shied and backed away in fear. I feel strongly that a horse absorbs the fear of its rider so I put the horse and the owner on **Grey Spider Flower** *for two weeks. The horse improved so much that the owner stopped giving the Essence to it and gave the rest of the bottle to another horse who was also very fearful. However, the first horse had not had enough of the Essence to really fix the problem so next time I went there I visualised her completely covered in Grey Spider Flowers. After that all her fear disappeared and the owner now rides her without any problems.'*
– Ilana Shapiro, Elands, New South Wales

Chapter 6

STRESS, DEPRESSION and OTHER PROBLEMS

One may not reach the dawn save by the path of the night.
'THE PROPHET' BY KAHLIL GIBRAN, 1923

STRESS

Just like their human owners, animals are very susceptible to stress and this can be a cause of poor health and unacceptable behaviour. Stress is often, though not always, associated with fear. Like fear, there is a direct connection between stress and the hormones of 'fight or flight' which are produced by the adrenals glands. These glands, situated above the kidneys, produce hormones which stimulate the heart to pump more blood to the muscles in preparation for some physical action. This results in rapid heart beat, greater alertness and

increased blood supply to the muscles involved in movement, and so less blood is available for digestion and other body systems. If there is long-term stimulation of the adrenals they cease to function well, resulting in adrenal depletion and a subsequent inability to deal with stressful events. An animal that is always primed for action can become confused and anxious. Long-term stress can weaken the body physically and reduce the effectiveness of the immune system. This can lead to many physical ailments including allergies, recurrent infection, thyroid disease, Cushing's syndrome and irritable bowel syndrome.

Symptoms of stress-induced anxiety vary in different species and in individual animals within a species. In dogs they can include repeated grooming, chewing of feet or other body parts, continual pacing or other obsessive behaviour. Anxious dogs will often be clingy, upset if separated from their owner, continually demanding attention or over-excited about ordinary things. There may be nervous shaking, starting at any noise and blinking eyes. Cats may stop eating, meaow excessively, stop grooming themselves, spray or urinate in the house, or even develop bladder problems. Horses may whinny as though in distress, sway, crib-bite or repeatedly pace up and down the length of their enclosure. Birds who lose their feathers or continually pick at their bodies are often suffering from anxiety. Parrots are particularly susceptible. However, feather loss can also indicate hormone imbalance.

The level of anxiety that an animal exhibits will be influenced by its current situation and its past experiences. Animals that are left alone for long periods can experience real stress. Ongoing fighting in multi-pet families, owners or trainers who are inconsistent, children who tease, a new home, new family member or being left in unfamiliar surroundings can all contribute to an anxious state in any animal. In fact any change in circumstance, environment or routine can cause stress, as can ongoing irritation or interference from other people or animals. Emotional turmoil in its human family can also upset an animal.

There are a number of Australian Bush Flower Essences that are excellent for relieving stress.

Black-eyed Susan is *the* Essence for stress and emotional burnout. It is a component of the **Calm & Clear Essence** blend. Like **Macrocarpa**, which deals with physical stress, **Black-eyed Susan** has an energetic association with adrenal glands. **Calm & Clear Essence**, as its name implies, can create a sense of calm in an otherwise agitated situation.

Boab is for breaking family patterns of reacting badly to stress.

Boronia will help to break nervous or obsessive behaviour associated with stress.

Bottlebrush and **Bauhinia** will help an animal accept and adapt to change.

Cognis Essence can help where hyperactivity is causing stress.

Confid Essence is to increase an animal's confidence in its ability to handle any situation; it is also good for the owner.

Crowea will help if the animal is a worrier.

Dog Rose is useful if the animal always seems to be slightly anxious about something and that anxiety is ongoing.

Emergency Essence, plus Essences for anger, grief, fear or adapting to change, will help an animal cope in a stressful situation.

Freshwater Mangrove will help an animal move into completely different ways of behaving and responding to situations.

Illawarra Flame Tree will ease any feelings of rejection.

Meditation Essence supports the relaxation process. It is possible to teach any animal to relax using massage or established relaxation and meditative techniques, which relieve stress and anxiety.

Wedding Bush will help an owner stick to a routine and be consistent in his handling of his animal.

POST TRAUMATIC STRESS

Animals which survive accidents, extensive surgery or other distressing experiences may mend physically, but often remain traumatised emotionally. The shock of the incident and subsequent treatment can create fear, anger and depression, changing a normally active, happy animal into a subdued, sullen, frightened one. Trauma can damage the energy fields around the body, resulting in imbalance in the physical energy of the body and also a gradual depletion of the finer energies surrounding it. When this happens, it is also possible for an animal to absorb the negative energy of other people, animals and situations. This can be detrimental to its physical and emotional well-being. Bush Essences will help in such cases, working energetically to process the underlying trauma and repair the energy fields.

   Emergency Essence is the first one to think of. It eases the distress, trauma and fear and gives courage to the animal to start living again. **Fringed Violet** and **Angelsword**, both components of the **Emergency Essence**, deal specifically with the effect of trauma on the energy fields – repairing them and replacing lost energy.

   Other Essences to help with post traumatic stress include the following.

Boronia reduces the incidence of obsessive or repetitive habits that develop after the trauma.

Bottlebrush will help an animal adapt to change, to let go of the past and move on.

Bush Iris, **Illawarra Flame Tree**, **Black-eyed Susan** and **Macrocarpa** help to boost a weakened immune system.

Calm & Clear Essence will relieve stress and help the animal relax and find peace, from which state it can heal.

Confid Essence brings out positive qualities of self-esteem and builds the animal's confidence.

Dynamis Essence can help restore an animal's physical energy and joy for life.

Grey Spider Flower will help deal with nightmares resulting from horrific events.

Mulla Mulla or **Electro Essence** is good for an animal that has been exposed to radiation from X-rays or other sources. **Mulla Mulla** also helps if the animal was involved in a trauma related to fire or excessive heat.

Pink Flannel Flower enables an animal to find deep peace and acceptance of the present situation.

Pink Mulla Mulla will help to overcome fear of the repeat of past trauma.

Purifying Essence is used to clear the body of toxic emotions. Because of its energetic association with the organs of liver and organs of excretion, it will also help to flush out chemical or other poisonous substances, and remnant drugs used to treat damage or disease in the body.

Sturt Desert Pea is for letting go of deep hurt and pain, and using the energy of that experience to move forward with joy.

Slender Rice Flower, applied either topically or taken internally, can help restore the flow of energy through any scarred tissue.

Sundew or **Red Lily** will help ground an animal that has had anaesthetic, has been in a coma or has been otherwise traumatised.

Lorraine Henderson, of Packenham, Victoria tells the story of Millie the Keeshond who went through a traumatic experience when she was only eight weeks old.

*'Millie was locked in the laundry in our house when we had a house fire. The house was full of thick black smoke and water was flooding through it. It was very hot by the time I was able to get her out. She was not physically burnt and I doubt that she would have seen any flames but she would have been subjected to a lot of cracking noises of the fire burning in the kitchen, glass windows exploding and a lot of activity going on around the house as neighbours tried to break in. As a result she became a really nervous dog. If anyone raised their voice or something was dropped that made a loud noise she would either hide in the en-suite, a poky little room far away from the living areas, or she would literally try to jump on someone's lap, despite not being a lap-sized dog. She was also nervous when going for a walk and when trucks thundered by she would stand still, with her ears down, until the truck passed. She was not afraid of flames or heat. She was quite happy to sit in front of an open fire going at home or when we were camping. Nor was she afraid to go into the laundry, where she was trapped at the time of the fire. When making my selection for Millie, I first matched the Essences to the emotional needs that were presented; I also spread the Flower Essence Insight Cards out on the floor and Millie paid particular attention to **Mulla Mulla** and **Dog Rose**, bypassing the rest of the cards. Using numerology I noted that she has the Arrow of Hypersensitivity, so when selecting her Essences I took account that she would be very sensitive, a psychic sponge, absorbing the feelings of others. The Essences in the mix were:*

Crowea to calm and relax her and to help her not to become agitated during stressful situations; Fringed Violet for the trauma and for any damage to the energy fields as a consequence of the fire; Mulla Mulla for any fear of heat and fire, which she would have experienced as a part of the fire; Dog Rose for shyness and nervousness; Dog Rose of Wild Forces to stop her taking on the disturbed emotions of her owners or agitated situations.

I gave her the Essences morning and evening for 19 days. Since then Millie has become a lot calmer and more relaxed in general. She tends to sleep a lot more as well, especially at night time when, in the past, I used hear her moving around the house and barking at noises. During the day she now sleeps outside the study when I am working or actually under my feet, instead of taking herself off to the en-suite. She now follows me around everywhere, whether it is to the toilet or outside to get the mail. She is a lot more confident in herself and she seems to walk taller with her head held high. I feel that she has learned to accept that the noises of trucks are not going to hurt her; she seems to process the thought that the truck is there but now realises that no harm is going to come to her and does not feel the fear so much. Last night when we were walking she was swooped by a magpie. This would normally send her scuttling back to me, but this time she didn't react negatively, instead choosing to chase the bird herself. Keeshonds are also known as "the Smiling Dutchman" because when they are really happy they raise their lips and give you a cheeky smile. We have been very fortunate to have been on the receiving end of many of these smiles lately. Millie is a different dog, she is lot happier in herself, not so frightened by loud noises and has the sparkle back in her eyes.'

Mary Cooper from the UK has a story about a dog that had experienced trauma.

*'This dog had been viciously attacked by three other dogs and since then Tom, her owner, had real problems. If they met another dog when out exercising, this dog would freeze, cower and almost go into a coma. In such a situation Tom had reverted to carrying her over his shoulder. This was not very practical as she is a big dog. I prescribed **Grey Spider Flower** and six weeks later the dog was happily socialising and running around with all the other dogs again.'*

EXTERNAL TRAUMATIC EVENTS

Animals can be affected by traumatic events happening in other parts of the world. Esther Faggianelli, of Moonee Ponds, Victoria told of her dog Lola in the RSPCA book *Smarter than Jack*. It is a fascinating example of animal awareness.

'Lola is a seven year old Maltese terrier. It was a quiet evening on September 11, 2001 in Melbourne, Australia. My husband and I decided to watch a DVD movie. Lola was asleep in her basket beside us. Three quarters of the way through the movie Lola became distressed. She started barking, howling and running from one corner of the house to the other. I thought there may have been fireworks or thunder outside but there were none. The howling became loud and my husband and I became very worried because we had never seen her in this state before. We did all we could to calm her but nothing really did the trick. After about 20 minutes or so, she went back to her basket and looked very disturbed and very sad. It was about 11.30 pm AEST. My husband turned on the TV and we witnessed the World Trade Centre in New York on fire and a second plane hitting the South Tower. It was a tragedy that would never be forgotten. I later rang Rupert Sheldrake, a man who has studied the psychic ability of dogs and asked him whether Lola's reaction could be an unexplained power that enabled her to sense a disastrous event such as the World Trade Centre towers collapse. His research assistant agreed with a simple "Yes"!'

Emergency Essence or **Fringed Violet** and **Angelsword** could have helped this animal through this experience.

Unconditional love and confident support from the owner can go a long way towards helping an animal deal with fear, anxiety and stress. The animal wants to know that the owner, its leader, can cope with whatever arises. Give it a safe space and your quiet but unobtrusive presence. In this environment an animal can gradually gain courage and overcome its fears. Give positive treats at times when it is likely to become fearful, and support the animal with the Bush Essences.

DEPRESSION

Depression is surprisingly common in domesticated animals. They become lethargic and lose interest in what is going on around them. Depression may stem from untreated anxiety but can also be triggered by trauma or loss of any kind. Sometimes the cause is something that might not seem important to us as humans, but is very important to the animal.

Extra attention, distraction with new activities, gentle touch and exercise can help some animals if the depression if not severe. The symptoms of depression result from chemical imbalances in the brain and any animal suffering from on-going depression should be examined by a health professional. The Bush Essences can certainly help with mild depression and will support medical treatment for the more severe forms of the disease.

Essences to consider for depression include the following.

Alpine Mint Bush is useful for animals who are carers, such as guide dogs, companion dogs, horses for the disabled or any animal who is continually in a situation where it has to virtually look after someone else. Like human carers, these animals can burn out if too much is demanded of them.

Dagger Hakea and **Mountain Devil** are good if an animal has been hurt or frightened but has been unable to express anger because of the fear of further punishment or it knows that the expression of anger would be seen as unacceptable.

Flannel Flower helps an animal respond to touch and gentle massage, and so helps the body produce endorphins and other pleasure producing hormones.

Illawarra Flame Tree is good where there are feelings of rejection.

Kapok Bush is for the animal that is apathetic and unresponsive to outside stimuli.

Little Flannel Flower can help an animal who is in low spirits to be more playful and joyful.

Mint Bush is useful where there has been a long period of prolonged confusion and chaos.

Pink Flannel Flower can bring joy and contentment, happiness and peace with the present situation.

Sturt Desert Pea helps with ongoing grief and deep hurt.

Waratah, Sunshine Wattle, Tall Yellow Top, Black-eyed Susan and **Red**

Grevillea are Essences used in a general formula for ongoing or severe depression.

Wild Potato Bush is useful where an animal is depressed because of restricted movement when it is ill or has sustained physical injury. It can be used with **Tall Yellow Top** for prolonged confinement in a cage, kennels or stables.

CATS AND ANXIETY

Although many cats can be completely relaxed and seemingly impervious to what is going on around them, they generally do not deal well with stress and can be very upset by change of any sort. Their inability to relax easily is particularly obvious in elderly cats. There is some research that suggests that many elderly cats eventually die as much from stress as from renal failure or other problems. A study done by Professor Ben Hart of the University of California indicates that, at a hormonal level, old cats have trouble turning off their stress response. Death is sometimes caused by an excess of gluco-corticoids, the stress hormones produced by the adrenal glands. If we can relieve their stress then we can improve their well-being and, in theory at least, ultimately increase their healthy life span.

Emergency Essence is always a remedy to consider when an animal is stressed or overly anxious short term. But if the anxiety goes on for a long time then other Essences should be considered.

Black-eyed Susan will help an animal who is normally very active to relax.

Bottlebrush and **Bauhinia** can help the cat adapt to change and to be open to doing things differently.

Calm and **Clear Essence** given orally or as a mist sprayed around the animal's living and sleeping area will help create a calm environment.

Macrocarpa or **Dynamis Essence** would help to energetically balance the adrenals.

Pink Flannel Flower can engender a sense of deep, inner peace.

TREATING THE WHOLE FAMILY

Animals often refect the emotional or physical problems of their owner or family. There are times when both animal and human will develop similar physical symptoms. Western Australian vet Clare Middle tells the story of one of her clients, an elderly dog and his elderly master, who both had cartilage problems in their knees. There have been cases where an animal would not heal completely until its owner had recovered. Situations even arise where problems diagnosed in a pet have consequently been uncovered in a member of the owner's family. Vets occasionally find that they need to treat animal and owner together, as a unit, and so there will be times when a Flower Essence practitioner will need to treat the whole family – human and animal – not just for emotional or behavioural problems but sometimes also for associated physical disease.

The way in which the different animals within a household interact with each other will affect how they behave and how they feel. It is good to be able to treat them all at the same time if there is any disharmony. By talking to the owner about the animal and also about what is going on with other family members, it is often possible to gain a broad picture of the situation and identify the problem and how it is affecting animals and humans alike. It is wise to always keep in mind the possibility that there might be much more to any animal's problems than just its presenting symptoms.

Bush Fuchsia, taken by animal and owner (and practitioner), can assist in getting to the bottom of the problem by helping them all access their intuition, and by improving communications.

Green Spider Orchid will improve non-verbal communication.

Yellow Cowslip Orchid taken by the practitioner could help her to see the broader picture.

If the animal is taking on the worries of the family and this is a problem, then think of the following.

Alpine Mint Bush is especially useful if the animal appears to be in danger of burning out.

Crowea will help the animal who is a worrier.

Flannel Flower and/or **Sturt Desert Rose** are for establishing healthy boundaries; they would help the animal let go of its need to be over-responsible for his family members.

Fringed Violet will prevent the animal taking on the energy of others.

Old Man Banksia can help if the caring for the family is becoming a burden.

If on the other hand an animal and its family are happy with the animal's role as family carer then consider the following.

Relationship Essence or **Bush Gardenia** could help to deepen and strengthen the relationship.

Slender Rice Flower will increase group harmony within the family.

Chapter 7

RESOLVING BEHAVIOURAL PROBLEMS

When a man wants to murder a tiger he calls it sport;
when the tiger wants to murder him he calls it ferocity.

GEORGE BERNARD SHAW, 1856–1950

Any animal living in domestication has to learn how to live with humans and to adapt to their environment. With proper care and training most animals will settle in well with their human family and bring them great pleasure. However, behavioural problems in domesticated animals can and do occur. Quite often, what we see as bad behaviour can simply be an activity that we are not comfortable with but which might be perfectly natural for the animal. Marking and defending territory are obvious examples. Challenging for position of leader of the pack is another. Overt sexual behaviour of their pet can be intensely embarrassing to some people. By recognising what is in fact natural behaviour it is possible to come to terms with that behaviour and, if it is not appropriate in the domestic situation, find ways to work with the animal's natural instincts so as to remedy it. Understanding the factors involved is the first step towards dealing with behavioural

problems, and using appropriate Bush Essences with the animal, and sometimes the carer, can be the next.

An interesting case of using the Essences to moderate the natural behaviour of an animal comes from Bush Essence practitioner Jeni Pollak.

'I have some Siamese Fighting Fish. These fish are well known for their colourful flowing fins and also their serious aggression to their own kind. They are extremely territorial and when I put a new female in the tank she immediately started attacking one of my females with a ferocity I have never seen, not in fish anyway. I quickly put seven drops of **Slender Rice Flower** *(stock) into the tank and within ten minutes everyone was swimming around happily and we haven't had any major scraps since.'*

One of the qualities of **Slender Rice Flower** is that it helps to engender harmony within a group of people or animals, in this case the fighting fish.

Negative experiences encountered when an animal is very young can often lead to poor behavioural patterns in adulthood. The story is from Peter Mandregin of The Pinnacles, New South Wales, about a cat called Thomas.

'I was to look after a friend's house while she went on holidays. She had a cat named Thomas who, as a kitten was rescued from physical abuse (used as a football). The only way I could describe Thomas is that he seemed to be possessed. His eyes would change, then he would leap up and grab you with his claws and teeth, he would draw blood every time. He was a cat you could not cuddle and he did not come inside. Then the time came for Thomas and me to live alone together while I house-sat. Each morning and night I would warm some milk for him and add seven drops of **Crowea** *(which is for engendering peace and calm and bringing about emotional balance). After about five days I could pat and cuddle Thomas and he no longer made pin cushions of my legs. There is a nice side issue to this story. There was a stray cat around at that time. It was wild and I only saw it occasionally when it came in to drink milk left over by Thomas – the milk to which the* **Crowea** *had been added. This cat also became quite friendly and was eventually taken in by one of my neighbours as a pet.'*

EARLY CONTACT

An animal that is orphaned at a very young age can suffer from grief at the loss of its mother and its litter mates. More importantly, it misses the natural mothering – the touching, closeness, disciplining and general basic education – that a mother and, in some cases, other members of the social group would give. Good care from a foster mother, be it human or another animal, will help to overcome these problems but if the young animal is left to fend for itself it can be quite wild and difficult to manage, if it survives.

The young of wild animals, including urban strays, will remain wary of human contact unless they have regular interaction with people almost from birth. Even animals raised by top quality breeders can miss out on this essential handling. They may have received excellent physical care but lack ongoing touching, play and 'conversation' with their carers. Their brains do not develop the neural pathways that bond them to humans and to other animals. A young kitten brought up in a family that has dogs and other animals will accept those animals without question. However, an adult cat brought into a similar family will find it much harder to assimilate unless it has had contact with other animals earlier in its life. Anybody who has raised a pet lamb knows how different the pet animal is from a sheep of a similar age raised in the flock. The pet will respond positively to the touch and voice of its owner, and even the family dog. However, a flock-reared animal will run in fear if approached by a human or canine. Firm, gentle loving care from birth, with much touching, communication and socialising, is an important factor in instilling cooperative behaviour in any animal.

Bush Fuchsia can support animals that have missed out on early nurturing, by helping to develop new neural pathways.

Emergency Essence is good for dealing with the fear and trauma of first human contact.

Flannel Flower can help by increasing the enjoyment of touch.

Kangaroo Paw helps to remedy inappropriate conduct.

Rough Bluebell will help if the animal's behaviour is hurtful and manipulative.

Lilly was a horse that obviously lacked that early gentle touch.

'She was a three year old filly. As a result of prior treatment she had no trust in humans at all. She was hard to catch, cranky when being handled and very aggressive with her hind legs. After ten months she did no more than tolerate my touching her. She was obedient, but resentfully so, and even when I fed her she would avoid my hand when I tried to stroke her, rigidly pulling back onto the barriers. She was very nasty to two horses in her paddock – biting and kicking out at them for no apparent reason. **Flannel Flower** *changed her attitude within three days. She softened. After one week she rubbed her cheek against my shoulder. To the uninitiated, this is a gesture of affection and I regarded it as a major breakthrough. Five days later she voluntarily walked into the feed shed – a place she had never ventured into before. Since then Lilly has made rapid progress initiating physical contact with me, becoming more gentle towards the other horses and relaxing remarkably in her hindquarters. Yesterday she rested her chin against my chest allowing me to take the weight of her head and today when I was grooming another of my horses she approached me for her brushing, standing untethered while I ran the brush over her body and even following me for more when I had finished. In short Lilly is a different horse from the one she was six weeks ago.'* – Linda Clancy, Goulburn, New South Wales

TRUST AND REJECTION

Some animals that have come from pet shops can have difficulty settling into a new home, particularly if they have been left in the shop for an extended period. After suffering the initial shock of being removed from their mother they may then be left in a small cage with minimum contact with people for days or weeks. This type of treatment can traumatise an animal and leave it very confused about who it can trust and what is normal. Also, some animals endure cruelty either from restricted mobility, poor sanitation or rough handling by owners and customers. Obviously there are many good pet shop owners who give their animals the care and attention that they need, but the possibility of this experience contributing to poor animal behaviour needs to be taken into account.

Another cause of inappropriate behaviour is rejection. A breeder who feels that an animal is not good enough and who talks about this in front of the young animal, treating it as a lesser being, may inadvertently harm the animal's self-esteem. A young animal might not understand the words but it can understand the vocal expression and the body language. Rejection can also be experienced when a family takes in an animal but finds that it can't cope or just doesn't like the animal, and subsequently sends it back. This is most likely to happen with animals that come from animal shelters or adoption agencies and it can traumatise the animal. It may have already been rejected by its first owners, and then the adoption agency, and then the second family and so on. Some go to many homes before they are finally settled. They get to the stage of expecting rejection and not trusting or bonding with anyone. Many such animals become very aloof.

Bluebell, **Mountain Devil** and **Tall Mulla Mulla** are Essences that could help build up trust in such animals and help them to interact confidently with those around them.

Illawarra Flame Tree will assist in dealing with feelings of rejection.

After the devastating bushfires in Canberra, Australia in the summer of 2002, many animals became separated from their carers. One such animal was a three month old kitten named Ani. She was found abandoned in the street and was taken home by Christine Cobden, a Flower Essence practitioner.

'We already had an older male cat called Monty. He is a very easy going animal who loves food and is very peaceful and affectionate. From the moment she entered the household Ani made Monty's life miserable by continually attacking him and beating him up. The old cat was completely bewildered by this treatment. Ani gave him no peace; she was not respecting him at all. I decided to give her **Gymea Lily** *to help her deal with her need to be centre stage and to awaken her humility. After only one dose she retreated into a cupboard – an over reaction – but her behaviour improved and harmony reigned for a while. Then she started beating up Monty again. She would ambush him on every possible occasion, leaping on him and really giving him a bad time. If any member of the family gave Monty attention she attacked him and demanded attention for herself. I selected a Flower Essence Insight Card for her. It was* **Christmas Bell**. *I feel that this Essence helps where an animal has been relocated and feels a sense of lack. Ani was originally abandoned and was scared of losing her family again.* **Christmas Bell** *helped her know that there was no lack. After four doses I found her and Monty curled up together. I called the family in and we all made a fuss of her, rejoicing in her new behaviour and praising her. She felt that she had a family again. She responded very positively to this and has been a changed cat ever since.'*

Bluebell is another Essence that can be used where an animal believes that there might not be enough love to go around.

OTHER CAUSES OF BEHAVIOURAL PROBLEMS

Poor handling and lack of good training by the current or previous owner are other common causes of behavioural problems. If an owner or trainer does not make clear who is boss, is not firm, consistent and kind in handling the animal, and does not understand how it thinks and feels, then such an animal will become disobedient, destructive and difficult to manage.

Other matters to consider when dealing with behavioural problems include the age of the animal and the state of its physical health and the possibility of sexual frustration.

Diet is another factor that can have a big effect on an animal's behaviour. You can bring about quite amazing changes by altering the type of food that you offer to the animal. There is much evidence that dogs fed a diet of raw or freshly cooked meat and vegetables and uncooked bones, with added fish oil or other omega 3 oils, are much healthier and better-behaved than animals on dried or canned foods. A recent book by Beth Taylor and Steve Brown, *See Spot Live Longer*, discusses this matter in some depth.

If any animal in your charge shows ongoing unacceptable behaviour you should have it checked by an animal health or behaviour professional, to identify any physical, emotional and mental problem that might be involved. There are many Bush Essences which, along with informed handling techniques, can bring about positive changes in your pet.

Bluebell will help an animal to be open to giving and receiving love.

Boab breaks down patterns of unacceptable behaviour that come down the genetic line.

Calm & Clear Essence, either as a mist or drops, could help to calm any agitated situation.

Calm & Clear Essence or **Emergency Essence Mists** can be sprayed around animals that are fighting.

Confid Essence and/or **Five Corners** help to build the confidence of the animal and the owner.

Dog Rose of the Wild Forces can prevent an animal taking on the disturbed emotions of its owners, other animals, or agitated situations.

Emergency Essence is the first remedy to consider when dealing with behavioural problems. The owner could benefit from taking this, as well as the animal.

Flannel Flower is very soothing and can support the animal's ability to respond quietly to people and situations, and to accept gentle touch and handling.

Fringed Violet will protect the animal from negative energy picked up from its family or other situations.

Green Spider Orchid will improve communications when an owner is explaining to an animal what is going on, and so help it cope better.

Kangaroo Paw will remedy immature or inappropriate behaviour.

Mountain Devil or **Dagger Hakea** can help with jealousy or aggressiveness.

Pink Mulla Mulla helps overcome lack of trust based on the anticipation of repetition of a past hurt.

Red Helmet Orchid will help an animal accept the authority of the owner.

Rough Bluebell can be useful if an animal is deliberately controlling in its behaviour.

Space Clearing Essence Mist can bring about great improvement where an animal is spooked by a particular place. Spray it around the area that bothers the animal to clear negative or unwanted energies.

Sturt Desert Pea will help an animal process hurt and pain which goes a long way back in its life.

Any of the Essences for fear mentioned in Chapter 5 can be considered when dealing with behavioural problems.

> *'A de-sexed tom cat, a much loved member of the household, had taken to disrupting anything and everything from 2 am onwards. He was six years old, weighed 8 kg and was in excellent health, as his shiny black coat confirmed. The disruptive behaviour started shortly after the couple who owned him began studying for their degrees. His regular schedule had become totally disjointed by owners rising at any hour from 2.45 am onwards to study. Anywhere from 12 pm on the cat had taken to waking any sleepers, swinging from the tapestries, playing with the telephone cord or pulling all the books off the bookshelf. The Essence chosen for this problem was* **Red Helmet Orchid** *for rebelliousness. By testing with kinesiology, using a surrogate, it was decided to administer seven drops twice a day for three days. Placing the drops in his mouth was stressful and so the drops were added to the food and he consumed them happily. By the second morning things were calmer and by the third morning peace reigned. The cat remained calmly on the bed until the owners rose to study. Then he was quietly roaming the house until food bowls were rattled at 4.30 am. Books remained on shelves and tapestries remained straight. After two months the disruptive behaviour began again but milder than before. After testing, seven drops were given for three doses and calm returned.'* – Angella Cowley, Tanawha, Queensland

SOME SPECIFIC BEHAVIOURAL PROBLEMS

Adolescent behavioural problems

Although much is written about adolescence in humans, the similar 'teenage' period in animals is often ignored. However, there is a definite period as an animal is moving into adulthood where problems can arise in its behaviour. At this stage the playful and reasonably obedient young animal might suddenly start to defy its owner, often ignoring verbal commands. Male dogs in particular can be very toey as their hormones kick in, and can become aggressive to other dogs and to their human companions. This is not an animal going 'bad' but rather an adolescent testing the power structure of the household and vying for the position of leader. It is important for the owner to re-enforce their own position as the 'head of the pack' and firmly put the young animal in its place. Getting angry or punishing it after the event does more harm than good. It is much better to tighten the rules, insisting on obedience to all commands and avoiding situations where the animal is free to go its own way. Additional professional training at this stage could be a great help. If the problem continues it would be wise to check with a vet to ensure that there are no physical or psychological problems that are causing the animal to behave badly. There are various Bush Essences which ease this transition to adulthood.

Adol Essence is the obvious one to consider. Originally designed for use with human adolescents, it is equally helpful for animals going through a similar stage of development.

Calm & Clear Essence will help create a calm environment for owner and animal.

Emergency Essence is good for both owner and animal when behaviour of the animal is proving stressful.

Five Corners or **Confid Essence** for the owner could also help. Being defied or threatened by your own animal can be scary, particularly if it is big or aggressive. Added confidence in the owner can improve animal handling ability.

Mountain Devil is for anger and aggression.

Red Helmet Orchid helps where an animal rebels against the owner's authority.

Aggressive behaviour

Virtually all animals have some aggressive tendencies. Jumping ants and piranha fish attack with a ferocity that seems way out of proportion to any threat to their lives. In the breeding season the normally friendly male Australian Magpie swoops and sometimes attacks anyone it sees as a threat to its nest. In his book *On Aggression*, Konrad Lorenz proposed that aggression is one of the four main drives in animals – the others being hunger, reproduction and fear. He believed that the function of aggression was to balance the distribution of the species, to select the strongest, and to defend the young. He proposed that aggression was good for the survival of the species and that female animals will choose aggressive males as mates because they will better defend their territory and their young.

In the wild, animals jostle for the position of leader, and to protect territory, guard young, secure food and defend themselves and their family from attack and injury. Carnivores show most aggression in their search for food. Most have to kill to eat and even the scavengers have to be aggressive to get their share of the kills of other animals. Herbivores will kick and bite on occasion, sometimes doing serious damage. The degree of aggression and the amount of time when it is obviously displayed varies greatly between species and their place in nature. In domestication, those instincts still remain and will sometimes be triggered by external events.

The behaviour of individual animals will vary according to personality, training and environment as well as their physical and psychological health. Any animal needs a social structure that will enable it to live peacefully and without dangerous aggression. If this social organisation is disturbed or completely missing then destructive violence, as distinct from beneficial aggressive behaviour, can result. A mixed group of baboons in London Zoo, who did not come from the same 'tribe', had no social structure and fought continually and destructively. On the contrary, when baboons in the wild fight, they do this in a more controlled way with a definite dominance order.

Aggression in an animal always has a cause. Good training can help to deal with this problem but it is also important to have a basic understanding of the contributing factors. These include:

- cruelty by owners or other people
- aggression from other animals
- apprehension about the repeat of traumatic incidents, previously experienced pain or fear of pain
- an owner who won't or can't move into the role of leader
- excessive timidity
- sudden loud noise or other disturbance which can terrify animals so that they can behave aggressively to escape the perceived threat
- the arrival of a human baby or another new family member in the house. Lone parrots can become very aggressive to what they perceive as a threat to their exclusive relationship with their owner
- defence of family or family property can bring out aggression in some animals
- irritation in old animals who may growl, scratch, kick or bite simply to protect themselves because of tiredness or painful body parts
- injury or trauma may lead an animal to become aggressive to protect itself from further pain or injury
- a female animal that has recently given birth will aggressively defend her offspring
- many male animals behave aggressively in the breeding season. If an animal is not going to be used for breeding, it is probably kinder to have him de-sexed
- allergies caused by wrong diet can bring out aggression in some animals
- animals such as fighting bulls, guard dogs and fighting cocks have been bred for their aggressive characteristics

- more rarely, a genetic fault or some brain or nervous disorder or injury makes the animal unreasonably aggressive.

An aggressive animal is not acceptable as a pet. We must deal with any aggressive tendencies that arise so that our animals will fit comfortably into human society. Careful selection of a pet, good training and ongoing caring will help avoid many of these problems. But if some aggressive behaviour does occur there are many Bush Essences which can bring about positive changes in an animal in conjunction with support training and behavioural therapy. It is possible to solve the problem by dealing with the emotional factors behind it. In crisis situations however, the aggression needs to be dealt with immediately and the causes worked on once the crisis has passed. **Emergency Essence** will always help to some degree, given to animal and human.

Never take aggressive behaviour in an animal lightly. Aggression in any animal can be dangerous. If it is ongoing, get professional help.

Vicki Rodgers from Western Australia had a worrying experience with her dogs.

'I have three dogs, a Poodle, a Maltese Terrier cross and a Siberian Husky. From the moment the Husky arrived in the house he attacked the Poodle; it was as though he considered the Poodle irrelevant. I had to keep the two dogs separated. However, one day the Husky got to the Poodle and attacked him so viciously that the Poodle went into shock. He was standing head down, hardly breathing. I gave **Emergency Essence** *in the mouth and the dog took a deep breath and everything started to work again. However, the animal was still in shock so I took him to the vet. I drove while my son sat with the dog in the back of the car. Half way down, the dog almost stopped breathing again. We gave him more* **Emergency Essence** *and again there was this kick start of a deep sigh and then breathing returned to a more normal pattern. When we got him to the vet he was put on a drip but it was the* **Emergency Essence** *which kept him alive till we got there. He subsequently recovered. I then muscle tested for all three dogs and made up a mix of Essences to give to them all to help them get on better together. Since then there have been distinct behavioural changes for the better between the Husky and the Poodle.'*

Many of the Essences suggested earlier for dealing with behavioural problems can be used with an aggressive animal but there are some Essences specifically for aggressive behaviour.

Flannel Flower and **Wisteria** can be considered for gentling a male animal.

Isopogon or **Gymea Lily** help where an animal is overly dominating.

Mountain Devil is *the* Essence to use where there is jealousy, anger and aggression.

Rough Bluebell is useful where the animal is manipulative or destructive. It can also be considered if there could be damage to the front part of the brain from an accident or disease.

Ludwig, a two-year-old desexed male Affenpinscher, responded well to the Essences prescribed for his aggressive behaviour.

*'As a breed, these dogs tend to be devoted to their owners but are disinterested in casual strangers. However, Ludwig began to display extremely aggressive tendencies towards strangers, even biting a well-meaning hand held out for a sniff. I could see there was no physical pain involved with the aggression and I found that his mother had also been aggressive while his father had been more friendly. I felt he lacked confidence and was really frightened by unfamiliar people. I made up a combination of **Dog Rose** and **Grey Spider Flower** for the fear, and **Boab** to break the family pattern. By the eighth day Ludwig still barked at a stranger but his attitude lacked the terror of his earlier reaction to visitors and he continued to improve. With his second bottle I wanted to calm him more and build up his self confidence. I also wanted to improve his ability to interact with invited guests and increase his trust. I felt that he needed to be more open to change. So I selected **Bauhinia**, **Flannel Flower**, **Freshwater Mangrove**, **Pink Mulla Mulla** and **Tall Mulla Mulla**. He became more accepting of people coming into the home, allowing them to pat him, even allowing one guest to hold him on her lap!'*
– Kerry Wyburd, Glenbrook, New South Wales

Boredom

If animals are going to be left alone for long periods, boredom can become a serious problem. It can be eased by having a variety of activities available but there are also Essences which will help a bored animal.

Dynamis Essence will encourage activity and help to overcome lack of energy and enthusiasm.

Illawarra Flame Tree will help if the animal feels a sense of rejection each time it is left alone.

Kangaroo Paw is good if the animal is destructive when bored. It helps reduce anti-social behaviour.

Kapok Bush helps where there is general apathy or lack of interest in life.

Little Flannel Flower is the Essence to engender a sense of fun, playfulness and joy.

Pink Flannel Flower can help an animal accept and enjoy its current situation and environment, whatever it is.

Peach-flowered Tea-tree helps to maintain interest in what is available for the animal to do.

Tall Yellow Top helps to deal with the feeling of being abandoned and alone.

Cruelty

Animals that have experienced cruelty before coming to you need special care. They are carrying a huge amount of emotional baggage as well as loss of faith and trust in human beings.

Emergency Essence or **Fringed Violet** and **Angelsword** should be the first Essences to consider with such animals, to clear the old or recent trauma and to re-vitalise the energy fields.

Little Flannel Flower can help the animal enjoy life instead of always being on the defensive.

Pink Mulla Mulla will help remove the apprehension of an old hurt occurring again.

Red Suva Frangipani will help if the cruelty is very recent.

Sunshine Wattle gives hope of a brighter future.

Sydney Rose and **Bluebell**, Essences for love, will help any animal who has suffered cruelty.

Waratah and **Bush Iris**, Essences for trust, could also help, as would Essences for fear, anger, confidence, touch and adapting to change, which are mentioned elsewhere.

Obsessive behaviour

Stressed, anxious, bored or grieving animals can occasionally indulge in obsessive behaviour. They may continually groom themselves, chew paws or lick skin till it is raw. Some pace up and down incessantly or become so attached to an object that they will never let it out of their sight. Crib-biting, wind-sucking and swaying can become chronic behaviour patterns in some horses. Dogs may chase their tails or continually snap at imaginary flies. In many animals such behaviour is just a habit they have slipped into but it can also be a symptom of an emotional or neurological problem and if it persists should be properly diagnosed and treated. Luckily there are several Essences that can help break an obsessive habit.

Boronia helps break obsessive behaviour patterns and would be the first Essence to consider.

Bauhinia and **Freshwater Mangrove** will help an animal to be open to new ways of doing things and could help if the animal is insistent on always doing something the same way.

Bottlebrush is for helping to let go of something that is no longer needed.

Monga Waratah will give the animal courage to get on with life without the support of its obsessive behaviours.

Spraying to defend territory

This is not only a problem with cats. Any animals that are territorial will mark their territory in some way. It usually only becomes a problem if their living space is too small or poorly designed or if another animal is introduced or comes uninvited into what is their personal domain. Reorganising the areas in which the animals live can allow each animal the space it needs to not feel threatened. Sometimes, however, an adult cat will never settle in a home with other cats and the only option is to adopt it out to another family with no cats. Neighbouring cats coming through cat doors is a common problem in city living and cats can become extremely stressed if stray animals repeatedly invade their space. It is worthwhile taking this into account if a cat suddenly starts spraying in the house. Trapping and relocating stray animals is often the first step to take in dealing with this situation. Having a male animal de-sexed can often remedy excessive territorial behaviour but it is not the complete answer and, of course, can create new trauma of its own. Addressing the emotional problems that are behind any spraying, urinating or defaecating in inappropriate places is crucial to solving the problem. Essences to consider for animals that are overly defensive of their home territory include the following.

Confid Essence or **Five Corners** is useful for building the animal's confidence and can improve the situation.

Flannel Flower and **Sturt Desert Rose** for setting healthy boundaries can help the animal come to terms with the limits of its own territory and adapt to the space needed by any new family animals.

Kangaroo Paw is for inappropriate behaviour generally, and spraying in the house is certainly not acceptable.

Slender Rice Flower for group harmony is another Essence to consider in assisting the resident animal to accept any new animal into the household.

Some of the Essences for fear can also help if the animal is obviously fearful.

Stubbornness
Some animals have very strong views on what they will and won't do. In older animals, stubbornness is particularly prevalent. Obviously, this is partly due to their personality, but if it becomes a problem then there are some Essences that will help.

Bauhinia can help overcome a resistance to embracing new ideas and different ways of doing things.

Freshwater Mangrove will open an animal to trying something new.

Isopogon will help if an animal is trying to control its carers, but with no malice present.

Rough Bluebell is for the animal who is deliberately trying to manipulate its owner by its stubborn behaviour.

Treating animals as humans
If we treat our animals as though they are humans, feeding them what we eat and generally treating them as a pampered child, the animal will become confused about its position. This can create behavioural problems. The dog or cat may become demanding or destructive if it doesn't always get its own way, and jealous of other household members or visitors. Also, many of the foodstuffs that are good for us are not necessarily good for our animals. Incorrect diet can lead to overweight and diabetic animals, and if we happen to be lounge lizards and encourage this in our pets, then lack of regular exercise can contribute to health and behavioural problems.

Dynamis Essence for both carer and animal will help if they are lacking in energy.

Flannel Flower and **Sturt Desert Rose** could be good for the owner and animal, so they can establish healthy emotional boundaries.

Suggested Essences for other specific behavioural problems are listed in the Repertory of Symptoms on page 149.

Chapter 8

GRIEVING and LOVE

I had bought two male chimps from a primate colony in Holland.
They lived next to each other in separate cages for several months
before I used one as a [heart] donor. When we put him to sleep
in his cage in preparation for the operation, he chattered and cried
incessantly. We attached no significance to this, but it must have
made a great impression on his companion, for when we removed the
body to the operating room, the other chimp wept bitterly and was
inconsolable for days. The incident made a deep impression on me.
I vowed never again to experiment with such sensitive creatures.

CHRISTIAN BARNARD, HEART SURGEON, 1922–2001

GRIEVING

All animals grieve to some degree over loss. While they may mourn differently from the way humans mourn, there will certainly be some behavioural changes as they make adjustments to the gap that the loss has created in their lives. Most animals will come to terms with such change in a short time, but the death of a family member, change of residence, loss of a role in life and certainly a change of ownership can result in quite serious grieving. Some will slide into depression, stop eating and grooming themselves, and generally lose interest in life. Animals have been known to lose the will to live and to die from grief. In an article found on the Messy Beast website Sarah Hartwell tells the story of a pair of cats who were put in a shelter when their owner had died.

'The cats refused to eat while in the shelter. To reduce stress, they were fostered in a household and the vet prescribed appetite stimulants. One cat recovered but remained withdrawn for a long period of time. The other continued to pine and became critically ill until it had to be euthanised (prolonged fasting results in liver damage.) Its behaviour was so severely affected that the foster carer considered force-feeding unsuitable; the cat had no interest in life. Post mortem showed no sign of disease except for that caused by failure to eat.'

It seems that this cat died of grief.

There are many stories of dogs grieving over the death of their owner or an animal member of the family. Probably the most famous of these is the story of Greyfriars Bobby. This version of the story was recorded in Wikipedia.

'Bobby was a Skye Terrier dog that became famous in nineteenth century Edinburgh, Scotland. Bobby's owner John Gray was a policeman who died in 1858 and was buried in Greyfriars Kirkyard, the cemetery surrounding Greyfriars Kirk in the Old Town of Edinburgh. Bobby, who survived John by more than a decade, is said to have spent the rest of his life sitting on his master's grave. A more realistic account has it that he spent a great deal of time at Gray's grave, but that he left regularly for meals at a restaurant beside the graveyard and may have spent colder winters in nearby houses. In 1867, when it was pointed out that an un-owned dog should be put down, the Lord Provost of Edinburgh, Sir William Chambers (who was also a director of the Scottish Society for the Prevention of Cruelty to Animals), paid for a renewal of Bobby's license making him the responsibility of the city council. While Bobby himself could not be buried in the cemetery proper, since it was consecrated ground, he was buried just inside the gate of Greyfriars Kirkyard, not far from John Gray's grave.'

There are some well documented stories about wild animals going through specific death rituals for one of their kind. These rituals have many of the characteristics of a grieving process. Elephants have been seen to stay with a dying animal until it has died. McBride and Berrill, in their book *Animal Families*, record the story of a herd observed in the Serengeti National Park in Tanzania. These animals expressed concern and grief to an extent seldom seen among animals. The dying elephant stood apart, anxiously watched by the rest of the herd. When she finally collapsed the rest of the elephants screamed and trumpeted, hurrying to her side. The bull even tried to raise her and put grass into her mouth but all in vain. *'The death throes of this elephant produced not just distress in its herd-mates, but a frenzy of shrieks and the kind of helpless fury that is sometimes seen in hospitals when a bereaved human being is suddenly confronted with death.'* Throughout the rest of the day the bull repeatedly laid his trunk on the body of the dead cow and tried to rouse her. And one by one the family units, each led by a large cow, returned to the body to trumpet and sniff. Finally in the late afternoon, the herd shuffled away. For animals in the wild, grief is a natural cycle. They process it and move on. They live in the moment.

Farm animals also appear to grieve for community members who have died. In the book *Smarter than Jack*, Gia Toovey tells the story about cows in a paddock in Victoria. She noticed that there was a dead cow some distance away. About 15–20 other cows were forming a tight circle around the dead cow. They were preventing the young calves, which were obviously curious, from entering the circle by closing ranks and mooing at them. Once the circle was tightly formed, with all the cattle facing inward towards the dead one, the bull moved to the dead cow. He looked, smelt and circled round it before resuming his position in the circle. One by one the cows then moved forward and did the same, each resuming her position in the circle. This continued until all the cows had gone through the procedure, all the while keeping the calves at a distance. This took about an hour. They all then walked away slowly at which time the calves had a quick look and a sniff and left also. Whether this was in fact grieving or part of the grazing animals' natural instinct to protect a weak animal is not clear. But as with the elephants, once they had acknowledged the death then they left the dead animal, accepting the situation and moving on.

Most cows bellow for several hours after having their calves taken away, but a story from Scottish vet and author James Herriot tells of a dairy cow who took this a step further. This cow's previous five calves had been removed soon after birth. When the sixth one was born she left it in a grassy ditch and returned to the barn without it. The farmer didn't even know she had calved until the vet did an internal examination. When the calf was eventually found the cow gently nudged it back into the ditch as it tried to join her. She certainly appeared to be hiding it. Was this animal anticipating the repeat of a previous loss? **Pink Mulla Mulla** could have helped her as it removes the fear of facing something that has happened previously and is likely to occur again. Maybe there are times when an animal owner might break with normal farm practice and allow an animal to keep its young beyond the usual time. **Bauhinia** for flexibility or **Hibbertia** for moving from head to heart could help the owner make a decision like this. Many 'normal' or acceptable animal husbandry practices can deeply influence some animals emotionally. It can be worthwhile talking to the animal, using **Green Spider Orchid** and **Bush Fuchsia**, and then deciding what will be the best action.

The level of anxiety an animal experiences when it is grieving varies with personality and situation. Dr K Houpt DVM PhD, physiologist and animal behaviourist from Cornell University, records that there is a big variability in the way any two horses will react to separation. Some hardly seem affected by the loss of a herd mate but others bond very closely and if one dies or moves away then the one left behind can become very upset and slip into serious depression. He feels that if a horse dies then the other members of the 'herd' should spend some time with the dead animal. If this is done then the 'grief response' seems to be less and the time taken to return to near normal behaviour much shorter. Bruce Fogel, in his book *Natural Cat Care*, supports this thinking. *'When an animal death occurs, whenever possible let the survivor see and scent the body of the recently deceased animal.'* He also believes that in the weeks following the death of a family member it is important to give remaining animal(s) greater attention and increased activity.

Death of an owner

Although much has been written about the grief an owner experiences upon the loss of a loved animal, there is very little about how an animal feels upon the death or separation from its owner. Some recent research in this area has been done by animal behaviourist Dr Sharon Crowell-Davis at the University of Georgia, using PET scans to measure brain activity in humans and animals. She used various stimuli to induce a number of different emotions, including grief, in her test subjects and she has found that the pattern of brain activity for each emotion stimulated was the same in both humans and animals, and that the brain chemistry was also identical. She felt it logical to assume that both were experiencing similar feelings. She also came to believe from her research that horses had a real concept of death.

Animal Communicator Caroline Pope from Victoria has come across several horses that were grieving after the death of their owner.

'One horse I met only briefly a few years ago. I commented on his beautiful condition and his owners said, "You should have seen him a few years ago". Apparently this horse was owned and very much loved by an elderly but very active lady. She died whilst riding the horse (of a stroke I think). While the estate was being wrapped up the horse was left in his paddock and cared for by neighbours. The horse dropped a considerable amount of weight and condition, and although the vet was called he couldn't find a reason for the horse's decline. He suspected it was grief, as he knew the strong bond that had existed between the horse and its rider. A clairvoyant medium, who knew the dead woman's family, received a message in the middle of the night from the deceased owner of the horse (rather like Alison in "Medium") telling her where the horse had to go. She described the property well and told her that this was to be the new home for the horse. The family recognised the description of the property instantly – the owner had taken the horse there for riding lessons on a number of occasions.

The horse was loaded up and driven there the next day. It settled in well, but didn't put on weight, was still miserable and had now developed cancerous lesions where the saddle sits. He told an animal communicator that he blamed himself for his owner's death and wasn't ever going to allow that to happen to someone else. No one could ride him if the cancer was there. The new owners were wonderfully switched on people. They allowed the horse time to grieve, supported him emotionally and physically with herbs and Flower Essences (I'm not sure which ones) and simply gave him the time to work through his issues. The cancers receded with no further treatment. Eventually the horse was ridden again and has gone from strength to strength with his new family. He is truly a magnificent animal, with an incredibly close bond with the two people who now care for him.'

If an animal is obviously unhappy, listless or disinterested in what is going on around it after any change in its life, and if there seems to be no physical cause, consider the possibility of grief. Flower Essences to assist grieving can be given to the animal and also to the owners or carers. They include the following.

Bluebell will support the expression of feelings and coping with denial, maybe more for owner than animal, but many animals have also learned to suppress their emotions.

Boronia helps where there is pining for a person or animal who has died or from whom they have been separated.

Bottlebrush is for adapting to changes that death and separation inevitably bring.

Dagger Hakea dissolves anger that may arise around the death of, or separation from, a loved animal.

Emergency Essence will help get through the initial shock and hurt of a loss.

Little Flannel Flower can help bring back joy and child-like exuberance for life.

Red Suva Frangipani will help the raw emotions immediately after a death or separation.

Sturt Desert Pea is for ongoing, long term grieving.

Sturt Desert Rose can help if there is any guilt associated with the death or other loss.

Separation anxiety

Many animals suffer from separation anxiety when separated from their owner or other animals. Horses, however, are particularly prone to this problem. They can become very attached to another horse and become frantic when separated. It is natural behaviour in a herd animal in the wild – to stay with the herd no matter what. But with animals in domestication it can become a problem when a horse becomes seriously upset if taken away from the rest of the herd. Princess was a six year old riding pony who had a fear of being left alone. Her owner, Caroline Hamilton, felt that this was a consequence of her abrupt weaning from her mother and subsequently being left in a stable in which she could not see out.

*'When she came to me I paddocked her with another mare and a pony. Princess became very attached to the mare and fretted badly whenever the mare went out for a short spell. Princess was never quite relaxed, eyes always on the alert for something scary. Although her situation had changed for the better in that she had come to a more caring home, it was still a change and Princess needed support for this. Her constant timidity affected her eating which in turn had a detrimental effect on her whole health. It did not allow healing to take place. I wanted Princess to feel safe and secure and "at home". I wanted her to have enough of this feeling inside herself that she would continue to feel safe when the mare left the paddock. The Flower Essences I made up for Princess were **Waratah** for courage and **Dog Rose of the Wild Forces** for further confidence and courage. This Essence would also deal with the feeling of things going out of control. **Crowea** was included for worry and to help her acquire peace and calm. It was also for muscle repair, as Princess had an ongoing shoulder problem. **Tall Yellow Top** was added to deal with loneliness, for the sense of feeling at home. I felt that all four Essences complemented each other for what she needed. She was on this blend for two weeks and, with a regular routine, a calmer pony emerged and a lovely cheekiness began to develop in her personality. Seven months ago, the mare*

had to move away to a larger pasture due to drought conditions. I gave Princess the same blend of Essences again for about three weeks to help with any separation issues she might feel. She accepted the mare's departure with ease. Princess has now been off the drops for about six months. Her health is very good and she is certainly feeling at home.'

Cheering up a grieving household

When an animal is brought into a family to cheer up a grieving household after the loss of another animal or a family member it can take on the emotions of the family. An animal being cuddled by a crying or obviously very sad family member is receiving very confusing signals. Such an animal can become bewildered or even depressed by the reactions it is receiving from its new carer. Strong clear messages of love and acceptance from the family to the animal will help clear the bewilderment, as will the implementation of basic rules of behaviour for the animal. Such an animal can also sense the 'weak' energy in the household and may try to move into the role of leader with the problems that can be associated with this. It is not wrong to bring an animal into a home to help restore happiness. In fact some animals can work miracles in such a situation, but it can create emotional patterning which needs to be recognised. It can set up ways of behaving that can influence the future emotional and physical health of the animal. This is another reason why it is important for practitioners to carefully investigate the history of any animal they treat.

Fringed Violet will protect the animal from taking on the energies of the family.

Paw Paw given to the animal will ease feelings of confusion.

Red Helmet Orchid taken by animal and owner will clarify just who really is the boss.

Sydney Rose, taken by the family, will encourage unconditional love.

SOME THOUGHTS ABOUT LOVE

Because aggression, hatred, anger and jealously are the flip side of love, many of the Essences that help process these emotions also bring through the love vibration and can be used by animal and owner simply for that experience, even when no aggression or other anti-social behaviour is present.

The unconditional love that our animals need from us is more than the warm fuzzy feeling we experience when we sit with a favourite dog, watch a new foal stagger to its feet or pat a soft, purring cat. Love includes that feeling but it is much grander than that. It is a positive, completely supportive energy and also an act of will to work with that energy. It is trust and true forgiveness. It is just being there for an animal come what may. Unconditional love is not about giving them whatever they want whenever they want it, but rather accepting and enjoying them for being what and who they are. It is taking the responsibilities you agreed to take when they moved into your family, even when you are tired or when your animal is behaving badly. People and animals need love most when they are being unlovable! Animals have no trouble loving unconditionally but in times of great fear and trauma their instincts for survival can temporarily override, not their love, but their training as domesticated animals.

Having a much-loved animal can sometimes bring up dependent love in the owner, who can't bear the thought of having to live without the animal. The strong emotional need in such cases can be suffocating for the animal. A loving animal will always support its master or mistress emotionally and help them through difficult times, but long term it is not good for the animal to have a dependent 'leader'. What the animal needs is a reliable, consistent carer who loves it. Even a therapy or guide dog, while supporting its owner physically and emotionally, still needs strong, consistent leadership.

The following Essences help with issues relating to love.

Bluebell is for opening the heart to love, joy and sharing.

Dagger Hakea creates loving forgiveness and releases resentment.

Dog Rose helps to let go of fear and so let in love.

Five Corners can help with self love.

Flannel Flower helps to express love to others with words and through gentle touch.

Monga Waratah can help a dependent owner to stand alone and love their pet without expecting anything in return.

Mountain Devil and **Rough Bluebell** both bring through the love vibration as well as clearing anger and manipulative behaviour.

Pink Flannel Flower is about gratitude and acceptance for the present situation whatever it is. It creates a sense of deep peace and love.

Sydney Rose works on developing unconditional love and acceptance of people and animals as they are, without trying to make them into what we think they ought to be. It is *the* Essence for unconditional love.

Chapter 9

BREEDING and FERTILITY

A kitten is a rosebud in the garden of the animal kingdom.

ROBERT SOUTHEY, 1774–1843

BREEDING

Most mammals and birds care for their young until they are able to fend for themselves. The family group, whatever that may be, offers a natural sanctuary – a powerful, protective environment that enhances the infant's chances of survival. Many larger mammals stay within their family group for up to two years or even longer. The raising of lion cubs is shared by several of the females in the pride. Young male lions stay with the pride for up to three years, while females usually remain even as mature animals. A female Emu (*Dromaius novaehollandiae*) lays her eggs but leaves it to the male to incubate them and raise the young. He stays with them for around 18 months.

The Eastern Grey Kangaroo will often have a young joey at foot and a younger one in the pouch, with milk being provided from different teats at different strengths to suit the varying ages of her young offspring. She also carries a fertilised ovum within her body which stays in a quiescent stage until the current occupant of the pouch is ready to leave. Then it starts to grow and, while still at an embryonic stage, the animal is born and crawls up through her fur into the pouch where it continues its development. During this time the kangaroo and her young are associated with others of her species. There is much interaction between the younger animals and, as with most kangaroos, they are very gregarious.

With breeding animals, owners take on a range of new responsibilities and move into roles that would originally have been filled by the animal's family group. Carers also have to provide the food and health remedies that the animal would normally find for itself in the wild. In most cases, care even extends to finding it a mate.

Planning to breed from your animal

There are many things to consider if you plan to breed from a domesticated animal. You need to take into account the physical space available and the time and energy needed for dealing with the pregnancy, birth and subsequent care of the babies. It is important that you discuss the idea with other family members. You need to be honest with yourself about your commitment – physical, emotional and financial. You also need to consult with an animal health professional to ensure the animal is healthy and ready to be mated. It may help to try talking to your animal. You don't have to be a fully-fledged animal communicator to get an intuitive feeling for what it wants. Another factor is what to do with any potential offspring. Unless you are certain you can place them, it is unwise to consider breeding from your pet. It is far kinder to have your animal de-sexed than to produce unwanted animals.

Health and maturity of the mother

It is important that the mother animal is physically and emotionally mature. Be careful that any young female animal that comes into season before she is fully grown does not have access to males. Very young mothers often have birthing problems and are sometimes not sufficiently mature, either physically or emotionally, to be effective mothers. A young bitch may leave her young unattended and unfed, or suffocate them by lying on them. I had a Poodle/ Labrador cross who loved riding in the car. At little more than a year old she had just given birth to her first litter of puppies when she heard the car start. She leapt out of the birthing box and into the car without a thought for her very new pups. She eventually became a good mother but it was a rocky start.

Your pet must be healthy and happy before becoming pregnant. Make certain that she has the vaccinations or other protection from infectious diseases that she needs before she is mated, so she will pass some of that protection onto her babies. And ensure that the she is free of worms and on a healthy, nourishing diet. Get advice about any possible mineral supplements that might be needed.

Check that the male is also healthy and comes from a line of sound and well-behaved individuals, with no obvious genetic problems. If possible, inspect him and his parents to get an idea of the type of temperament that his offspring may inherit. Also, make sure that the male is of a similar size to the female. Big offspring from a small mother can result in birthing complications that may necessitate medical intervention.

Some female animals that are kept continually indoors will not come into season because they do not have sufficient exposure to sunlight. The pineal gland, that produces hormones which trigger the ovaries, is stimulated in many animals by the lengthening of the daylight hours. Research carried out by Patrick W. Concannon of Cornell University, with mares kept indoors over winter, has shown that they will come into season earlier if exposed to artificial lights. Chicken farmers use the same procedure to encourage their chickens to lay eggs over a longer period.

Making the experience a positive one

Animals that are being used for breeding and are being mated with unfamiliar animals in an unfamiliar environment can suffer from extreme stress and anxiety. Do what you can to make the experience a positive one and explain to your animal what is going on and that there is nothing fear.

There are many Bush Essences that can help with breeding.

Boab can help to clear negative genetic patterns or behaviours coming down through the family line.

Bush Fuchsia might be considered because it energetically supports the function of the hypothalamus which is associated with triggering hormone production. This is particularly helpful if the female animal has been on some form of contraceptive medication.

Bush Fuchsia and **Angelsword** together could help male and female animals who have had little contact with other animals of their own kind to identify with and respond to each other when they are brought together for mating.

Bush Iris works on the pineal gland and can help an indoor animal adjust its body rhythms despite the lack of regular exposure to sunlight.

Dynamis Essence helps to boost the energy of a lethargic or disinterested male.

Emergency Essence should always be on hand when animals are being mated, to deal with any trauma that may arise.

Five Corners or **Confid Essence** will increase an animal's confidence when placed with its mating partner.

Flannel Flower improves enjoyment of physical contact and energetically can help balance the hormones of a male animal who is an unsuccessful breeder.

Pink Flannel Flower enables the animal to accept the present situation, whatever it is.

Pink Mulla Mulla will help overcome the fear of repeating a previous bad mating experience.

Purifying Essence will help to cleanse the body of emotional and physical toxins before mating takes place.

Relationship Essence, given to both animals, could help improve their interaction.

She Oak energetically supports the ovaries and so helps balance the hormones in a female animal. If, after mating, the female does not become pregnant, think of putting her on a course of **She Oak** to help increase her fertility. Try a regime of four weeks on and two weeks off for several months.

Sensuality Essence Mist or **Calm & Clear Essence Mist** sprayed into the area could improve the atmosphere and enhance the animal's emotional state. Though keep in mind that the animal's natural pheromones are very important in their sexual interaction and the perfume of the essential oils in these two products could be counter-productive in this situation.

Sexuality Essence given to both animals could enhance sexual performance and also the enjoyment of the interaction.

Space Clearing Essence Mist will clear any agitated energies remaining from previous animals and people in the area where the animals mate.

For a sexually frustrated male animal, **Calm & Clear Essence** could calm down the whole situation, while **Wisteria** and **Flannel Flower** will balance the male hormones.

A female on heat can become very unsettled and unpredictable in her behaviour. Try **Calm & Clear Essence** in drops or mist to calm the animal. **Pink Flannel Flower** for acceptance of what is, rather than what might be, is certainly worth trying.

As ovulation is a natural process there are no Essences that will work as a contraceptive; however, individual Essences to deal with the particular behaviour of an animal could be used to settle the animal.

PREGNANCY

A pregnant animal is not a sick animal. Reproduction is a normal event of life and with nourishing food, a clean and healthy environment and exercise the mother animal normally moves through her pregnancy with ease. Even so, it is wise to have your vet check the animal during the pregnancy to rule out any health problems. This becomes essential if there is any indication of something amiss.

Numerous studies have shown that unborn animals, including humans, pick up on what is happening in their immediate surroundings. A Canadian orchestral conductor tells of his ability to recognise and play some pieces of music even though he had never seen the music before. He knew what was coming up in the cello line before he turned the page. When discussing this with his mother she un-covered the secret. She was a cello player herself and all the scores that he knew sight-unseen were those that she had played to him when she was pregnant.

Donald Shetler, a professor of music education at the University of Rochester, has studied the effect of music during pregnancy on human infant development. He believes that prenatal music may, in fact, give babies a head start. At the University of California, Marion Diamond, a neuroanatomist, placed pregnant rats in an environment with mazes and toys, to stimulate learning. The offspring of the mothers who had this experience while in utero had larger brains than the control animals raised in plain cages. They also had higher levels of neurotransmitters and an increase in connecting fibres between brain cells.

It seems that creating a nurturing, peaceful, but stimulating and loving environment around the mother during her pregnancy can be of benefit to the unborn animal as well as helping the mother herself.

Australian Bush Flower Essences can help support this natural process and will greatly enhance the magic of bringing new life into this world.

Bottlebrush will help the mother animal deal with the major transition in her life that pregnancy brings.

Calm & Clear Essence either as a mist or drops will create a peaceful environment.

Five Corners and **Dog Rose** will help the mother animal who is fearful or confused at what is going on, something most likely to happen towards the end of a first pregnancy.

Flannel Flower or **Relationship Essence** will enrich the relationship between carer and pregnant animal as you move into a supportive role.

Fringed Violet will protect the pregnant animal from taking on the energies of those around her particularly if they are engendering fear or anxiety.

Green Spider Orchid or **Meditation Essence** could be taken by the owner if she wants to try communicating with the unborn babies or their spirit beings.

Hibbertia, given towards the end of the pregnancy, could help keep the calcium levels balanced at the time of the birth and also while the mother is nursing, because of this Essence's energetic association with the parathyroid glands.

She Oak will assist in regulating the hormonal balance.

Sydney Rose engenders unconditional love so this would be a wonderful Essence for both animal and owners to take at any stage of the pregnancy.

Wild Potato Bush, given towards the end of pregnancy will address the sense of being burdened by the physical limitations of her body. Also, for the unborn young, it will greatly help with their physical restrictions within the womb before birth. Some practitioners may want to use this Essence to address any frustration felt by spiritual beings coming into these new, restrictive animal bodies. By rubbing **Wild Potato Bush** on the mother's belly, both she and the offspring will benefit.

BIRTHING

Most animals give birth easily and without human intervention. It is important to interfere as little as possible while an animal is giving birth and also while the offspring are still very young. But if there is any extended delay in the birth once labour begins then professional help should be sought. A cat will usually produce her first kitten within 15 minutes of the onset of labour and, depending on the number of kittens, labour will last two to three hours. A dog will usually produce her first pup within 20–60 minutes of the commencement of labour. If the animal is obviously in ongoing pain or if there is much pushing with no results for more than half and hour, then you should quickly contact your veterinary health professional. A horse going into labour will be very restless and sometimes exhibit symptoms resembling colic. If this stage continues for more than eight hours without any obvious signs of labour, call the vet. The first stage of real labour takes approximately two hours and the actual birth of the foal happens quite quickly after that. If the foal isn't expelled within 30 minutes then get veterinary help. All female animals can tire very quickly if the labour is prolonged. Sometimes a big kitten, pup or foal can be positioned badly or get stuck in or across the birth canal and the mother may need intervention, maybe even a Caesarean, to deliver, and to survive herself.

The mother's natural instincts about caring for her young usually ensure the best care the young animals can have. Owners only need to step in when it is obvious that the natural system has broken down.

There are times when things can certainly go wrong. Ian White's Sydney Silkie, Pixie, had just given birth to her first litter of two puppies.

'She was assisted in her labour with **Emergency Essence** *and was very satisfied with herself and what she had just achieved. At first she kept a very diligent eye on her two pups; however, shortly afterwards, she lost all interest in her own babies and instead wanted to mother and bond with our collection of Beanie babies – small stuffed toys. She went to every room where she knew they were and barked until she was given them. She took them back to her whelping box and was very protective of her ten beanie babies but oblivious of her own pups. I was concerned for the well-being of the two pups but a few doses of* **Bottlebrush** *had the desired effect and Pixie re-bonded with her pups and resumed her mothering.'*

Ilana Shapiro from Elands, New South Wales, tells of a pet dingo called Sasha.

'She had previously had one litter of pups but had attacked them at birth. She was now pregnant again and nearing the end of her gestation and her owner was concerned about how she would cope. I could see she was ready to give birth but she was restless and would not settle. I gave her one dose of **Emergency Essence** *and she lay down immediately and gave birth to five puppies and she licked them and bonded with them and was a very good mother, raising them all successfully.'*

If the mother is lethargic after the birth or is obviously ill, discharging from the vagina, running a fever, not eating or not showing interest in her young, you should contact your vet. Retained placenta, mineral deficiency and infection of womb or mammary glands are common in mammals.

Horses, being nervous animals, are particularly prone to shock and this should be taken into account when a mare has given birth. If a mare rejects her foal, a vet may give tranquillisers which can sometimes help by reducing stress and trauma and so encourage bonding between mother and young.

Emergency Essence, **Black-eyed Susan** and **Bottlebrush** could help a nervous mare who is obviously upset after the birth.

Other Bush Essences that can help when caring for birthing animals include the following.

Bauhinia, **Bottlebrush** and **Crowea** will expedite the move from the first to the second stage of labour – **Bauhinia** for welcoming change, **Bottlebrush** for letting go and moving on and **Crowea** because one of its functions is supporting muscle tissue. The uterus is one big muscle!

Bottlebrush supports bonding between mother and babies. It may help where the mother is reluctant to feed and care for her young.

Bush Iris, **Illawarra Flame** and **Macrocarpa** can support the immune system and aid healing where there is an infection. They are also helpful after antibiotic treatment, which can suppress an animal's natural immunity.

Emergency Essence can help if an animal seems distressed when giving birth. It is also good for the attendant owner. This Essence is also useful if an animal has to have surgery or other intervention. Add **Macrocarpa** to the **Emergency Essence** to counteract the effects of any anaesthetic.

Flannel Flower added to a base cream can help sore teats. **Emergency Essence Cream** or **Face, Hand & Body Essence Cream** could also be considered for this condition.

Fringed Violet and **Sundew** applied to the top of the head of the newly born young will help ground the spirit into the body and protect this new animal/spirit being from any negative energies.

Macrocarpa or **Dynamis Essence** can help keep up the mother's stamina and energy levels.

Mountain Devil could support treatment for any inflammatory infection.

FAILURE TO THRIVE

Some newborn animals just don't do very well. They are pushed from the 'feed bar' by stronger brothers and sisters and are roughhoused and picked upon by their bigger siblings. Some were in a poor position in utero or had a less than perfect placenta and so have not developed as they should have before birth. Others are just naturally timid or small of stature. Sometimes mothers favour the bigger, healthier babies which have a better chance of survival. Many animals fail to thrive because their spirits are not sufficiently in their bodies. Rudolph Steiner believed that it takes a long time for an animal to be fully incarnated. You should ensure that any young animal that is failing to thrive is checked by a vet to rule out any health problem. If there is nothing seriously wrong then there are some Essences which could help.

There is wonderful story from Pennie Telford of Westbourne, England, about a pup who wasn't thriving but who responded well to treatment with the Essences.

'My Samoyed bitch produced five puppies in her third litter, just before Easter in 2002. After a couple of days of feeding, one little bitch, Tia, had actually lost a little weight, although she appeared to be suckling with gusto. I took her to the vet for a check up and was assured that there was nothing wrong with her. I gave her some **Emergency Essence** *three or four times a day for the next couple of days and started to hand feed her with a dropper. Even though she was still apparently suckling well, milk was coming down her nose. After a week she had hardly gained any weight. She was not being pushed away from the mother and the other pups were all gaining weight. She was getting weaker and dehydrated.*

I dowsed to select an Essence mix for her. It was **Bottlebrush, Bush Fuchsia, Pink Mulla Mulla** *and* **Sundew**: **Bottlebrush** *to help her bond to her mother;* **Bush Fuchsia** *to help align right and left brain;* **Pink Mulla Mulla** *to give her the deep spiritual healing and* **Sundew** *to ground her into her physical body. She had this mix for three weeks.*

I continued to supplement her feeds and she seemed to be taking in the milk more easily and began gaining weight. Tia was the most active pup in the litter, even though barely half the size of her siblings. At three weeks of age she had a very bad infection in the nose, with a lot of green mucous coming out of both nostrils and breathing was a struggle, so back to the vet and antibiotics. Three days later she was very thoroughly examined by a senior homoeopathic vet who found she had a deformity of the soft palate – not a cleft palate, but a foreshortened palate with bilateral notches. There was the possibility of having to have plastic surgery, which would be rather experimental as this condition is rare, and it would have to be supervised by a human ear, nose and throat specialist. Because the deformity was already clearly visible at such a young age, it was felt to be a particularly severe case and would definitely get worse as she grew and her nose lengthened. The operation could not be done until the puppy was six months old and even then the prognosis was very poor with only a 25% chance of success. Also she was likely to be in and out of the vets' frequently with various infections, so I would need an open-ended cheque book! I was told that really she should be put to sleep. I could not afford the surgery, let alone the constant vets' bills thereafter. But fate definitely took a hand and the next day I received a totally unexpected cheque for virtually the same amount I had been quoted for plastic surgery, so I decided I was being told that the puppy should be given a chance. The vet recommended getting her weaned as quickly as possible as more solid food would be less likely to come down her nose.

Next I dowsed to select a new Essence mix of **Bauhinia, Isopogon, Mountain Devil** *and* **Yellow Cowslip Orchid**. *By this time she was eating and gaining weight though she was still taking in smaller quantities of food than her litter mates, and milk and water still came down her nose. She was also constipated. So I had to smile when* **Bauhinia** *appeared in the mix and I read of its effects on the ileocaecal valve (***Bauhinia** *helps the ileocaecal valve to function correctly – to open when needed and then close completely – so preventing leakage from small to large intestines).* **Isopogon** *(which as well as boosting memory is good for those who are bossy, trying to control others) – well she was certainly the boss of the litter, she was small but she would grab the others by their tails and drag them around ruthlessly while they yelped for mercy.* **Mountain**

Devil (one of the Essences for anger and suspicion) – she became angry and frustrated when her bigger siblings knocked her over in play and she would launch herself into the attack. **Yellow Cowslip Orchid** *– to stimulate the pituitary to produce growth hormone and hopefully encourage her shortened palate to grow. One week later I added* **Illawarra Flame Tree** *to the bottle because it deals with rejection and works on the thymus gland which is important for any young animal. I also wondered if on some level Tia might have felt rejected because although she was getting plenty of milk from her mum, she wasn't getting the nourishment she craved. She continued to flourish although she had not caught up with her siblings in size before they went off to their new homes at eight weeks. I decided I had to keep her; she was such a gutsy little character.*

Her nose had been producing a lot of mucous again, so before going to the vet for more antibiotics I decided to treat this as a sinus infection, allergic rhinitis, caused by all the milk in her nasal passages. So her next Essence mix was **Bush Iris**, **Dagger Hakea** *and* **Fringed Violet** *(the Essences recommended for allergic conditions) to deal with this. Tia never barked, yet Samoyeds are renowned for being vocal. A speech therapist informed me that children with foreshortened palates often have problems learning to speak and maybe Tia would not be able to bark. So* **Flannel Flower** *(for expressing emotions) was added to the mix to deal with that. She took this for two weeks. Her mucky nose cleared up and she started barking occasionally.*

Possibly because of smaller amounts of water flushing through her system she seemed to get either mild vaginitis or urinary infections, so I made her up a mix of **Dagger Hakea** *(for irritation of any kind),* **Mulla Mulla** *(for anything to do with heat and redness) and* **Sturt Desert Rose** *(can help with sexual problems) to help with this. I ensured she took in more water, even if I had to sometimes syringe it down her throat!*

Tia was really coming on well now but before going back to the vet to consider surgery I decided to try re-enforcing the good already done by the Essences. I dowsed again and came up with **Bush Iris**, **Dagger Hakea**, **Flannel Flower**, **Fringed Violet**, **Illawarra Flame Tree** *and* **Yellow Cowslip Orchid**, *all of which she had had before. She took this mix three times a day for a month. At the end of August the vet examined her and really struggled to detect her short palate. It is still there, but only slight, and she can cope with it very well. So Tia never had the plastic surgery. She is now the same size as a couple of her sisters. I have shown her and she not only qualified for Crufts Dog Show, but came second in her class of 14 bitches. I think we can say she has grown to her full potential!'*

Recent research on monkeys, noted in the BBC documentary *Primal Instincts*, has found that if an animal is orphaned at a young age and does not receive care, attention and discipline from other adults, it is likely to develop unacceptable behaviour as an adult. These orphaned animals tend to live with other young monkeys, and are virtually raised by their peers. They grow up with little respect or moral sense in relation to family members and are often aggressive in their interaction with other animals in the group. Other monkeys may carry a gene that is known to result in aggressiveness, yet these animals remain gentle and non-aggressive as long as they receive the needed nurturing. A 2002 report of a human study in New Zealand has come up with similar findings. Gregory Carey, geneticist at the University of Colorado, studied 1,037 young New Zealand males for 30 years and found that children who suffered abuse and who also had a common variation in a gene linked to behaviour, were much more likely to become aggressive, anti-social adults than other children. However, children who had the faulty gene but had good caring attention when young grew into balanced non-aggressive adults. Nurturing when young is obviously essential for the emotional health of animals.

If a young mammal or bird has to be raised by hand, because it has been removed from its mother, or the mother has died, the carer needs to provide the attention that the creature would normally receive from its natural mother. Feeding and keeping the animal warm is not enough. It also needs close contact with another living being and regular touching and grooming. With very young kittens and puppies, stimulating urination and defaecation by stroking the anus and urethra with a damp cloth or tissue after each meal is also important.

There are many Essences which can be considered at this stage.

Bottlebrush, given to mother and baby, would help the bonding process. It would also help a young animal adapt to change and bond with its human carer and help the carer bond with the baby animal.

Bluebell could be considered for mother and offspring to open the way to the loving of all.

Dynamis Essence could give the animal more energy, more strength and stamina.

Fringed Violet or **Emergency Essence** will support a young animal in dealing with the shock of separation from mother and siblings.

Illawarra Flame Tree helps if the baby is feeling rejected.

Paw Paw and **Crowea** could help the animal adjust to digesting the different type of milk. If there is diarrhoea you should check with your vet but also give **Bauhinia**, **Bottlebrush** and **Kapok Bush**.

Sundew assists in bringing the spirit into the physical body so can help a young animal to be more focused on surviving.

Tall Yellow Top will help the young animal that is adopted by another animal or human to get over the feeling of being the 'odd man out'.

Waratah could give courage to a timid young animal.

Many animal stories were circulating on the internet in the months following the Asian tsunami which resulted from the Indian Ocean earthquake in 2004. One story involved a baby hippo and a big old tortoise. Owen, a one year old baby hippo weighing 300 kg, had been swept down the Sabaki River, into the Indian Ocean and then back to shore after the giant waves struck the Kenyan coast. The dehydrated hippo was found by wildlife rangers and taken to the Haller Park animal facility in the port city of Mombassa. Pining for his lost mother, Owen quickly befriended a giant 120 year old male Aldabran tortoise named Mzee –

Swahili for 'old man'. When Owen was released into the enclosure, he lumbered over to the tortoise, which has a dark grey colour similar to an adult hippo. Haller Park ecologist Paula Kahumbu said that the pair were now inseparable.

'After it was swept away and lost its mother, the hippo was traumatised. It had to look for something to be a surrogate mother. Fortunately, it landed on the tortoise and established a strong bond. They swim, eat and sleep together. The hippo follows the tortoise exactly the way it would have followed its mother. If somebody approaches the tortoise, the hippo becomes aggressive, as if protecting its biological mother.'

Hippos are social animals that like to stay with their mothers for four years. Owen was left at a very tender age. His chances of survival in another herd were very slim, as it is most likely that a dominant male hippo would have killed the lone baby. While **Emergency Essence** would have been the obvious Essence to use here to help the young hippo, **Red Suva Frangipani** for grieving, and **Bottlebrush** for bonding and adapting to change, could have supported this animal through such a traumatic experience.

WEANING

Weaning is a natural procedure and will usually happen without intervention from the carer. Puppies and kittens are normally weaned between eight and twelve weeks of age. With horses it is later; while some foals are weaned as early as four months, if left to themselves weaning often doesn't happen till around eight months.

It is best for a young animal to be completely weaned before it is given to a new owner. It lessens the double trauma of losing its mother and siblings *and* being weaned, and can also help the mother to avoid the problems of over-supply of milk. However, there are times when you have to abruptly wean an animal, such as when the mother is ill or dies, when animals have to be sold or given to new owners on a specific date or when the babies do not wean themselves naturally after a reasonable time. It is important that the newly-weaned animal is given plenty of attention so that it knows it hasn't been abandoned. There are some Essences that will help.

Bottlebrush will assist an animal to adapt to change.

Emergency Essence given frequently to a young animal during the first couple of days after weaning could help with the shock of the new regime.

Five Corners or **Confid Essence** could be considered to boost the young animal's confidence in its ability to live without its mother and its mother's milk.

Flannel Flower and **Mountain Devil** could be considered for the mother if she develops swollen teats or infection after abrupt weaning.

Illawarra Flame Tree deals with any sense of rejection in the baby.

Monga Waratah helps the young animal become independent of its mother.

Red Frangipani could help with the loss that some animals experience if the weaning is abrupt and premature.

Ian White suggests a combination of Essences to give to young animals when they are being separated from their mother. This 'separation mix' is: **Bottlebrush**, **Dog Rose**, **Illawarra Flame Tree**, **Tall Yellow Top** and **Waratah**.

DE-SEXING

The majority of companion and farm animals, male and female, are de-sexed unless they are being used for breeding. When you are considering de-sexing, discuss it with your vet. You might also try to communicate with your animal. Explain what you are planning and why, and see if you get any intuitive response about what the animal wants. It might be important to this animal to breed, once or many times. On the other hand the animal might be quite content to go along with sterilisation. Respect for the animal at this time is essential and any fear or apprehension needs to be acknowledged. Your openness, reassurance and calm will flow onto your animal. If the animal feels that you are in control and not anxious, it will sense that there is nothing to fear.

Most animals do well after this operation, particularly if **Emergency Essence** is used at the time. However, some de-sexed animals have problems with hormone imbalance, lethargy, weight gain and the effects of the trauma of the procedure. Sometimes bladder dysfunction or other side effects from the surgery can occur. Any of the Bush Essences mentioned for dealing with trauma in Chapter 6 could be of help, working at the emotional level and processing the underlying fear and hurt. There are also some Essences that will deal with specific aspects of this experience.

Crowea could energetically support the sphincter muscle in the bladder.

Dog Rose and **Red Helmet Orchid** can ease problems of incontinence.

Dynamis Essence can help restore energy to an animal that has become lazy or lethargic.

Emergency Essence can be given before the operation and for up to two weeks afterwards to deal with any trauma and so reduce recovery time. Add **Macrocarpa** to counteract the effects of the anaesthetic.

She Oak will energetically support hormone imbalance in females and **Flannel Flower** in males.

Slender Rice Flower restores the flow of energy through scar tissue. It is particularly effective where the scar runs across an energy meridian. This Essence can be given internally immediately after the operation to help resolve emotions associated with the surgical wound and later applied for up to two weeks to the healing scars.

Wild Potato Bush could be considered after the operation for the loss of a body function.

One animal who did not respond well emotionally to being de-sexed was Mollie.

'Mollie is a female pedigree Bullmastiff aged five. She came to us when she was two and a half years old, from a breeder who had kept her as a pet. She was a nervous dog, vulnerable and needing constant reassurance. According to the previous owner Mollie had been a very friendly and gregarious puppy – but she never seemed to be the same after she was transferred out of the puppy area. I believe that she suffered emotionally from this, from being de-sexed and from other unnerving experiences that happened to her before she came to us. The Essences I selected for Mollie were:

__Fringed Violet__ to repair Mollie's aura, damaged from de-sexing and to help to clear her anxiety from old distressing events
__Crowea__ to dispel and remove worrying feelings and bring about a sense of balance within her
__Jacaranda__ to assist Mollie to think more quickly and realise that she is not in danger
__Little Flannel Flower__ to bring back the playfulness that is a part of her true self.
__Red Suva Frangipani__ to bring about a feeling of inner peace and allow her to cope with everything more easily.

The response was so quick that by the second day we could see a more lively and interested Mollie, and the improvement continued. She is now much happier. When she is being really playful she holds her ears in a certain manner as she runs towards us. We call them her 'silly ears' and we see them every day now. The treatment was successful and the outcome was as I had hoped.'

Chapter 10

AGEING, SLOWING DOWN and DYING

Old Deuteronomy's lived a long time; he's a Cat who has lived many lives in succession. He was famous in proverb and famous in rhyme a long while before Queen Victoria's accession.

FROM 'OLD POSSUM'S BOOK OF PRACTICAL CATS', T.S. ELIOT, 1939

One of the sad things about living with animals is that, with the exception of a few species such as tortoises, elephants and parrots, we humans usually have much longer life spans. We will almost always outlive our animal friends. One small boy, when asked why dogs live much shorter lives than humans, is quoted as saying, *'Everybody is born so that they can learn how to live a good life – loving everybody and being nice, right? Well, animals already know how to do that, so they don't have to stay as long.'* Whatever the reason, it follows that throughout our lives we are going to have to come to terms with our animals becoming old and eventually dying. This is part of the life journey we move into when we take an animal into our care.

OLDER ANIMALS

As they age, animals require more attention. Some of the bodily systems may begin to break down, and various ailments occur. Carers need to provide extra attention to assist aching joints, ageing hearts and failing kidneys and keep a careful watch kept on the creature's well-being.

With age, animals become less tolerant of extremes in temperature, so shelter from the sun and cold, wind and rain becomes more important. Dogs and cats, because they are unable to sweat, are particularly intolerant of extreme heat as they get older. They may benefit from being sprayed with water on hot days to let the evaporation cool them. Adding **Mulla Mulla** to the water can increase the cooling effect.

As an animal ages its digestive system becomes less efficient. The animal can benefit from being fed more frequently, with smaller meals and quite often different food. A diet that is good for a young active animal many not be suitable for an ageing one. Food supplements can also be helpful.

However, an elderly animal doesn't need to be mollycoddled – sensible care is called for, with any symptoms of deteriorating health dealt with. A persistent cough, for example, or increased thirst, an unexplained lump, obvious pain, or a change in the coat condition all need to be checked. Teeth may become covered with scale and the ears dirty. The eyes may change in colour or become opaque rather than transparent. Animals are generally creatures of habit so any change in an animal's way of doing things should be investigated. Presuming that a marked behaviour change is just 'old age' might mean that you miss a health condition that needs attention. Many conditions can be checked if seen early enough, and pain and discomfort can be relieved. Delay, because of fear of what the vet might say, can result in unnecessary pain and discomfort for your pet.

Dogs, cats and horses often try to do more than their ageing bodies can cope with. The spirit remains strong even though the body is starting to wear out. I remember a Border Collie I used to care for. She was addicted to retrieving balls and in her youth could keep chasing them all day. As she grew older she would sit with the ball for longer and longer times, until she caught her breath, and then she would bring it back to me, always wanting one more throw. It was I who had to stop the sessions. In the weeks before her death, one or two very short throws were all she could cope with but she still loved the game. Exercise is important at all times of an animal's life and as it gets older this should still be encouraged, though monitored according to the animal's condition and ability to enjoy. Shorter walks and easier terrain are advisable.

An animal's behaviour may change as it ages. An old animal can become stubborn and reluctant to follow commands. It may become listless and disinterested in life. The Bush Essences can bring about amazing changes.

Magic was a very old dog belonging to Kate Mancham from the Seychelles.

'Magic had been depressed for weeks and could hardly be bothered raising her head in greeting. She had an inoperable tumour, but her main problem was a lack of interest in life. I squirted **Emergency Essence** *into her mouth one night and again the next morning. I felt that it might help while I gave some more thought to what other Essences to give her. Each morning I used take my other two dogs swimming far out in the sea. Magic had not been swimming with us for four years. So you can imagine how astonished I was when I saw her later that morning, swimming*

*out with the others. I was a long way out and she was coming right out to join me – she'd been almost dead the day before. And this, after just two doses of **Emergency Essence**. I continued with the **Emergency Essence** for a week, thinking of the **Waratah** for her depression, and two months later, although the tumour was still there, she was still quite happy and enjoying life.'*

Some ageing animals can become irritable and even aggressive because of pain or because younger animals or children keep worrying them. Their only means of defence is to bite, kick or scratch. It is wise to arrange your older animal's accommodation so that it is protected from too much attention from people or other animals and so that it has an escape hole when it wants to avoid them. Another thing to note here is that if you have more than one animal, the second pet might defend the weaker one, so be aware of the possibility of defensive aggression from the younger, fitter animal. It does happen sometimes.

However, don't be tempted to put the ageing animal in seclusion. As much as any period in its life, this is a time when it needs the company of its human and animal companions. Basic every-day activities like gentle grooming, quiet companionship or gentle walking will mean much to an ageing animal. Avoid unnecessary change and keep routines as regular as practicable. Keep new people or animals at a distance and try not to change vets at this time. Keep the whole environment as peaceful and normal as possible.

Some Essences to consider as your animal is ageing are listed below.

Bottlebrush will help with the acceptance of ageing – to be taken by the owner!

Calm & Clear Essence, either as a spray or as drops, will help to create a peaceful environment.

Crowea and **Black-eyed Susan** will help where there is chronic worrying and anxiety – as happens with old cats especially.

Dagger Hakea will reduce irritability.

Dog Rose is for general fear and anxiety.

Isopogon will help to restore poor memory.

Little Flannel Flower is useful for retaining joy, playfulness and flexibility of mind and body.

Macrocarpa encourages stamina and muscle strength and helps with exhaustion.

Mountain Devil is useful for dispelling anger and aggression.

Mulla Mulla and **She Oak** can help skin that is drying out and becoming inflexible.

Any of the Essences described in other chapters, or in the Repertory of Symptoms, for treating specific illnesses or behavioural problems may also be useful with ageing animals.

CHANGING PACE

Just like some humans, some animals do not cope with 'retirement' very well and all of them need help adjusting to their new life style. All working animals – whether they be therapy animals, show dogs, performance or zoo animals, racing or coursing animals and hunters – live most of their lives to fairly rigid and often busy routines. They are out working with their owners or trainers for many hours every day, or being groomed or otherwise prepared for the work they do. They often travel and mix with other animals and people. Their lives are full of excitement, change, companionship and stimulation.

Then suddenly old age approaches and everything changes. Racing animals are put out to pasture. Show animals are replaced by younger and more attractive animals. Some very old zoo animals are given special quarters behind the scenes where they are no longer seen by the public. Whether they are happy with these new arrangements depends on the individual animal. Guide dogs that have spent all their adult lives being very important to their owner suddenly are without that dimension in life. Even if they stay with their owner they are replaced by another dog to carry out the guiding work. Many such animals need Essences for depression and acceptance of change, and sometimes there is jealousy of the new animal brought in to replace them.

Some animals revel in the new conditions as they slow down and many owners make sure that their 'retired' animals get plenty of love and attention. But some former working animals can become restless and impatient to get going again. They become bored or lose interest in life, and they can develop obsessive habits as they try to deal with the loss of routine and the new regime of compar-atively empty days. It is important to be aware of this and make arrangements for new stimuli in their day. Try to find new activities or games for dogs to enjoy. The company of other animals or humans can help, together with walks and visits. This is a time to devise new roles which will add interest and routine to their activities but fit within their now limited physical capabilities. Old horses do best if they can exercise at will, with an open stall adjacent to an open paddock. If left in a stall for a long period, arthritic joints can seize up and be painful to get going again. Horses that can no longer be ridden can be taken for a walk or a swim on a lead rein. A companion animal can bring new life to a retired horse. Donkeys have proven very effective in this role but a goat can also be a good companion animal – though goats are traditionally very difficult to fence in.

There are many Essences to consider using with an ageing animal.

Bauhinia will encourage the animal to be open to new ways of doing things and to new experiences generally.

Banksia Robur supports an animal that is normally active and energetic but has become tired and lethargic.

Boronia can help with repetitive or obsessive habits. It could be useful for those animals that pace up and down an enclosure or paddock.

Bottlebrush is for adapting to change and letting go of the old ways of doing things.

Dagger Hakea or **Mountain Devil** can help if there is jealousy of a new younger animal usurping an old animal's role.

Five Corners helps to boost flagging self confidence and self-esteem.

Illawarra Flame Tree is for the animal that feels rejected by its owner or trainer.

Kapok Bush will help the animal that loses interest in life.

Little Flannel Flower could help animals who have spent much time working and maybe not enough playing.

Pink Flannel Flower can help any animal to be happy with the status quo, whatever that may be.

Silver Princess is for helping to find a new direction in life.

Tall Yellow Top can help where an animal's sense of identity, which has been connected with its work, no longer exists.

Also consider using spiritual-type Essences which are discussed in Chapter 11 – Spirituality. This is a time in their lives where animals that were previously very busy and occupied with their human handlers have time to see again the animals that they truly are.

DEATH AND DYING

Supporting an animal when it is dying is very important. Obviously be guided by your vet concerning pain relief and other medical matters. But there are other ways to improve the quality of this final period in your pet's life.

Spend time with your animal. Its body will no longer respond as it used to and this can engender confusion and fear. Your regular presence will bring reassurance, and gentle stroking and communicating will make this final period less stressful.

A story about an animal dying, from the *Smarter than Jack* book of animal stories, is worth repeating here.

'I got Goldie from an animal shelter and loved her at first sight. She was a warm and affectionate friend not only to the family but also to visitors and neighbours. She was special. When she was about 12 years old she became ill with a weak heart. On her thirteenth birthday, at about three in the morning I was awakened by something cold and wet on my face. Goldie never came into our bedroom so I knew something was wrong. I got out of bed and Goldie led me to the back door, where we sat together for a while looking up at the stars in a beautiful night sky. I told Goldie what a wonderful friend she had been and how much she meant to me. She looked at me and we both understood this meant goodbye. In the morning Goldie had died. We buried her at sunrise that morning in the bush near our home.'

Seeing an animal die is always painful but knowing that you are doing all you can to ease that process will make it easier for both of you. Keep it as comfortable and peaceful as possible. And whenever practicable allow the animal to die in a familiar environment with someone it knows in attendance. The use of Essence mists will help to create a peaceful environment and **Transition Essence** will certainly ease the dying process.

Sometimes a quite young animal will give up after suffering trauma or severe illness and will sometimes die simply because it loses all interest in life. Jan Fowles from Caloundra Pet Kennels tells how loving care and the Bush Essences can bring about change in such an animal.

'Bianca the cat was the victim of rat bait poisoning. I met her after she had had extensive vet treatment. She was emaciated and many organs were damaged. She was fearful and not eating. Her owner thought that she had lost the will to live and was told to expect a sad outcome. Bianca's eyes told us a different story. They conveyed the message of wanting to continue in this life. The first steps were **Emergency Essence** *and Reiki. We added the Essence to her drinking water. There was a slight shift in her mental outlook – she was more interested and less stand-offish. We then decided on the* **Purifying Essence** *to assist the body to eliminate any toxins from the bait she had eaten, and also from the medications she had been given. To this mix was added* **Bauhinia**. *It was important that the body was not only eliminating toxins but also rebalancing body, mind and soul. After four weeks of caring she went home and we had no word from the owners about her condition until twelve months later when she came back for minding – a happy, feisty, fat cat!'*

The question of euthanasia may come up when dealing with a very old or very sick animal. Consultation with your vet is essential to discover the amount of pain or other discomfort your animal is experiencing. Its quality of life in general must also be taken into account and it is important to try to get an intuitive sense of how and when the animal wishes to die. If you decide that your animal should be euthanised, the same rules apply about staying with the animal. It might be tempting to leave your animal with the vet but in doing so you and your animal miss the enriching experience that dying can be.

Transition Essence is *the* Essence for this final stage of any animal's life. Animal communicator Caroline Pope tells the following story about the use of this Essence.

'In the past 12 months we have seen two of our dogs return to Spirit. In both cases we used the **Transition Essence** *and then Essences for the grief (***Red Suva Frangipani** *and* **Sturt Desert Pea**). *I was amazed at the impact the* **Transition Essence** *had in preparing both dogs, as well as our other remaining dogs, for their passing. We noticed it especially with Billie, a 7 year old English Mastiff, because she was completely calm and had already begun to move out of her body hours before the time came for her to be 'put to sleep'. I know she was able to see the spirits of other animal companions, which made her passing less traumatic for her, for us and for our other dogs as well. For both dogs, the transition was very quick and gentle*

*and the **Transition Essence** was largely responsible for this. When the time came for them to leave us, our other dogs simply lay down around them. They were very peaceful and quiet as the **Transition Essence** had also prepared them for their friends' return to Spirit. I gave the **Transition Essence** to the human and four-legged friends, not just the animals going to Spirit. We had been particularly worried about our two other dogs, Wookie and Malaika, as all four of the dogs had been very, very close. Wookie was Billie's litter sister and they had been inseparable. However, while both dogs were quiet and obviously sad for some days after Billie's passing, we regularly gave them the drops for grief and they were accepting of the situation. Because they had been so well prepared emotionally with the **Transition Essence**, the grieving drops were able to help them remain very calm and peaceful and increased their ability to cope emotionally with the loss of their companions and friends.'*

As well as dealing with the dying animal, owners also need to recognise, acknowledge and process their own grief. It can be very painful to watch a beloved companion fade away before your eyes. Outsiders might comment that it is only an animal, but animal/human relationships can be as deep and beautiful as any. Talk with someone who cares, take some Essences to help you cope, and be open to feeling the sadness, loss, anger and sense of emptiness that the death of an animal can bring. Go through some ritual to mark the passing of your animal friend. It could be a funeral ceremony or it could be a poem written for the occasion or you could write the story of its life and death, just for you if you wish. You could set up a little shrine with a photo and candle and try to communicate with the spirit of your animal. Do something that feels right to you and give yourself the luxury of settling into your emotions and gently working through them. You will feel all the better for the process. There is much emotional adjusting to do and there is no point in suppressing or trying to rush through the grieving process.

As already mentioned **Transition Essence** is *the* Essence for death and dying. Its purpose is to help the animal release its spirit from the physical body though it doesn't hasten death, but simply makes it easier if the animal is ready to die. Jan Fowles has used it often with her dogs.

*'Since the **Transition Essence** was released it has shown me its special qualities many times. I have said goodbye to several of our dogs and have given the **Transition Essence** to all of them as they got ready to leave us and go on their spiritual journey. But instead of leaving, on more than one occasion, after being given the Essence they went into a deep sleep after which they started to improve and responded to treatment or just simply got up and went about their business. I feel that this Essence allows the animal to go to that space where, unhindered by emotion, they can reconnect with the animal devas and honour their spiritual contracts either to come back to us mere mortals and teach us more lessons, or accept that their work is done and it is time to move on.'*

Transition Essence can help relieve tension and support the animal in letting go without fear. Treating the owner and animal at the same time is often very helpful. Often the owner is more upset and confused than the animal. Animals seem to accept death as just another stage of life, but they get concerned when the owner gets distressed or doesn't accept the process. There are several other Essences that can help ease the pain of dying.

Calm & Clear Essence Mist, sprayed in the room where the animal is situated, can help to induce a place of stillness and calm.

Emergency Essence plus **Dog Rose** can help in reducing pain and discomfort by reducing fear and relieving trauma. These Essences can also help to give the owner courage and strength to cope.

Pink Flannel Flower can help an animal accept the present situation with deep peace and gratitude. This Essence used with **Dog Rose** could be particularly helpful to horses and other grazing animals who must feel very vulnerable lying down, often in the open, when they are dying.

Red Suva Frangipani will ease the intense upset and grief felt by all family members at the time of the loss of a beloved pet.

Sturt Desert Pea will process long term grief and hurt.

The story of Toothless Tibby wonderfully illustrates how the Essences can help ageing animals in often unexpected ways.

*'I had a most unusual result from your **Transition Essence**. A friend has an ancient Corgi cross dog with arthritic hips, very few teeth and large hairless patches on her back. She was 14 years old, the equivalent of 98 in human years. Tibby had a fast growing abdominal lump which the vet thought was a tumour. Tibby's owner knew her dog had reached the end of its life and asked me for **Transition Essence** to help it on its way. A month later Tibby looked healthier than she had for a long time – wait for it! Some months later I was asked to look after old Toothless Tibby while her owner was away. One morning Tibby wasn't in her usual place and didn't come to be fed. I looked for her rather apprehensively and found her, not dead, but having just given birth to two puppies! Giving birth at age 98 – no wonder she had a look of shock and horror in her eyes. So did I! Grannymother and one healthy pup survived and both are doing well. It is all true – when you use Flower Essences, magic happens.'* – Susan Wood, Cooran, Queensland

Chapter 11

ANIMAL SPIRITUALITY

The animal shall not be measured by man. In a world older and more complete than ours, they move finished and complete, gifted with extension of the senses we have lost or never attained, living by voices we shall never hear. They are not brethren; they are not underlings; they are other nations, caught with ourselves in the net of life and time, fellow prisoners of the splendour and travail of the earth.

HENRY BESTON, 'THE OUTERMOST HOUSE', 1928

How do animals fit into the grand universal plan of living and dying? And how are they placed on the evolutionary scale of spiritual development? What is their role in life generally and in our lives in particular?

The majority of civilisations, both ancient and modern, have acknowledged the important roles that animals played in the physical and spiritual world. Eagles induced a sense of wonder as they soared high in the sky. Wolves howled from hilltops in soul-stirring communication, inspiring fear and respect in those who heard them. Fully antlered deer displayed awesomely in forest clearings. Bees pollinated plants and produced honey, while browsing and grazing animals helped determine plant distribution and balance. Birds brought colour and song, while larger animals supplied material for homes, tools, clothes and personal decoration as well as being a source of food for humans and other animals. As some animals became domesticated they brought companionship, protection, physical warmth, pest control and even modes of transport and power for farm implements. They were recognised as being a significant part of daily life and respected for being the creatures that they were. And some were held in reverence because of their special spiritual qualities.

Animals are an integral part of Australian Aboriginal spirituality. Dreamtime stories tell of a time when great ancestors roamed the Earth. They were human, animal and bird all at the same time. The Rainbow Serpent is a universal symbol in Aboriginal stories and is a consistent theme in paintings and rock art, going back many thousands of years. It is represented as a large, snake-like creature, whose Dreaming track is always associated with billabongs, rivers, creeks and lagoons. It is the protector of the land, its people, and the source of all life. The Rainbow Serpent is a powerful representation of the creative and destructive power of nature.

In American Indian teachings, animals are seen as pathways to power. The Indians believe that animals have lessons to reveal to us, each type of animal having a slightly different emphasis or focus. They portray the concept that we gain understanding from members of the animal kingdom and that this learning can be a healing process. Animals are seen as helping us to understand our role in the great mystery of life by our recognition that every living thing is a teacher that enables us to find deep connection with Spirit. The buffalo was of special significance to many of America's native people. They saw it as a Spirit Being blessing the people with all they needed to survive, both physically and spiritually.

In practically every civilisation, animals have been involved in religious philosophy. The ancient Babylonians saw their gods in the signs of the zodiac and ascribed animal names to each of these stellar constellations – the Ram, the Bull, the Crab, the Lion, the Scorpion, the Fish and so on. In the Chinese horoscope each of the 12 years in a cycle is named after an animal. There are many stories about the origin of this custom and one of them relates to Buddha. It is said that just before his death, Buddha summoned all the animals to him but only 12 answered his call. He honoured each of those 12 with the name of a year in the order in which they arrived. The Egyptians had cow, ram and ibis-headed gods, and one god which was a baboon. The cat was a very sacred animal in Egypt. In Western civilisations black cats, in particular, have been seen as magical right up to recent times. The Hindus placed the elephant and the lion above man in their hierarchy of beings. In Greek mythology, the god Zeus often took the form of a swan, a bull or an eagle. The Germanic tradition held that the boar, raven, horse and cat were sacred. The Celts placed animals at the centre of their religious rituals. Cernunos the Antlered was one of the gods of fertility and also the god of the untamed forces of nature. He was often depicted as being surrounded by deer, serpents and other woodland creatures. In a small village in England, the Abbots Bromley Horn Dance, which dates back to the thirteenth century, continues to this day. It is performed annually in September. Six 'deer-men' wear reindeer horns and follow a ten mile course performing a ritual at each of twelve locations, accompanied by music played on a melodian. The Celts honoured their dogs and crowned them with flowers on special occasions. The Galatian Celts are described as making a yearly sacrifice to the goddess Artemis of a sheep, goat, or calf and they believed that hunting and killing boar was a way of making contact with Spirit. Muslims believe that all living creatures were made by and loved by Allah and that they should be treated with kindness and compassion. In Christianity, Jesus is sometimes described as the Lamb of God.

ANIMA ... ANIMAL

During the 1960s, Aniela Jagge, an associate of renowned psychologist Dr Carl Jung, wrote about animal symbolism in early religions. She believed that it was about man recognising our own animal self and animal instincts. But might it not have been something more than that? Perhaps these early peoples recognised something of the Spirit of the animals around them. The English word 'animal' comes from the Latin word 'anima' which means soul. Was it the souls of animals that these early peoples could recognise and venerate? Do animals have a less complicated spirituality than humans? Does their apparent lack of questioning give them a more direct link with Spirit? Through them, could we possibly have a stronger, easier connectedness with the Divine?

Throughout the literature of the Western world, we find mention of the importance of animals in many rituals and societal processes. A chameleon would supposedly guard against evil eye, increase sexuality and ward off disease, while the owl was a symbol of wisdom and intelligence. Toads and bats were integral parts of witchcraft and the occult, and the mythical dragon and unicorn were central to many legends and fairy tales. Sailors used cats to predict the voyages they were about to embark upon. Loudly mewing cats meant that it would be a difficult voyage. A playful cat meant that it would be a voyage with good and gusty winds.

Quite early in the Christian Church, the concept that animals did not have souls was proposed and widely, though not universally, accepted. During the seventeenth century in the 'Age of Reason', philosopher Descartes again proposed that animals do not have souls. This caused a definite change in thinking, particularly amongst educated people. Animals were relegated to a much lower ranking in the scheme of things. The acceptance by a large section of society that animals did not have souls and so were lesser beings brought much sadness to people whose beloved animals died, leaving them with no hope of meeting up again in an afterlife.

Lila Devi, in her book *Flower Essences for Animals*, writes about the Indian teaching that each of the kingdoms on Earth evolves through five veils or koshas. *'God sleeps in the minerals, dreams and cries in the plants, begins to stir in the animals and is capable of fully awakening in humanity.'* Humanity has the capability of moving through the final veil of awareness, while in the animal kingdom the veil of discrimination is still in place. In the human kingdom we can make choices. We are able to override our instinctual nature. We have free will. We have imagination. We can picture what will happen tomorrow or next year. We can feel an instinctual response to a situation but can choose to ignore it. An animal, it is believed, cannot normally do these things.

But perhaps there is another side to this. Are the differences between humans and animals more like the differences between humans and angels or other Spirit beings? Animals have a greater awareness than we do in many areas and seem able to communicate more easily with each other – and with us, if we are prepared to listen. Perhaps they have a more direct connection to Spirit than we have. Like the angels who, according to tradition, do not have free will as we know it, animals lack free will. But, unlike the angels and nature spirits, they do incarnate into physical bodies. In that sense they are more like us than other Spirit beings. Their role in creation is different from ours – not better or worse, or greater or lesser, just different. We can help them and learn from them and they can help us and learn from us. All living things are evolving – humans, other animals, plants, even the Earth itself. As inhabitants of this planet, we are all becoming more aware and, in theory at least, more enlightened in our own particular ways. We are all going through life experiences, then returning to our source with the added awareness and maturity of an existence on Earth. Interaction between species, as well as between individuals, has the potential to deepen and broaden life experience and spiritual evolution for all of us.

A slightly different view is that, as humans, we are involved in taking animals further along their evolutionary path. By associating with us they are learning to expand their level of awareness and move beyond their natural instinctive behaviour. Our interaction with them helps to progress them to a higher level of being. Whatever the reality, animal and humans have a very powerful connection.

Caroline Pope sent in this story about some dogs she was associated with.

'George was one of three Bull Arab dogs and was the son of Jamilla and Rhuarc. Rhuarc was seven years old and had been off colour for a week or so and wound up in the Werribee veterinary teaching facility for an overnight stay. When his owner, Mairi, went to pick him up next day she was told that he had a tumour on his heart and there was nothing that could be done about it. Rhuarc was a wonderful dog and everyone was upset at the verdict; even the veterinary nurses were in tears. Mairi took him home and out into their back yard with her partner and the other two dogs. Earlier a bottle of **Emergency Essence** *had been left on the kitchen bench. They were all standing in the yard with, Rhuarc and Jamilla, feeling very miserable when George trotted back to the house. He soon returned and dropped something at Mairi's feet. She figured that it was a stick and took no notice. When she failed to respond George pushed it towards her with his foot. Mairi still did not respond so he pushed it towards her again and barked – he rarely barks. Mairi looked down to find the bottle of* **Emergency Essence**. *George had taken it off the kitchen bench and brought it out to them! Mairi immediately gave some to the three dogs and to herself and her partner as well. In this situation George knew what was needed.'*

ANIMAL AWARENESS

There are many animal stories that support the concept of animals showing compassion and awareness beyond what we would see as 'normal'. They have shown that they care about their human and animal companions and respond to them emotionally. In his book *The Angel at my Side*, Mike Lingerfelter tells the story of his therapy dog, Dakota. Mike was suffering suicidal depression after two serious heart attacks left him with severe and unpredictable angina. No further medical treatment was available except drugs for partial reduction of the pain. From being a busy, active, reasonably fit business man, he became an invalid who was controlled by his disease. One of his doctors recommended a therapy dog to motivate Mike to live. Mike developed a deep and loving relationship with this dog and Dakota was able to predict the angina attacks, which enabled Mike to gradually extend his life beyond his home and doctor's surgery and, in time, to travel without a human companion. It was later revealed, via an animal communicator, that Dakota was in fact a Spirit guide. His role was to help Mike but also, in that process, to expand the view that people currently hold about animals: to help humans see animals as spiritual beings, to raise the status of animals in society and to show that they too have consciousness. While helping Mike, Dakota was also helping to get this message across and they both became well known public figures in many parts of the USA.

An edited extract from the RSPCA book *Smarter than Jack*, relates a fascinating story of a dog rescuing another animal.

'One hot Tuesday afternoon in February I had just reached my front gate after visiting a friend when my four year old Doberman cross, Tim, jumped the eight foot plus high fence surrounding the back yard and raced past me, across a four lane highway and down a long stretch of road and into the local golf course. With me in hot pursuit, she leapt over a quite wide creek, ran along fairways, ignoring the verbal abuse of golfers, and eventually ran into the creek. When I caught up with her I could see that she had picked up something white from the murky brown water. When she reached the bank she scrambled up and dropped a plastic bag at my feet. I crouched down and peered inside and saw what appeared to be a lifeless grey and white kitten. I picked it up and began rubbing it with my windcheater. "Meaow", the little creature cried as it looked up at me with its big yellow-green eyes. How did Tim know about the kitten? It was dumped a kilometre and a half away from my backyard.'

Another story, from Reuters in Thailand at the time of the Indian Ocean Tsunami disaster in December 2004, demonstrates animals' sensitivity to the environment and also their compassion for human kind. Dang Salaangam and his wife Kulada ran an eight-elephant business offering rides to tourists at Khao Lak beach in eastern Thailand. At first light on the morning of the tsunami, the elephants started trumpeting in a way that could only be described as crying. This was something they had never done before. The mahouts calmed the elephants but the huge animals started wailing again about an hour later and this time they could not be comforted. They ran for the gently sloping jungle-clad hill behind the beach, some with tourists on their backs. The elephants who were not working broke their hefty chains and also ran. The big wave then became visible and people started running away from the water. Some elephants, with the help of their mahouts, stopped and lifted tourists from the advancing water. The elephants charged up through into the jungle, then stopped. The tsunami drove up to one kilometre inshore but stopped short of where the elephants stood. At least 3,800 people, more than half of them foreigners, were killed at that beach that morning, but those who went with the elephants survived.

Some reports tell of animals responding over distance to family situations in ways that were little short of miracles. English biologist Dr Rupert Sheldrake has come to believe that animals and their owners may be linked together by a flexible, invisible, energy field which he terms a 'morphic field'. This field of energy connects things separated by distance. He compares it to an elastic band that can stretch over a great distance without breaking, whenever animal and owner are separated. In his book *Dogs Who Know When Their Owners Are Coming Home* he describes this phenomenon.

> *'Morphic fields are not the same as gravitational or electro-magnetic fields. They are more like quantum matter fields where two particles that have been part of the same system and then move apart, retain a mysterious connection at a distance, called quantum non-locality'.*

At Dudley Zoo in England, in 1937, the actor Sabu who was star of the film *Elephant Boy*, was coming to visit. He wanted to see two elephants with whom he had worked as a child in India and had not see for many years. Remarkably, when he arrived at the zoo, long before he reached their enclosure, both elephants began trumpeting excitedly. Dr Sheldrake believed that this was an example of a morphic field connection.

THE ANIMAL–HUMAN CONNECTION

The area of animal spirituality is complex and our understanding of it is still at an embryonic stage, but the connection between humans and animals is so strong that it cannot be ignored. Even animals in the wild sometimes care for human beings with whom they come in contact. Legends of wolves raising human children have been around since stories have been told. The most famous of these tales is the story of Romulus and Remus, the founders of the city of Rome. These twin boys were supposedly raised by a mother wolf by the Tiber River, but there were many other such stories. Semiramis, for example, the semi-legendary queen of Assyria who lived around 900 BC, is recorded as having been fed by doves. According to Greek mythology, Telephus, the son of Hercules, was suckled by a doe and Hippothous, son of Poseidon, was suckled by a mare. But there are many modern stories of children apparently having been raised by animals. A 1993 report by John McCrone relates the tale of two girls in India aged, about three and five, who were found in a wolf's den in 1920, along with two wolf cubs. Their hair was matted and they walked on four 'legs' but were otherwise quite healthy. It was believed the two girls were not sisters and had probably been abandoned soon after birth and taken at different times by the mother wolf and raised by her. Whether this was compassionate behaviour on behalf of the wolf or a distorted mothering instinct is unknown.

Tales abound of dolphins swimming with humans and rescuing or even healing them. An article by Anupama Bhattacharya in *Life Positive* magazine tells the story of a Belgian woman who went to live at the Human–Dolphin Institute in Florida, USA. This woman was suffering from leukaemia and had been told that she had only a few months to live. She swam with the dolphins, who seemed to recognise her fragile state and interacted with her very gently. Her leukaemia went into remission and five years later she was still alive and well.

Animals can and do warn humans of danger. In relatively recent times 'war' dogs have been trained to recognize booby traps, mines tunnels and weapons caches. They warn troops about ambushes and have been known to save lives by dragging wounded soldiers to safety. During World War II, many families in Britain and Europe depended on the behaviour of their animals to alert them to air raids. The animals started to act differently long before the planes could be heard or the sirens were sounded.

SPIRITUAL AGREEMENTS

Before we are born, or even conceived, in a space or time between lifetimes, some people believe that we make agreements at a spiritual level with other people who will play key roles in our lives. Medical clairvoyant Caroline Myss describes these agreements as 'sacred contracts'. Michael Newton in his book *Journey of Souls* and Brian Weiss in *Many Lives, Many Masters* also explore this area of time between lives. The idea behind spiritual agreements is that we are born for a special purpose, always to learn something, but also to help others in their life journeys. Our main contracts are with our parents, siblings, spouses and children, but we also make contracts with other people such as work colleagues, neighbours, teachers and pupils. We agree to interact at various times, not in predestined events, but rather in setting up scenarios so that a particular lesson can be learned. If we miss one opportunity to learn then it will be set up again at another time to give us another chance. These are the repeating patterns in our lives. We are in fact Spirit beings in body suits and all the things that happen in our lives are at one level human experiences, but at another they are pre-conception agreements being acted out by Spirit beings. It seems probable that animals also make such contracts with us.

If we can accept the idea that animals do make sacred contracts then we can see that our time with a particular animal or group of animals is part of an agreement we came to before their arrival in our care. It is not coincidental that we end up with a beautiful pet that brings us much joy, or a difficult animal that pushes all our buttons and forces us to learn new skills and awareness as we cope with its behaviour or health problems. It can be beneficial to become conscious of the terms of these contracts and look for the lessons we can learn from interaction with our animals. By living with this added sensitivity we can more fully appreciate the richness that animals bring to our lives – another layer of learning and development without which we would be lesser beings. We need animals to complete our sense of self, just as animals in domestication need us as their family and maybe as their Spirit teacher or pupil.

AUSTRALIAN BUSH FLOWER ESSENCES AND SPIRITUALITY

We cannot separate body from Spirit. They work as one. It is through the body that we experience Spirit. There are specific areas of the brain that become active when we meditate deeply or achieve awareness of higher Spirit beings. This results in bodily sensations, images, sounds and/or the stimulation of emotions. Beauty can also excite our emotions and open us to the Divine. The focus of our awareness will, of course, vary from moment to moment. In periods of deep meditation, consciousness of our body will be minimal. When we are in physical or emotional pain or agitation it can be difficult to be aware of Spirit.

Before we can hear our intuition, our Higher Self, our God, we have to calm our minds and settle our emotions. Emotions are the bridge between the spiritual and the physical. All Australian Bush Flower Essences deal with emotions and although the early information about the Essences focused on emotional, behavioural and physical problems, all the Bush Essences also work at a spiritual level. Some have special focus in this area, addressing the spiritual aspect of being in unique ways. Whether we work directly at the spiritual level or through the emotions and the physical, the Bush Essences will take us to great heights if we allow them to.

Like us, animals will also respond well to the spiritual aspect of the Essences. The Bush Flower Essences help animals to reconnect with nature. They help to increase animals' awareness of themselves as spiritual beings and to improve their connection with us as co-con-spirit-ors. The Essences will protect them from negative energies, strengthen their connection with their God and help them live fully as spiritual as well as animal beings. The Bush Essences will also help us, as humans, to work at a spiritual level with our animals.

Angelsword helps with recall of past life knowledge and skills. It will revitalise energy fields.

Bush Fuchsia or **Meditation Essence** can enable animals that have little contact with other animals to reconnect with their Spirit selves and with their animal-ness.

Bush Iris strengthens connection with Spirit.

Crowea will help align the subtle energy bodies of an animal who is touched or otherwise disturbed and has to come quickly back into its body when astral travelling or dreaming deeply.

Freshwater Mangrove can help humans overcome preconceived ideas about what animals are and open us to the larger picture.

Fringed Violet provides psychic protection. It also repairs damage to aura after shock or trauma or after psychic attack.

Green Spider Orchid will help animal and human to communicate better at a non-verbal level. Once we can see our animals as Spirit beings in furry, scaly or feathered coats, we can interact on a more equal level.

Mint Bush can help when an animal is striving to fulfil its role on Earth only to be met by obstacles that seem beyond its control.

Meditation Essence can help animals and humans move into a meditative state. Many animals love to sit in a meditation room and soak up the energies present. This Essence can create an ideal environment in which to communicate with our animals.

Pink Flannel Flower moves animals and humans into a space of deep gratitude, love and joyful peace. When in this state it is much easier to work together at a spiritual level.

Space Clearing Essence can help to clear negative energies that are attached to an animal's energy fields. It also can clear areas which spook an animal or human.

Southern Cross can help us and our animals to learn life lessons.

Finally, any of the Essences for love are good for strengthening spirituality – **Sydney Rose**, **Pink Flannel Flower**, **Bluebell**, **Mountain Devil** and **Rough Bluebell** all help to bring in the love vibration. Where there is unconditional love there is connection with our God-ness. Animals naturally love without judgment or conditions, so being with animals in a harmonious relationship can strengthen our connection with the spiritual aspect of our lives. Love is a state in which spirituality will flourish.

Chapter 12

LIVING IN ZOOS, FARMS or THE WILD

*Those who wish to pet and baby wild animals love them.
But those who respect their natures and wish to let them live
normal lives, love them more.*

EDWIN WAY TEALE, 'CIRCLE OF THE SEASONS', 1953

CAPTIVE BEHAVIOUR

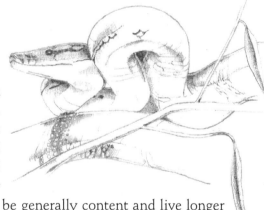

Opposition to keeping animals in zoos has increased in recent times, and with good reason. Animals kept in small cages, often in isolation and in unsuitable climates have been subjected to nothing short of cruelty. However, many animals in well-run modern zoos appear to be generally content and live longer than their brothers or sisters in the wild because of their improved living conditions. It needs to be recognised that, even in the wild, most animals have invisible but well marked boundaries to their territories which restrict their movement almost as much as do the boundaries of a zoo enclosure. Wild animals are also limited in the distances they can travel. Competitors, predators, available food and the amount of energy they have to expend all exert an influence on their range. Ideally, all animals would be able to roam freely in their natural habitat, but zoos do exist and many do magnificent work in breeding and releasing endangered species. They also house injured animals or those bred in captivity that cannot easily be released back into the wild. In addition, zoos play an important role in educating the public about animals, both native and exotic.

The term 'animal ambassadors' is being used to describe animals that cannot be released and which are used to better educate the public about wildlife and conservation. Many such animals take to this role enthusiastically. Perhaps at Spirit level this is their destiny?

The needs of mammals, reptiles and birds vary dramatically, as do those of aquatic species. The thoughtful design of animal habitats in zoos is more important for the well-being of the animals than the size of the enclosures. Ideally, replication of the natural environment of each species is desirable. Some modern animal enclosures have interesting design features including waterfalls which drown out the sound of zoo visitors as well as providing entertainment and fresh running water for the animals. Native vegetation provides shade and helps to create a familiar environment. Flamingos respond well to mirrors in their enclosures giving them the impression of the presence of many more birds than there really are and so encouraging breeding. Toys that will release minute amounts of food will keep an animal entertained for long periods. Polar bears enjoy big iceblocks packed with food titbits which cool them down as well as giving them entertainment over a long period.

Animals in the wild generally go to great lengths to avoid confrontation with other animals and although they need to defend their territory, their food, their mate and their young, they will rarely fight violently or to the death. Marking their territory is one behaviour that mammals use to avoid conflict and it works well as long as there is plenty of space for all the animals in the area. If an animal in captivity can similarly mark its territory without overlapping the space of another animal and the enclosure is designed to give room to move, places in which to retreat and a variety of features that encourage activity, then the animal can live contentedly. Of course the animal must also be well fed and cared for.

But where zoo accommodation is poorly designed or overcrowded, animals can engage in a continual struggle to establish their territories and fighting can be frequent. Apart from the obvious danger of injury, this constant need to defend an over-small territory can result in permanent stress which often results in an animal becoming neurotic, ill or even dying. Where there are many animals in one enclosure, it is important to have places for the subordinate ones to hide from the aggression of the more dominant animals. This is especially so during the breeding season. A subordinate animal can die from stress if it can't escape constant harassment.

The majority of captive animals will benefit from having animals of their own species nearby, or any other animals with which they would mix in the wild. It is important, however, to keep carnivore enclosures away from those of prey animals – the smell of a lion or tiger can seriously upset an antelope or zebra. Even animals who are loners by nature don't like to be solitary all the time. Animals like lions, sloths and koalas, who are usually reclusive and are inactive for much of their day, will usually settle well in captivity. Those that are inquisitive, active and curious need a rich and diverse habitat to be happy in their restricted quarters. Naturally playful animals such as otters and monkeys need a stimulating and varied environment. Frequent enjoyable interaction with keepers can be an important factor in the contentment of captive animals. Animals that are gregarious by nature, such a gorillas, macaques and dolphins, can become very depressed if left alone for long periods and some will never settle well into captivity. Richard Farinato, Director of Captive Wildlife Protection for the US Humane Society and a former zoo director, believes that some species, including marine mammals, polar bears, great apes and elephants, are unsuitable to be kept in captivity as display animals because their physical and mental needs cannot be met in a zoo environment.

Some Essences to consider for captive animals are listed below.

Bush Gardenia (or **Relationship Essence**) will help to improve the interaction between different animals.

Calm and Clear Essence, in mist form, will help to create a peaceful atmosphere within an enclosure.

Dynamis Essence is good for promoting energetic enjoyment of life.

Flannel Flower and/or **Sturt Desert Rose** can help set healthy boundaries.

Little Flannel Flower is the Essence to engender playfulness in animals that have lost their sense of play.

Mountain Devil can help where there is fighting and jealousy.

Pink Flannel Flower can bring about deep inner joy and peace and help an animal accept its present situation, whatever it is.

Slender Rice Flower can help animals to get on better together as a group.

Space Clearing Essence will clear the energies of previous animals or trauma from an enclosure.

Wild Potato Bush helps where the animal is obviously distressed by the restrictions of its enclosure.

Captive animals can adopt repetitive, obsessive habits. Abnormal behaviours such as pacing, swaying or head bobbing can develop because of fear, boredom, stress or sexual frustration. Some animals will resort to stalking, baiting and sexually harassing other animals in the same enclosure. Others may harm their own young or indulge in self-mutilation, biting and chewing fur, feathers or toes. Some even bite off pieces of flesh. Other behavioural problems with captive animals include throwing faeces at the public, begging even when not hungry, or playing with their food – anything to break the monotony and create a situation that will stimulate activity around them. Even in open zoos, animals that have come from places with small, bare enclosures will often continue these habits long after the move to more spacious surroundings. They do not easily give up their ritualistic behaviour.

Black-eyed Susan could help a normally active animal that is frustrated because of its living conditions.

Boronia and **Bottlebrush** can help to let go of obsessive, repetitive behavioural habits.

Dog Rose or **Grey Spider Flower** can be useful where an animal is frightened.

Emergency Essence will help an animal that has been traumatised by a frightening experience.

Flannel Flower with **Wisteria** could reduce sexual aggression in a male.

Kangaroo Paw could help where behaviour is not appropriate, particularly in adolescent animals.

Peach-flowered Tea-tree could help to ease the boredom of a routine existence.

Also consider some of the Essences for depression described in Chapter 6.

Poor sex drive in captive animals

Poor sex drive, common in some zoo animals such as pandas and elephants, can be helped by putting animals with others of their kind in a more natural environment. In a current experiment in China, 16 young pandas are living together in 'panda kindergarten' so that they can get used to playing together and interacting with each other in the hope that this will improve their receptiveness to mating when they are mature. However, a report from the Bronx Zoo in New York suggests that too much time spent together can reduce the sex drive of zoo animals and that keeping male and female animals apart until the breeding season can encourage reproductive activity. This report also suggests that obesity in zoo animals can reduce their libido. Animals that have been hand reared sometimes have trouble breeding because they imprint on their human carers and also because they have had no role models to follow regarding sexual behaviour and caring for their young.

Bush Fuchsia enables an animal to see itself as an animal and not as a surrogate human.

Dynamis Essence could help if the animal seems lacking in sexual energy and enthusiasm.

Flannel Flower would help boost hormones in a male animal.

She Oak encourages breeding in a female animal.

Where some animals are over-abundant in a zoo, they are given a contra-ceptive drug to prevent unwanted pregnancies. **Bush Fuchsia** and **She Oak** can help keep the hormones of such animals in balance when they come off the birth control medication and are wanted for breeding again.

Caring for captive animals

Zoo wardens and other animal carers need to do more than just feed their charges and clean out their enclosures. They need to spend time interacting with the animals, enriching their social environment.

Alpine Mint Bush could help the carer who is in danger of burning out.

Confid Essence or **Five Corners** would help to enhance the keepers' confidence in their role.

Flannel Flower helps in the giving and receiving of gentle touch.

Green Spider Orchid and **Bush Fuchsia** will encourage understanding and communication between animals and keeper. All these Essences could be given to humans and animals.

Macrocarpa or **Dynamis Essence** could help an animal carer maintain enthusiasm and energy.

Where it is the keeper's job to be the boss of their particular group of animals, then **Red Helmet Orchid** given to the animals can help them accept that relationship.

Relationship Essence, **Red Helmet Orchid** or **Bottlebrush** could be considered for bonding between animal and carers. Any of the Essences for love could always be helpful in this situation.

The carers of captive newborn and young animals usually become very attached to the animals they are working with. As in any relationship, there is a fine line between the giving of self and maintaining the professional independence of carer and her charge. Unlike pets, wild animals in refuges and some animals in zoos are being cared for so that they can be returned to the wild or released within an enclosure with others of their own kind. Well-meaning 'smother love' can be damaging in the long term to the animal's natural socialising skills with others of its own species. It is always in the animal's best interest to bring in other animals and keep human-to-baby-animal contact to a minimum. There are Essences which will help carers to give the animals all the contact, love and attention that they need but, at the same time, to keep a degree of separation between themselves and the animals they are working with.

Angelsword can disconnect the energy cords between people and animals where that is desirable. It could help, for example, where the animal is draining the carer of energy or where physical separation has to happen and the carer is having difficulty coming to terms with that.

Bottlebrush can help bonding between the carer and the young animal while at the same time balancing the mothering instinct and preventing a dependent relationship developing. It can help the carer to let go when time comes for release of the animal in her care.

Flannel Flower helps with the enjoyment of touch by both carer and the young animal and, with **Sturt Desert Rose**, will help establish healthy boundaries.

Fringed Violet could protect the carer from taking on the energy of the animal or vice versa.

Gymea Lily is beneficial if the carer has a need for the love and adoration of the animals in her care.

Monga Waratah could be considered if the carer is using the animal/human relationship as a prop for her own sense of well-being.

Old Man Banksia is for the human who willingly takes on the mothering role with many animals but who has become drained or even resentful from the constant ongoing caring.

Need for sedation

Captive animals are often anaesthetised or heavily sedated for even minor medical treatment or for moving from one location to another.

Emergency Essence with **Macrocarpa** added, given before and immediately after a procedure, can help the animal deal with any trauma and to quickly return to its conscious state.

Mulla Mulla can be considered for helping an animal to regain normal body temperature if it rises above normal while the animal is being anaesthetised. In major surgery the body temperature is sometimes lowered to minimise bleeding. In these circumstances **Tall Mulla Mulla** could be given to energetically boost circulation once the danger of bleeding had passed. **Bush Fuchsia** has an energetic association with the hypothalamus, which is involved in the control of body temperature. It could support other treatment of a young animal if its temperature is found to be lower than normal after a medical procedure, or immediately after birth.

Purifying Essence can help clear drugs from the animal's system after such procedures because its component Essences work energetically on the organs of excretion – the intestines (**Bottlebrush**), the kidneys (**Dog Rose**), the lungs (**Sturt Desert Pea**) and **Wild Potato Bush** helps prevents toxins settling in the tissues and so helps to remove them from the body.

WILD ANIMALS

Many of the ideas already discussed will apply to wild animals just as they will to pets and zoo, farm or working animals. However, there are a few special circumstances that occur when dealing with rescued wild animals where Australian Bush Flower Essences could help. Shock is the number one killer of rescued animals, whether native or feral, so using **Emergency Essence** can improve the survival rate. Handle the animal as little as possible, keep it warm and quiet, preferably in a dark place, and allow it to deal with its trauma.

There is evidence that the purring of cats is of such a vibration that it helps to heal the animal. Certainly cats have a high survival rate after the physical trauma of accidents. Cats will purr when badly injured or coming out of anaesthetic after surgery. It seems that the measurable frequency of a cat's purr is in the range of 25–150 Hertz. Various investigations have shown that sound frequencies in this range can improve bone density and promote healing. Professor Leslie A. Lyons from the University of California feels that this association between the frequencies of cats' purrs and improved healing of bones and muscles may provide help for some humans – a purring cat sitting on your knees might do a lot more than make you feel happy! Other animals have their own survival strategies and keeping them quiet, undisturbed and calm will allow that healing to happen. Of course, where there is serious injury this must be dealt with, but **Emergency Essence** will support the animal through the experience of being handled by humans and undergoing anaesthetic and surgery. Where an animal is trapped or not easily accessible, **Emergency Essence Mist** can be sprayed in the vicinity until rescue is possible.

There is a lovely story illustrating the imaginative use of Emergency Essence with wild animals. Paula, a Bush Flower Essence practitioner, was involved with a whale rescue at Busselton on Western Australia's south-west coast in May 2005.

*'I made up a mix of **Emergency Essence** to deal with the shock and trauma, with **Macrocarpa** added to deal with exhaustion and to provide stamina. I made the Essence up using just water, no alcohol. After I put on my wet suit I poured half the bottle of Essence down my front and immediately went in with the whales. I stayed in the water for two hours which is normally the maximum time allowed in such conditions. I was then told by the rescue organisers to come out and have a break. I did leave the water for a short while but, after pouring the other half of the **Emergency Essence** on my wetsuit, I returned and was able to stay in with the whales until they were shepherded out to sea over two hours later. This was an amazing rescue. All but one of the whales survived and they did not return to the beach as they often do. Nor did they beach themselves further along the coast as can sometimes happen. It is thought that the one who did die was already ill or injured before beaching and that the others had followed it in. I was amazed at my stamina at being able to stay in the water so long. But I also felt that it was the **Emergency Essence** that helped the whales and enabled this rescue to be such an outstandingly successful one.'*

Ongoing care of wild animals has other problems. Many survive the initial shock, but succumb to the stress of the injury or disease and the unfamiliar environment, food and regular close contact with humans.

Calm & Clear Essence or just **Black-eyed Susan** by itself can reduce the stress factor. Some animals move through stress into depression and eventually just give up and die.

Emergency Essence, or **Fringed Violet** and **Grey Spider Flower**, both components of **Emergency Essence**, can be used as ongoing treatment for shock and terror.

Kapok Bush supports the animal that is in danger of giving up because it is all too difficult.

Waratah can help a sick animal recall survival strategies of its species and draw upon those energies. It will give the animal the courage to live.

Many rescued wild animals have trouble digesting their food. Very young koala infants need the mother's gut flora to establish their own flora and so digest their food. They can die of hunger while waiting for it to become available from another koala, sometimes from a fresh road kill.

Bauhinia, **Bottlebrush**, **Crowea**, **Paw Paw** and **Peach-flowered Tea-tree** are all associated energetically with the various stages of digestion and should be considered to support other treatment for any animal that has digestive problems.

Essences to boost the immune system should help the animal fight infection, particularly if they have taken antibiotics. **Bush Iris**, **Black-eyed Susan**, **Illawarra Flame Tree**, **Macrocarpa** and **Pink Flannel Flower** can be a good mix for such animals because it helps them deal with their emotional turmoil, engen-dering a state of inner peacefulness, which is a strong place from which to heal. Contact with other animals of their own species can also encourage an animal to thrive and the Essences **Bush Gardenia**, **Slender Rice Flower** or the **Relationship Essence** can help animals to get along with each other in this situation.

Releasing wild animals

When animals are ready for release back into the wild, Australian Bush Flower Essences can be used to ease the trauma of release. Kangaroos and wallabies can panic when first let out of intensive care into an outside enclosure. They have a strong instinct to get back to their home range and their family and will crash into fences in blind panic in an effort to do this. Anne Cullinan, who works at Waratah Wildlife Park, in Sydney, uses a special blend of Essences to help animals that have been raised in captivity when they are released into the wild. The Essences included in this combination are as follows.

Bush Fuchsia helps with tapping into natural instinctive behaviour.

Dog Rose is for fear and anxiety.

Dog Rose of the Wild Forces is for fear of losing control and for embracing instinctive behaviour.

Fringed Violet offers protection.

Slender Rice Flower encourages the ability to merge and connect to animals in that same species and group.

Tall Yellow Top counteracts the sense of being alone.

There are other Essences that could also be considered.

Confid Essence or **Five Corners** will boost an animal's confidence to start living in the wild again.

Emergency Essence is always good to have on hand, both for the animal being released and for the carer.

Emergency Essence plus **Dog Rose** will help to deal with the panic.

Flannel Flower and **Sturt Desert Rose** support the newly-released animal in establishing healthy boundaries.

Macrocarpa will address the stamina needed to get through the first couple of days back in the wild.

Monga Waratah gives the strength to step out and stand alone without the support of carers.

TOXIC ENVIRONMENTS

Animals that live with humans are in danger of absorbing, breathing or consuming physically toxic substances. Many of the substances used to treat animals for internal and external parasites can be very toxic if not used with extreme care. Crop sprays can also be toxic to animals if they come in contact with the spray drift or eat plants that have recently been sprayed. Rodent and snail baits are notorious for poisoning cats and dogs. Household cleaning agents can poison many animals as can insect sprays, engine exhaust and other substances that form part of our day-to-day living environment. If an animal is obviously ill, then get professional treatment immediately.

Emergency Essence will assist in keeping the animal calm.

Electro Essence is good where there has been exposure to electro-magnetic radiation from personal and household equipment, overhead powerlines and X-rays. It is also beneficial if the animal has had X-rays or radiation treatment.

Purifying Essence can support the body energetically in cleansing toxins from the body.

Mulla Mulla or **Solaris Essence** can be used where heat or fire is involved in the trauma.

A story received from Bush Flower Essence user Peter Mandregin of T, tells of a pet diamond python that came into contact with termite spray.

*'This snake became very ill, was quite limp and was frothing at the mouth. It was doubtful that she would last through the night. The vet was called and the only advice he could think of was to wash the snake with soapy water. The Essences **Bush Fuchsia**, **Crowea** and **Bottlebrush** were added to plain water and sprayed over the snake so it would be absorbed through the skin. Next morning the sick snake was much healthier and within a few days was back to normal.'*

Bush Fuchsia would have supported the health of the nerve endings, **Bottlebrush** would enable the snake to let go of the poison from her body and **Crowea** would have helped bring the body into balance.

Animals can also be affected by energetically toxic environments – places like slaughter houses or war sites where traumatic events have occurred. Agitated households and chaotic situations such as accident sites or natural disasters can also upset an animal. Even a vet's operating room, where many other animals have been frightened and some have died, can upset an animal as it picks up on the energy of those who have been there previously.

Calm & Clear Essence Mist can help create a peaceful environment where an animal has been previously upset or agitated.

Emergency Essence Mist can be used in a similar way where there is trauma, terror and upset.

Space Clearing Essence Mist can be sprayed around an area where there is a sense of disturbed or negative energy.

SHOW, RACE AND PERFORMANCE ANIMALS

Animals that perform for an audience, race against other animals in front of a crowd or who are regularly on the show circuit have some special pressures of their own. Preparation, training and rehearsal, together with the stress of the owner's expectations can all be very demanding. There is the need for focus and the ability to understand and carry out commands. Repeating a routine over and over again to get it just right can be taxing, resulting in boredom and disinterest. The excitement and hype of pre-performance and then the actual time on stage, in starting gates, or in the judging ring, is usually distracting as other animals around become agitated and human carers become tense and even angry. There can be a sense of confusion and rejection as an animal picks up on the emotions of its owner if the animal does not come up to expectations or fails in a particular performance. And the stress of travelling and staying temporarily in unfamiliar surroundings can all add up to a lot for an animal and its carer to cope with.

Of course many animals enjoy the ongoing attention. They thrive on the activity, the constant stimulation, the adulation, and being with the owner so much of the time. However, there are always moments when everyone is tired and exhausted, when focus wanders and when things go wrong. Essences can work wonders here to calm the situation and maybe save the day.

Calm & Clear Essence, either as oral drops or in the form of a mist, can be used to create a sense of calm.

Christmas Bush will help in the manifestation of the plan of a performance or show appearance. There is a lot of preparatory work involved and this Essence can help a dream become a reality.

Cognis Essence is a helpful combination for performance. It improves communication, focus and coordination, and helps with remembering routines. It could also be useful if the animal tends to be hyperactive.

Confid Essence is to be considered where an animal, and maybe its owner or trainer, is lacking in confidence.

Creative Essence is good for the period of preparation to help engender a creative and original way of presenting an animal, or when preparing a routine or other performance.

Dog Rose is good for the animal that is shy or timid when in the spotlight.

Dog Rose of the Wild Forces helps when an animal is in danger of taking on the agitation of other animals and people in a disturbing situation.

Dynamis Essence is beneficial where an animal needs strength and stamina. It can also help owners and riders.

Emergency Essence should be available all the time either as drops for a nervous or stressed animal or owner, as a cream for tense, tight muscles and as a mist to defuse tense environments. **Emergency Essence** will help with extreme performance anxiety. However, some animal carers feel that **Cognis Essence** is the best Essence for routine, normal nervousness before performance where the extra adrenalin rush is a positive factor for peak performance.

Grey Spider Flower can help where there is terror on stage, when an animal freezes or goes to pieces in front of an audience.

Illawarra Flame Tree is beneficial where there is a sense of having failed, or of being rejected by a disappointed owner.

Pink Flannel Flower will help an animal achieve a sense of deep peace and satisfaction with the current place and time, wherever that may be.

Space Clearing Essence can clear a space, an arena, a transport vehicle or any area where other people and animals have been and where an animal will be housed for short or long periods. This Essence is also good in motel rooms for the owners.

Travel Essence Mist or **Cream** can help when travelling is extensive and tiring.

FARM ANIMALS

If we can accept the possibility of animals making sacred contracts then it is logical to believe that some animal spirits choose to come to earth as farm animals that provide humans with meat, milk and eggs and other animal by-products, or maybe to be a working companion and four legged labourer. Within those parameters it is up to us, as animal carers and the co-signers of the sacred contract, to provide those animals with the best possible conditions for life and also for death. The thinking is similar if our belief is simply that we are all part of nature and that animals used in agriculture are part of that very complex natural arrangement. Of course, many people believe that no animal should be used to provide meat and other products and that will be dealt with later in this chapter.

A good farmer or grazier will normally have a satisfying interactive relationship with their animals. The farmer respects them for the important role they play in their life. They provide not just an income but also companionship and the satisfaction of seeing a job well done. The farmer will provide them with the best possible conditions for their comfort and well-being and they in turn will cooperate with them in their farming practices. It is a special relationship.

Many Essences can help to support this relationship including **Relationship Essence**, **Bluebell**, **Bush Gardenia**, **Red Helmet Orchid** and others which have been covered in detail earlier in the book.

It is a good idea to keep Essences on hand for dealing with the day-to-day experiences that living on a farm with livestock can bring. Olwen Anderson of Tyalgum in northern NSW tells the story of a very young dairy calf which responded well to the Essences. The calf had simply arrived one morning, from an adjoining dairy farm. It was barely one day old and was in bad way, obviously having been separated from its mother for quite some time, and was covered with ticks.

> 'We administered seven drops of **Emergency Essence** and were able to get the calf to drink some milk from a bucket. Our neighbours arrived an hour later and were amazed to see the calf in such good condition as its mother was sick and the baby had been missing for many hours. However, it was now in such good form that it took four adults to hold it down to remove the ticks. Enquiries made a week later revealed that the calf was continuing to thrive. I feel that the calf's recovery was largely due to the action of the **Emergency Essence** in removing a great deal of the anxiety it was experiencing.'

Dosing large numbers of animals

As mentioned in Chapter 2, dosing large numbers of animals need not be a problem. The Essences can be added to drinking water or to food. Obviously, when dosing a whole group of animals in this way, the quantity of Essence each animal receives cannot not be very specific. But being a form of energy medicine, the dosage of the Essences does not have to be as accurate as with a drug or herbal preparation. Listen to your intuition. Watch the results you get and you will soon work out what is the best dosage for your animals. To begin with, 10–20 drops in a water bucket or small trough is a good guide. In Britain, homoeopathic vets spray into the mouth or, with a head shy animal, under the tail – any mucous membrane will do! Unlike homoeopathics, the Bush Flower Essences do not necessarily need to be applied to a mucous membrane. They can be applied anywhere on the body or sprayed into the energy fields.

Being sent to market

Animals that are being sent to market need special attention. Certainly **Emergency Essence** will help the animals cope with the unfamiliar cattle truck and sale yards, but many of these animals, particularly if they have had close contact with their owner, will really grieve when sold on to another owner. This needs to be taken into account and communication with the animal will help it to understand and adjust. Essences for grief, for change and for fear and anxiety could all be considered.

If animals are going to be slaughtered then they should be prepared for that experience. **Transition Essence** given in several doses before the animal leaves the farm, and if possible on arrival at the slaughter house, will take some of the sting out of this premature death experience.

For animals who are housed indoors all the time, and there is no way to easily change that system, there are some Essences to consider.

Flannel Flower and **Sturt Desert Rose**, relating to healthy boundaries, could help.

Pink Flannel Flower would engender a joyful acceptance of the present situation.

Wild Potato Bush for frustration at the restrictions of physical movement is another to use in these circumstances.

Handling groups of animals

If there is unrest amongst any group of animals the following may help.

Calm & Clear Essence Mist, sprayed around the enclosure, could reduce the disturbances.

Emergency Essence Mist with **Slender Rice Flower** would also help.

Where animals in herds or flocks are moved from paddock to paddock or over a long distance, Essences could be added to the drinking water before the move.

Dynamis Essence or **Macrocarpa**, for stamina, could be good for animals that are on a long trek. It would also support the handlers, giving them the endurance to keep working in exhausting and often difficult conditions.

Green Spider Orchid and **Bush Fuchsia** would be good when communicating with working dogs or horses. These Essences could be taken by animal and owner.

Slender Rice Flower would help the group to move together harmoniously.

Sydney Rose will enhance the sense that all animals are one with each other. It could help the group move as one as a loose conglomerate instead of as a collection of disconnected individuals.

A story from practitioner Sally Rashbrooke tells how the Bush Essences helped cattle caught in big bushfires near her home early in 2006.

'Friends of mine were affected by the bushfires around Moyston/Pomonal at the foot of the Grampians in western Victoria. They have a well-pastured area, set up with 30 breeding cattle, and the fires passed through their property at both a canopy and ground level, (the wind unexpectedly turned), at about 30 kilometres per hour. Eighteen of the cattle died and the remaining 12 were adversely affected though burns, primarily to the underbelly areas. They were

*very uncomfortable and couldn't easily lie down. These friends commenced daily vitamin/mineral feeding and dressings with zinc and Paw Paw cream. I worked with my Guides in making up a dose bottle of Australian Bush Flower Essences for use in the cattle's drinking water – approximately half a bath-tub in size that is continuously fed, with a stop cock to prevent overflow. The dose bottle consisted of **Paw Paw**, **Mulla Mulla**, **Spinifex**, **She Oak**, **Mountain Devil** and **Dagger Hakea**. My instructions for the administration of these were 21 drops into their drinking water at each visit, and they drank their first dose on Sunday morning. I received a telephone message two and half days later, which I would like to share with you. "Thank you very much for the rescue drops. The cattle, after I put them in the first time, all drank from the trough. The very next day it was so amazing to see them – they were all lying down relaxed together – all close up together – even the little ones. It was amazing – the feeling was absolutely beautiful – thank you." Maybe you can imagine the goose-bumps I had when I heard these words – and the realisation of the power of the Bush Essences.'*

Eggs laying in poultry
For poultry there are some other Essences to consider.

Bush Iris, for birds who aren't laying, will help adjust their body clocks by energetically supporting the pineal gland, and so triggering the egg-laying cycle once again.

Bush Fuchsia and **Yellow Cowslip Orchid** work in a similar way on the hypothalamus and pituitary gland, and could also help to start this hormonal action.

She Oak has a beneficial effect on the ovaries, which produce the eggs, so is certainly an Essence to use here.

In the wild, chickens would not lay all year round, so an Essence such as **Macrocarpa** for stamina and physical energy could support animals that are kept under artificial lights to prolong their egg laying period. A similar situation occurs for milking cows or goats that are expected to produce milk for very long periods.

Farm surgery and other intrusive practices
Animals that have to face farm surgery or intrusive practices such as drenching, castration, de-horning, shearing and artificial insemination, could all benefit from the Essences.

Emergency Essence will always help. Even with a large flock of sheep, each one could be sprayed as it passes through the gate. Or consider adding the Essences to the worming or spraying mixture.

Slender Rice Flower is good for removing the effects of trauma from scar tissue at an energetic level and so helping the incisions to heal.

Spinifex has a particular affinity with the skin and can support the healing of fine cuts, skin lesions, blisters, and also damage to nerve endings.

Essences for other specific problems with farm animals can be found in earlier sections of this book or in the Repertory of Symptoms on page 149.

TRAVEL

Travelling can seriously upset some animals so **Travel Essence** is to be considered where an animal is travelling, especially by plane. There are other Essences which will also help.

Bauhinia will open an animal to doing things in ways that are outside its normal routine.

Bottlebrush can help the animal adapt to change.

Emergency Essence can be used if the animal is obviously fearful and upset in any situation when travelling.

Space Clearing Essence Mist could be good in horse floats, farm animal transport vehicles or live-sheep container ships to clear the energies of animals that have been transported in these vehicles in the past.

Travel Essence Mist would take some stress and discomfort out of the travel.

Wild Potato Bush should be considered to deal with the frustration of limited space to move when an animal is travelling.

Maggie from Adelaide sent in this story about Possum, a 13 year old Chihuahua, who had a great fear of travelling.

*'This dog suffered from spinal problems and was under treatment from a vet so could not be left with anyone whilst the owners had to travel interstate. I gave the owner **Emergency Essence** for the dog. She forgot to give it to him first thing at their 5 am departure and Possum had bulging eyes and ears pinned right back trembling all over from entering and sitting in the car. The owner ran back and got the Essence and gave Possum her first dose. As they moved off the symptoms subsided and she settled immediately and did not need another dose from Adelaide to Bendigo – a distance of almost 700 kilometres. Her owners had always dreaded any time Pos had to travel in the car. On the return trip one dose was administered and that was all that was needed. The whole family was delighted, amazed and relieved, and so was Pos.'*

OPPOSITION TO THE FARMING OF ANIMALS

If you feel that animals should never be used for their meat or other body products then your thinking in this area obviously has another dimension. Certainly, what has been suggested earlier still applies. Even though you don't believe that animals should be farmed, it does happen. It is up to you to help the animals to be as comfortable and well supported as possible in that situation. Working at improving the housing of commercial poultry, pigs and cattle, and also the preparation of these animals, at a spiritual and emotional level for slaughter, are certainly areas where you can help them – as can lobbying for humane conditions in abattoirs and on animal transport vehicles.

If you feel passionate about animals not being used in agriculture, then there are Essences which will support you.

Calm & Clear Essence will help where you need to keep a clear head and controlled emotions.

Confid Essence will give you the confidence to do what you set out to do.

Cognis Essence will assist when you have to talk in public or read and understand a lot of information.

Dynamis Essence helps when you need physical energy and stamina.

Freshwater Mangrove will enable you to be objective when looking at the situation, not blindly taking on board the beliefs and prejudices of others who have gone before you.

Green Spider Orchid could help you learn to communicate with the animals and find out exactly what they want.

Gymea Lily will help you follow your passion, have the courage to go out on a limb, take the flack, and keep pursuing your drive to stop a particular practice.

Illawarra Flame Tree can help where you feel rejected or ridiculed for your actions and beliefs.

Peach-flowered Tea-tree is good in the situation where you start off enthused about a plan of action but find yourself losing momentum.

Sturt Desert Rose is another Essence to consider. It will help you to stick to your beliefs even when others are disputing what you say. It will also encourage you to follow your own beliefs and not eat meat or wear animal products, if that is your conviction.

Always have **Emergency Essence** on hand for times when you are stressed or find animals that are stressed or going through trauma and crisis.

Making a difference

Don't forget about love. Going in with anger and aggression might energise you temporarily but it will create more aggression in the long term. No matter what anybody else is doing, sending love rather than hate will achieve much, much more. So consider the love Essences.

Bluebell is for opening the heart to love.

Pink Flannel Flower is for accepting any situation with love and joy.

Sydney Rose is for seeing us all as one.

And remember *The Hundredth Monkey*, a story by Ken Keyes. In 1952, on the island of Koshima in Japan, scientists were providing monkeys with sweet potatoes which were dropped onto the sand for the animals to eat. The monkeys liked the taste of the potatoes but found the sand that stuck to them was unpleasant. A young female named Imo washed her potatoes in a nearby stream. Other monkeys started to copy her. Over the next four years all the young monkeys learned to wash the sandy sweet potatoes although only a few of the older animals did this. Then something startling happened. One day there were, say, 99 monkeys on the island who had learned to wash their sweet potatoes. Then later that morning the hundredth monkey learned the process. By that evening all the monkeys on the island were washing the potatoes. The added energy of this hundredth monkey somehow created an ideological breakthrough. What was even more amazing, all the monkeys on other islands in the area and the nearby mainland troop at Takasakiyama began washing their sweet potatoes. Thus, when a certain critical number achieves a new awareness, this awareness may be communicated from mind to mind without actual physical contact. You might be the hundredth monkey on your mission!

Chapter 13

PHYSICAL AILMENTS

One thing that especially saddened
me [as a child] was that unfortunate
animals had to suffer so much pain and misery.
It was quite incomprehensible to me why in my evening prayers
I should pray for human beings only. So when my mother had prayed
with me and kissed me good night I used to add silently the prayer
that I had composed myself for all living creatures –
'O heavenly Father, protect and bless all things that have breath:
guard them from all evil and let them sleep in peace.'

ALBERT SCHWEITZER, 1875

The Australian Bush Flower Essences work essentially on emotional problems. However, because of the close connection between the emotions and the physical state of the body, the Essences have proved to be useful in helping to relieve physical problems in both humans and animals. Once any emotional block or disturbance has been cleared, the body is then better able to heal itself and the physical symptoms will usually dissipate.

Good history-taking is essential for providing clues as to what might be behind the animal's physical symptoms. The more you know about the animal's medical and behavioural history, its background and its current environment, the clearer will be your assessment of its condition and the more accurate your Essence selection. Examine the animal physically, paying particular attention to its demeanour, the expression in its eyes and its body language. Then consider any emotional problems that might be behind the presenting physical symptoms.

There is much information available that can help in making this connection. In traditional Chinese medicine the emotions are connected with particular organs in the body – the lungs with grief, the kidneys with fear, the liver with anger, etc. In her book, *Heal Your Body*, Louise Hay suggests that colic, for example, is associated with impatience and annoyance with one's surroundings. Annette Noontil wrote in *The Body is the Barometer of the Soul* that a tumour is associated with lack of trust in self and others. Caroline Myss's books *Creation of Health* and *The Anatomy of Spirit* work with the chakra system to connect the physical and the emotional. She sees congestive heart failure as being associated with the fourth or heart chakra and with the emotions of love and hatred. These publications deal with the human body, but in most cases the information can be moved sideways to accommodate animal anatomy. None of these books can give you an exact diagnosis of the emotional problems behind the physical symptoms of a particular animal, but they will give a good general indication of what might be going on. Having come to an understanding of the possible causes of the animal's symptoms, refer to the appropriate chapter or look up the Repertory of Symptoms (on page 149) for suggested Essences to deal with the presenting emotional and physical symptoms. Use your learned knowledge and your intuition to make your selection of Essences.

If, for instance, your animal has a kidney problem, look to Essences that deal with fear, such as **Dog Rose** and **Grey Spider Flower**, because kidney disease is usually associated with fear at some level. If the animal has a poor immune system, consider Essences such as **Black-eyed Susan** and **Macrocarpa** to deal with physical and emotional stress which reduces the functioning of the immune system. Also, look at Essences such as **Illawarra Flame Tree** and **Bush Iris** which deal with feelings of rejection, abandonment and lack of faith, all of which contribute to a weak immune system. **Pink Flannel Flower** can also support the immune system because it creates a sense of deep peace and satisfaction with the present situation. As mentioned earlier you can also use muscle testing or dowsing to support your selection process and the Flower Insight Cards are another excellent selection tool. (See Chapter 2)

To make up a dosage bottle with more than one Essence you add seven drops of each selected Essence to a mixture of one part brandy and three parts purified, spring or mineral water in a 25 ml or 30 ml bottle. It is recommended that the number of Essences included in any one bottle be limited to four or five (though there will always be exceptions) and that the Essences all address the same broad area. It is best to deal with only one problem at a time.

Always consult a vet for accurate diagnosis and recommended treatment for any serious or ongoing problem. The Essences can be used to support any veterinary or other alternative treatment.

EMERGENCY ESSENCE

As mentioned in earlier chapters, **Emergency Essence** is *the* Essence used most often with animals. It is a wonderful remedy and should be in everybody's first aid kit and car. It is particularly helpful when dealing with accident or crisis situations where some immediate treatment is needed. It is a combination of seven powerful Essences:

Angelsword to recharge energy fields; to cut energetic cords connecting us to others; to help retrieve past wisdom and abilities and to connect more fully with Higher Self; to release negative energy or entities.

Crowea to balance and centre the body and energy fields; to ease worry.

Dog Rose of the Wild Forces to prevent an animal taking on the agitated energies of other animals, people or places; to deal with the feeling of things going out of control; to ease the panic of loss of control.

Fringed Violet to process shock and trauma; to repair damage to energy fields around the body.

Grey Spider Flower for terror, nightmares and nightmarish situations; it engenders a sense of trust.

Sundew for grounding and disconnectedness; for regaining focus after shock or trauma.

Waratah for courage; for enhancement of survival instincts; for deep, dark despair.

Emergency Essence can be used to help get an animal through any traumatic situation, while getting veterinary help as soon as possible. This Essence can be given quite frequently – seven drops into the mouth every hour (or more often) until a crisis has passed. It can also be patted onto the head or elsewhere on the body. It will help to ease the animal's stress and panic until medical treatment is obtained. If an animal is trapped or where dosing an animal is impractical for some other reason, **Emergency Essence Mist** sprayed in the general area will help ease the fear and panic until it can be released. **Emergency Essence Cream** can be rubbed into damaged joints or other painful areas to relieve tension and so reduce pain. This combination can be used for an animal that has to go through a surgical procedure, starting two or three days before the operation and continuing for two weeks after surgery. **Emergency Essence** can also be used for lesser dramas such as getting into an unfamiliar vehicle, staying at a pet motel or going to the vets, taking the fear and stress out of day-to-day activities. It can help an animal deal with minor injuries, insect bites and lesser fears and crises.

Emergency Essence Drops, **Cream** and **Mist** are available in a special economically priced Emotional First Aid Kit from Bush Essence suppliers.

This report from Caloundra Pet Kennels explains a further possible application of **Emergency Essence**.

'**Emergency Essence** is a wonderful First Aid kit in a bottle, especially useful in times of stress, when we have an injured or sick animal to care for. It is beneficial for the owner to take the Essence at the same time as the animal. If the owner feels the pet is in a serious state then the pet will pick up on the owner's distress and will react accordingly. This sometimes results in a deterioration of the animal's condition. By taking this Essence, the owner defuses the situation and the animal can then move into a space of healing without taking on the distress of the owner. So **Emergency Essence** should be part of the regime for everyone when going to the vet's.'

Emergency Essence has literally saved lives on many occasions as the following cases illustrate.

'I could not believe how fast-acting **Emergency Essence** was; it is truly powerful. My oldest dog, Sato, had a heart attack about three weeks ago. When we found her she was at death's door – convulsing, eyes sensitive to light, vomiting, frothing at the mouth and in extreme, extreme distress. I immediately gave her three doses of **Emergency Essence** in quick succession before putting her in the car and rushing to the vet. By the time we got there she was sitting up, eyes open, still very shaky, but a lot more aware of what was going on than what she was when we left home. The vet concluded that she had suffered a heart attack that was induced by a spider bite. The vet put her on heart medication. For the next three weeks I also had Sato on two different batches of Flower Essences: **Slender Rice Flower**, **Dagger Hakea**, **Spinifex** and **Bauhinia** – to deal with the toxicity in her system. **Bluebell** will help her heart to heal after the heart attack. I thought the **Bluebell** would lift the old sadness from the heart; help her release emotions more easily. She is now just about back to normal, running, playing and more of a sparkle back in her eyes. And she has a greater sense of companionship with our other two dogs than she had previously. She has been seen playing with them and voicing herself to them as well.'
– AH, Crabbes Creek, New South Wales

'We own a Jack Russell terrier called Zac. One day he was a bit wobbly on his legs and just not himself, and very quickly his back legs became paralysed and there was terror in his eyes. I sprayed him with **Emergency Essence Mist** which relieved his fear but he was not getting better. As we were driving him to the vet his eyes became cloudy and we thought he was dying. I kept spraying him with **Emergency Essence Mist** and I also gave him **Emergency Essence** by mouth. The vet found a large tick on him and gave him antivenene. However, he did not give much hope of recovery. He felt that Zac was on his way out. Zac was kept overnight at the clinic and we asked the vet to continue to spray him with the **Emergency Essence** spray. The vet was rather bemused at this idea but agreed to do it saying it would not do any harm. Next day the dog was greatly improved and soon recovered completely. The vet was very impressed. He did not expect the dog to live let alone get over the whole episode so well and so quickly. He felt that Zac would have died if we had not given him the Bush Flower Essences. When the paralysis gets to the throat the dog panics and the **Emergency Essence** calms him down and makes him more responsive to treatment.' – JT, Queensland

'I was out walking by a creek early one morning and found a young galah caught in the reeds. He was very wet and cold so I waded into the water and rescued him. I wrapped him up and put him under my arm for warmth and took him back home. We kept him warm and gave him

Emergency Essence drops frequently. One of his wings was drooping and he was in severe shock. We did not expect him to last the night. I decided to do Bowen treatment on his wing. I put **Emergency Essence** on my hands to do the treatment and put it all over his feathers. I also added it to water for him to drink. Within two hours of the treatment he was running around like a crazy thing and drinking lots of the treated water. He soon recovered completely but never flew away. We have him around to this day.' – Gillian Taylor, Wombye, Queensland

'My dog Sam, a big Shepherd/Rottie cross managed to eat some snail bait pellets and quickly became a very sick dog. I rushed him to my vet immediately, giving him doses of **Emergency Essence** on the way. By the time we arrived at the surgery, a journey of about five minutes, he was so ill I really thought we had lost him. The vet did not give me much hope of his survival and Sam was anaesthetised and kept asleep for nine hours. All this time I treated him with **Emergency Essence**, first every ten minutes and then periods longer apart. Sam not only survived but recovered so quickly that the vet was amazed. He said that survival from snail bait poisoning is very, very low.' – JW, Brisbane Queensland

The **Emergency Essence Cream** can also work magic. Zoe Hagon, who worked at an animal refuge, told of success using it.

'I want to share two success stories. The first was a small dog with a terrible skin condition. We tried special washes, cortisone creams and nothing was working. The vet was amazed to see this same condition almost cleared up after a few applications of **Emergency Essence Cream**. Similarly we had a cat with burnt paws come in. I was working in the vet room that day, and the vet was more than happy when I suggested applying **Emergency Essence Cream**, I left instruction for twice daily applications, and one week later, her paws had healed completely.'

KEEPING YOUR ANIMAL HEALTHY

Keeping an animal well nourished and fit will protect it from many health problems. Treating an animal for minor and major emotional upsets as they occur will keep it happy, interested in life and energetically involved in its environment. This will go a long way towards keeping the animal physically healthy. Don't wait for something to go wrong. Use the Essences as an everyday routine to deal with minor imbalances as they occur and to continually reinforce a sense of happi-ness, well-being and connection with the animal's spiritual self. **Purifying Essence** can be given to an animal for two weeks annually, as a preventative treatment.

Animals will occasionally camouflage an injury so if they are slower, quieter and not as interactive as usual look for a possible pain source. Do regular home checks. Run your hands along the animal's body so as to become familiar with what is normal and to pick up any lumps or other changes while they are still minor. Run your hands through the energy fields and see if anything feels out of balance. (See Chapter 2 for more details). Examine the gums for infection and check the teeth for cavities, damage or tartar. Start doing this while the animal is young so it accepts this from you as normal. Get to know the animal's body and energy and if you notice small changes get them checked out by an animal health professional.

PROTECTION FROM INFECTIOUS DISEASE

There are some serious diseases that need special attention, such as feline enteritis, parvo-virus in dogs and strangles in horses. Vaccination against these and some other diseases has been recommended by most of the veterinary profession for many years. The purpose of vaccination is to protect an animal from potentially fatal infections by injecting them with either a killed or a modified (non-pathogenic) live virus, which sensitises the immune system to that particular virus. Thereafter, if the animal is exposed to that disease-producing organism it will be able to respond quickly and vigorously, producing antibodies to overcome the infection. This usually gives good protection again the disease. However, this process is not without dangers, and side effects varying from mild to very serious, or even death, are not uncommon. The practice of regular boosters for vaccinations is being questioned as they can result in health problems in some animals. Many animal owners are looking for alternatives and one area to consider is the use homoeopathic nosodes as a means of protecting their animals.

A nosode is a homoeopathic preparation made from disease matter – such as respiratory discharges or diseased tissues – from a sick animal or person. Using alcohol, repeated dilution and succussion, the process of forcefully striking the remedy against a firm surface, the substance is rendered harmless, producing a safe product which is given to an animal to help build its immunity to a particular disease. It is thought that nosodes act at a deeper level in the body than vaccines. They are administered by mouth and they can be given to very young animals as they don't interfere with their maternal antibodies. The dose is repeated over several months, gradually building up the animal's defences against disease. There has been little long-term testing of nosodes to determine the effectiveness of this treatment, because of the difficulty of measuring results with the usual blood tests. (Their use will not register in a regular titre test). Any assessment of this system has been done with collation of clinical results. However, the use of nosodes for preventing disease has been employed in veterinary and human homoeopathy for many years. In places where vaccination is compulsory for a disease like rabies, homoeopathic nosodes are *not* a legal alternative. Also, many pet motels, boarding kennels and stables still demand allopathic vaccination. This is usually also the case when transporting an animal to another country.

VACCINATION CHOICES

The Australian Veterinarian Association has been looking into vaccination and its effects on animals. Dr Clare Middle, holistic veterinarian from Western Australian has commented on its findings.

'The Australian Veterinary Association has recently modified its recommendation to veterinarians, urging them to encourage individuals to make their own decisions about vaccination, rather than making one general rule that may not suit all animals.

Any individual vaccination programme needs to take into account maximum vaccination for any potentially life-threatening disease which is endemic where the animal lives. **Only vaccinate for serious and endemic diseases.** *For all Australian dogs this includes parvo-virus; for cats – feline enteritis; for horses – strangles and tetanus etc. It would* **not** *include diseases that are no longer endemic in your area, possibly viral hepatitis and distemper, but check with your local vet. In most cases it would not include non-serious disease such as kennel cough, canine coronavirus, feline chlamydia etc.*

It is also recommended that polyvalent vaccinations (i.e. three or five diseases all at once, for example "C5", "F3") are more likely to suppress the immune system and cause unwanted side effects, compared to monovalent (i.e. just vaccinating for one disease only such as parvo-virus by itself.

For this reason, it is far better to minimise vaccination for very young animals, when their immune systems are so delicate and immature. For example, where distemper and viral hepatitis are not endemic, vaccinating for parvo-virus is the priority. Any more unnecessary vaccinations may render the pup more likely to get side effects (allergy, infection, autoimmune disease) and also reduce the effectiveness of the parvo component against the parvo-virus.

Vaccinating for kennel cough at this young age is generally not warranted, as this is hardly ever a serious or life-threatening disease. Possible exceptions may be if the pup comes from a breeding colony or pet shop where there is an unusually strong strain or outbreak at the time. Kennel cough vaccination has a reputation amongst vets as being not really effective. This is because there are so many factors, other than antibodies, which contribute to kennel cough, and to cat flu for that matter. These two diseases are likely to occur due to stress, especially grief (in Chinese medicine the lungs are associated with grief) so weaning or boarding are likely to worsen kennel cough or cat flu, or make them a more likely problem. Vaccinating cats and dogs at the end of weaning, and not weaning until about eight or nine weeks can greatly reduce the weakening and stressing effects of weaning and vaccinating. Sometimes both are carried out too early. Maternal antibodies from the mother's milk not only help to protect the young animal but they can also stop the vaccine from working. It is important to check by blood test that the mother's antibodies are high, prior to breeding.

Another matter that needs consideration is that animals are often given their vaccination in the area between the shoulders which is the site of a chakra, found only in four legged animals. Squirt-on insecticides are also applied to this site. It is not known at this stage what damage that might do to an animal's energetic system.'

For booster shots it is recommended that a titre test be taken to check if the animal really needs the extra dose of vaccine. The more vaccinations an animal receives, the more likely it is to develop allergies and immune system problems. Quite often the animal's antibodies are at a high enough level to deal with any infection. Using Flower Essences for stress and grief (see Chapter 8) when an animal is being weaned or staying at boarding kennels can greatly reduce the incidence of kennel cough and cat flu. Using the 'separation mix' described in Chapter 9 could also help to ease any separation anxiety. Moving animals directly to their new home, not via a pound or pet shop, and giving boarding animals clothes that smell of their owner can also relieve their stress.

Bush Flower Essences to naturally help boost the immune system and help protect an animal against any infection include **Illawarra Flame Tree**, **Bush Iris**, **Black-eyed Susan**, **Macrocarpa** and **Pink Flannel Flower**. However these Essences are not a replacement for a vaccination regime. Always consult your veterinary professional about vaccination.

If an animal has a bad reaction to vaccination the following Essences could be of help.

Boab will help to clear any blocking in the cranial bones, which can often jam up after vaccinations; in severe cases they become very rigid – like blocks of steel.

Bush Fuchsia will help to relieve convulsions.

Bush Iris will assist in cleansing via the lymphatic system, boosting the immune system.

Emergency Essence before vaccination will help ease the trauma to the body, and should be given again afterwards if there is an acute reaction.

Mulla Mulla will ease the sense of burning in the body cells.

Purifying Essence helps to clean out toxins from the body.

WHEN IS IT ESSENTIAL TO TAKE YOUR ANIMAL TO THE VET?

Do not assume that Flower Essences or other alternative treatment will always deal with all your animal's health problems. It is important that your animal be taken to the vet when any of the following symptoms are present:

- all ongoing disorders of defaecation and urination
- depression apparently unrelated to environmental or circumstantial factors
- ongoing irritability in an animal, which could indicate an undiagnosed source of pain
- listlessness, which is often the first indication of uterine problems in female animals
- aggressiveness that doesn't quickly respond to changes in handling or other home treatment
- drinking large amounts of water
- lumps that persist anywhere in the body
- bleeding from any orifice that can't be explained by obvious injury
- fever, listlessness or poor appetite that goes on for more than 24 hours
- collapse or fever and obvious signs of poor health in a female animal who has very recently given birth, or hyperactivity, agitation or trembling which could indicate milk fever (low calcium)

- collapse in any animal
- when a birthing animal is in labour for an extended period, or if there has been longer than four hours between pups/kittens
- scabies and sarcoptic mange
- paralysis tick (*Ixodes holocyclus*) bite or snake bite
- poisoning – early signs of snail pellet or organophosphate poisoning are excessive salivation, then trembling – drop everything and phone the vet
- any serious injury
- hind leg lameness, even if not painful, for more than a few days. If there is rupture of the crucial ligaments, which link the tibia of the lower leg with the femur of the upper leg, early treatment can prevent arthritis later
- straining to urinate in a male animal – stones can easily block the narrow penile urethra and urine can cause back pressure to the kidneys in hours and lead to kidney failure
- vomiting water – dehydration can occur within hours.

The Repertory of Symptoms on page 149 gives detailed information of Essences suggested for other specific problems. We are not claiming that the suggested Essences will heal the problems referred to. However, from the reading of the energies of the Essences, testimonials from Flower Essence practitioners and our own experience, we believe that these Essences have the capacity to help in some way in the areas mentioned, at the very least.

CASE HISTORIES

We have received hundreds of case histories from Bush Essence practitioners who have used the Essences for dealing with physical problems in their animals. Here are some of them.

Kangaroo with a sore foot

'Happy Jack is a kangaroo who lives at the Barrington House nature reserve. When the owner found him he was doing very poorly and barely tolerated people around him because of his obviously very painful and swollen foot. I think the only thing more miserable than a kangaroo with a sore foot is a kangaroo with a sore tail! An X-ray indicated that he had had a broken bone for some time and there was a lot of calcification as well as swelling of soft tissue. The vet had no suggestions and a local zoo suggested putting him down and sending them the foot for testing!!!

I asked for a sample of fur to be sent to me. With a pendulum I chose appropriate remedies and thought, "no wonder he was in such pain". The Essences that came up for the kangaroo were **Dagger Hakea, Paw Paw, Tall Yellow Top, Billy Goat Plum, Spinifex** *and* **Sunshine Wattle**. *Jack responded very well; the heat and swelling were gone within days. His condition improved and he was at that time given his name, Happy Jack. He had taken up residence on the tennis court. The owner was alarmed one morning to find he wasn't there, but on turning around found Jack waiting for someone to open the gate and let him back in. He has become* *one of the favourites amongst the residents and visitors. He is friendly and gentle with children. He has moved from the tennis court to the house and now sleeps on a bed on the veranda. The transformation of his health had been remarkable and his appealing character goes a long way to make up for his forthright manner.'* – David Salamon, Bolton Point, New South Wales

Phooba's flea allergy

*'I have a dog called Phooba. She is a Border Collie and a beautiful dog. However, she had a skin problem, a rash which caused her a lot of distress. She was continually scratching and restless. She could never get comfortable and her sleep was broken by the irritation of the rash. She was very unhappy. The vet diagnosed it as a flea allergy though she had no obvious fleas on her. I gave her **Emergency Essence** frequently for two days – every hour, or as often as I thought of it, and at the end of the second day the dog went into a very deep sleep. After that I gave her **Peach-flowered Tea-tree** for allergies, **Dog Rose** for fear, **Fringed Violet** for shock or trauma – recent or past, **Dagger Hakea** for irritation and **Red Grevillea** for the sense of being stuck – itching to get out – by mouth, for two weeks. I also washed her in a bath of water to which I added seven drops of **Spinifex**, an Essence which is to be considered for any skin problem. She improved dramatically. The scratching stopped and her skin started to heal. However, after a few weeks she started to scratch again so I repeated the whole process and since then there has been no scratching, and her skin has cleared and hair has grown back. She is a much happier dog.'* – Ilana S, New South Wales

Cat free of internal parasites and fleas

*'About five years ago I began giving my cat **Green Essence**, two weeks on and two weeks off, because she'd been scratched on the eye by another cat which resulted in a recurring eye infection. Plus, I thought it would also help to keep intestinal parasites at bay without having to use a chemical worming product. Five years on, her eye infection still flares up from time to time, but she is completely free of intestinal parasites. But, the thing that is most pronounced is that she has also been completely free of fleas all this time! We live in a very sandy, bush area and before giving her the **Green Essence** regularly, I would comb her twice a day with a special flea comb and get on average thirty fleas each time! Now I just comb her to remove excess fur.'* – Karen Vidal, Sydney, New South Wales

Coffee the horse

*'Coffee is a 24 year old gelding who had had diarrhoea for about 12 months and within that time he had lost a lot of weight and was a very sad horse. He had a vet check which included his teeth being filed and a complete worming. Then the vet started him on cortisone which did not lead to much improvement. His owner tried a range of other products – Protexin, egg white, cider vinegar, rice flower and probiotics. He also had some Bowen Therapy which did help with his self-esteem but did not really have any effect on the diarrhoea. He was then started on the Australian Bush Flower Essences and it was found that he had parasites that had been eating at the wall of his bowel. The Essences prescribed were **Bottlebrush**, **Green Essence**, **Macrocarpa** and **Spinifex**. He was given 14 drops twice daily for two weeks. Within a short time on the Essences he was starting to improve every day with a slight setback around the full moon. His weight*

*gain was wonderful once all the parasites had gone. Coffee still had a bowel infection which was treated with **Mulla Mulla**, **Mountain Devil** and **Spinifex**; 21 drops were given twice daily, 2 bottles. He then went on to **Spinifex** and **Bottlebrush**, 14 drops twice daily, to give the bowel extra support for one month. He is now like a new horse. His bowel movements are back to normal. He is much more alert and his condition is improving every week. His coat and hooves have also shown great improvement. They now have life in them instead of being dull, dry and lifeless. They have shine and condition. His coat is much softer and smoother. His eyes are also sharp and clear.'* – Julie Tucker, Noosa Outlook, Queensland

A Dobermann with throat cancer

*'Khan was a 13 years old dog who developed swelling in his throat glands – like mumps. Within three days his face blew up like a football and I took him to the vet who diagnosed terminal cancer and gave him only three days to live. I took him home and worked on him with energy healing – if only to ease his passing. However, I also decided to give him Flower Essences that might help treat cancer. Khan was given five Essences together – **Sturt Desert Pea**, **Dagger Hakea**, **Mountain Devil**, **Slender Rice Flower** and **Kapok Bush** – seven drops twice daily. Within 2 days the swelling in his glands had gone and his face was back to normal. I also continued my energy healing. Two weeks later I took him back to the vet to check that he was not in pain. The vet was astonished, saying it must have gone somewhere else and she checked his lymphatic system. Her shock, disbelief and astonishment were great. Khan recovered totally and I had another wonderful seven months to lavish all the love and appreciation for his unconditional love, devotion and loyalty before he passed away from natural causes without the need for euthanasia. He died from kidney failure.'* – Jeanne Ivens, Norwich, UK

… also from the same practitioner

A Red Setter with paralysis of back legs

*'I was called to see Thomas when he was eight months old. He was displaying paralysis of the back legs, one in particular. The local vet was unable to find a reason for this paralysis and sent Thomas to the Flitwick Veterinary Referral Centre where he stayed for two days for spinal X-rays and various blood tests. No reason was found for the paralysis although cerebellum atrophy was suspected. I felt that Thomas had 'come into this life' with some 'old energies' not cleared up from a previous existence. I gave him some energy healing and put him on the Bush Essences **Angelsword** and **Fringed Violet**, seven drops twice daily, to repair his whole energy field and to clear shock and trauma from past and present situations, which I felt had caused the condition. Thomas was up and walking normally within an hour of his first treatment. His back legs were a bit wobbly because he had not built up muscles in that area. He still needed the treatment to continue to completely clear the energies and this continued for two weeks. I then prescribed **Boab** to release negative family patterns and **Wild Potato Bush** to give him the ability to move on in life, with freedom. Five weeks later Thomas was taken back to see his vet and he was very impressed – he had been quite sure of his prognosis of cerebellum atrophy with euthanasia the only possible outcome. I am now giving Thomas **Gymea Lily Essence** to ensure the spinal energy is flowing clearly, and also **Crowea** to aid the build up of ligaments and muscles. His improvement continues.'* – Jeanne Ivens, Norwich, UK

Horse with back problems

'I was approached by a friend requesting that I treat his horse which had lower back problems. This problem was affecting his performance on the trotting track. The horse would flinch when touched around the sacroiliac region, and had previously been diagnosed as having inflamed muscles to that area. After surrogate muscle testing I gave him **Wild Potato Bush** *and* **Crowea**. *A few weeks later the owner called to say that there had been a marked improvement in the horse's performance – he was more relaxed, responsive, winning races and not complaining of pain when touched.'* – Michael Menners, workshop participant

Emotional upset and a tumour

'Patty the dog had been through a difficult emotional time with her family. Her owner and his partner had broken up after a rather turbulent period in their relationship. This had very much upset Patty. As well as this, her owner's partner also had a dog who was Patty's best doggie friend. When this dog left with his owner Patty was doubly upset. Patty's owner is telepathic and is able to communicate with his dog. Patty told him that she was sick but three vets insisted that she was quite healthy. However, after a month a tumour developed on her side and vets said that it was too late to treat it as it had started to spread to the liver. Without treatment she had about three months to live. As she is an old dog, her owner knew that she probably wouldn't survive surgery or chemotherapy so decided to try Flower Essences. I worked essentially on the emotions which had caused the tumour. The Essences I selected to treat this dog were: **Spinifex** *to help reveal the underlying cause of physical problems;* **Tall Mulla Mulla** *– the little dog had been so distressed by the events in her life that she was withdrawing from social contact with others; this Essence could help overcome this problem;* **Yellow Cowslip Orchid** *to relieve her sense of aloneness; the loss of her best friend;* **Peach-flower Tea-tree** *for emotional turmoil resulting in mood swings and boredom at being alone;* **Tall Yellow Top** *to help deal with her feeling of isolation and loneliness;* **Red Suva Frangipani** *for the sadness of the relationship break-ups of her owner and of her own loss of her close friend. The dog was given the Essences morning and evening for three weeks. By the end of that period the tumour has almost gone and all the negative issues which caused it in the first place had been released. Patty is continuing only on* **Spinifex** *to remove the last remains of the lump.'* – Julie Tucker, Noosa Outlook, Queensland

Incontinence in dogs

'A dog I treated had suffered from incontinence for one year. Pills from the vet resulted in little long term improvement. I tried **Grey Spider Flower** *and* **Dog Rose**. *Two courses of these Essences made a big difference. But a course of* **Macrocarpa** *and* **Dog Rose** *finally cleared the problem completely.'* – Gerda Vel, Northern Territory

A dog with seizures

'Barry is a young Cavalier King Charles Spaniel. He started to have unexplained seizures at around two years of age and underwent a series of tests. The vets diagnosed that he was epileptic and suggested he go on medication. I chose not to accept this advice and kept Barry under close observation. I kept a detailed diary of his day to day routine and discovered that he tended to have his seizures after vaccinations, heartworm treatment, flea treatment etc. and also when he had too much protein in his diet. This led me to believe that his body could not breakdown, assimilate

*and excrete metabolic waste and toxins, and they were building up in his system and causing the seizures. So the course of action was to give him **Purifying Essence** in his water for one week to help detox his body. Then I made up a blend of **Bush Fuchsia**, **Crowea** and **Paw Paw**. The **Crowea** and **Paw Paw** helped Barry by improving his digestion and emotional balance. The **Bush Fuchsia** assisted in neurological conditions. He had this blend orally for six weeks and he remained well. About six months later he had a series of petit mals or small fits – so I used the blend again with the same success.'*
– Jan Fowles, Caloundra Pet Kennels and Cattery, Queensland

Featherless parrot

*'A parrot owned by my hairdresser had been featherless for four years – completely bald. I gave him **Sunshine Wattle** and he is now in the process of growing back his feathers.'*
– Jenny Halliday-Hall, Armidale, New South Wales

Cat with kidney problems

*'This cat had been diagnosed with kidney problems. She was not eating and her urine had a strong smell; she also sat around hunched up all day long. Her owner had been advised to have her put down. I made up some Bush Essences for her – **Dog Rose**, **Grey Spider Flower**, **Old Man Banksia**, **Fringed Violet** and **Waratah**. Within one day she started eating and sat properly. Within one week her urine lost its smell and she improved markedly. One month later she was walking around with her tail up and started playing with other cats. Two months she was back to protecting her territory against foreign cats while maintaining the above mentioned improvements.'* – Sue Brown, workshop participant

Barney the cat and brown snake bite

*'My cat Barney was found unconscious and paralysed as a result of being bitten by a brown snake. To our amazement the vet offered no advice, only the distressing information that cats rarely survived snake attack. Immediately we drenched him with water to lower his temperature and then phoned another vet. I frantically gave Barney **Emergency Essence** every 15 minutes for two hours. Following this I mixed up **Fringed Violet**, **Wild Potato Bush**, **Spinifex**, **Crowea**, **Jacaranda**, **She Oak**, **Southern Cross**, **Macrocarpa** and **Grey Spider Flower**. Twenty four hours on these Essences brought a remarkable change. His eyes opened and were alert, the paralysis was gone and he could meaow again. After 48 hours he showed a miraculous improvement. After 72 hours his body wriggled about and he was showing no pain. We added glucose to his drops because he was getting very thin. I took him to the vet and he was amazed at the cat's liveliness. We kept up the Essences for another day but then discontinued because of his speedy recovery.'* – Judith Collins, Thirlmere, New South Wales

Rocky's itchy problem

Rocky is a much loved Jack Russell/Poodle cross but he brought with him many problems, including a missing tear duct and a very wobbly lower back. The missing tear duct is a constant worry and has to be treated every day of his life with different creams and potions. As Rocky grew older he developed skin problems – he became so itchy that he scratched his tummy on the concrete until it bled and as well he had the problem of an itchy bottom. Over the years all alternatives have *bitten the dust to be replaced with the dreaded antihistamines and even cortisone. Being a member of the Bush Essence team I tried various Essences including **Dagger Hakea** and **Spinifex** but without success, but finally I thought of **Green Essence**. Well, the change has been dramatic – he does still occasionally scratch and rub his tummy but it is not as severe. The **Green Essence** also seemed to help his infected eye and lo and behold the 'scooting' to relieve the itchy bottom has lessened. We continued to add the **Green Essence** to his drinking water and will do so during the summer months when the itches tend to be worse.'*

– Sallianne MacGowan, ABFE Office, Terrey Hills, New South Wales

Disappearing lump

*Winnie, a 13 year old Welsh Springer Spaniel, had developed a benign lump on the top of his left paw. The lump had been growing slowly for a number of years and was the size of a golf ball. It had spread between his toes and had reached the pad of the foot. Winnie chewed and licked the skin off the lump, which was constantly open and weepy. As a result, Winnie had to wear an 'Elizabethan collar' to stop him from aggravating the lump and making it worse. Winnie's vet had prescribed antiseptic cream and antibiotics for the lump, which had only a short-term effect and did not reduce the size of the lump. His human companions were told that there was no other treatment available and nothing else could be done for him. By December 2000, Winnie was confined to wearing the collar all the time. Then I read an article about a terrier with a lump between his toes which disappeared after using the Australian Bush Flower Essence **Spinifex**. I immediately started using **Spinifex** to treat the lump. Winnie was given 7 drops of **Spinifex** twice daily in his water. Within a month, the lump had become noticeably smaller and after four months the lump had disappeared.'* – Karyn Hobby, Kenmore, Queensland

Disappearing skin cancer

*'Recently my pure white cat, Kimba, was diagnosed by a veterinarian as having terminal skin cancer on his nose. Kimba was all but written off as having six months to live before he would die painfully, and it was recommended that he be put down. Understandably, I was upset as I had had Kimba for eight years since he was a kitten. So I made him a dose bottle of **Spinifex** and **Mulla Mulla**, giving it to him on his paws, so he could lick it off very day. Then the miracle happened. Within a week the cancer went into complete remission and has not returned. Not even a scar was left behind. I took him back to the vet just to be sure and the vet was so astonished that he almost didn't believe me. But it was true. The Bush Essences cured the 'terminal' skin cancer.'*

– Faye Muldoon,(address withheld)

Harley's 'hot spot'

*'Using **Mulla Mulla** and **Emergency Essence** I have been able to put a stop to a very unsightly complaint referred to as 'hot spot', in my sister's Staffy called Harley. 'Hot spot' is a weeping inflamed area on a dog's skin that is intensely itchy and painful and resistant to treatment. We've kept it at bay now for two years and many other dogs and owners in Lismore are reaping the rewards. As Harley hadn't been to the vet since his last shots and he was due for more, the vet checked the computer and inquired about the hot spot. My sister told him we'd sorted it out and his words were, "Impossible, there's nothing that will." She mentioned the **Mulla Mulla** and he wrote it down!!'* – Lynne Rowlands, Lismore, New South Wales

REPERTORY OF SYMPTOMS

PHYSICAL AND EMOTIONAL

This Repertory contains an alphabetical listing of physical and emotional symptoms or problems. Its purpose is to help you select Essences for your animals. It also gives further insight into the emotional patterns and other factors behind physical and behavioural problems with your animals

To use this Repertory first find the presenting symptom of your client and then note the Essence or Essences recommended to treat it. Refer to the Essences listed in the 'Information about Individual Essences and Combinations' which starts on page 175, so as to obtain an understanding of the healing qualities of the suggested Essences. Also refer to the relevant chapter in this book for further information about the particular problem you are addressing. Look for those Essences that seem most helpful for the animal you are treating. You do not necessarily use all the Essences listed.

Note that the Essences suggested for each symptom are in alphabetical order, not in order of most appropriate Essence for the particular problem. For example under 'aggressive behaviour' the listing shows **Bluebell**, **Flannel Flower**, **Grey Spider Flower**, **Kangaroo Paw**, **Mountain Devil**, **Rough Bluebell**. Although **Bluebell** (which is for opening the heart) is listed first it is not usually the first Essence to think of for this problem. **Mountain Devil** would probably be seen as *the* Essence for anger and aggression but some or all of the other Essences will also help, depending on the animal and its particular personality and problem.

The information in this Repertory is a guide to the treatment of the symptoms listed but is not a claim that the Essences recommended will cure the disease. The Bush Essences should never replace the services of a qualified practitioner.

SYMPTOMS	BUSH FLOWER ESSENCES
A	
abandoned animals in shelters	Emergency Essence, Illawarra Flame Tree, Tall Yellow Top
abandonment, sense of	Illawarra Flame Tree
abdominal distension	Bottlebrush, Bauhinia, Crowea, Green Essence, Paw Paw, Peach-flowered Tea-tree
abscess	Billy Goat Plum, Mountain Devil, Sturt Desert Pea
absentmindedness	Isopogon, Jacaranda, Red Lily, Sundew
abuse, trauma, after… restore confidence	Five Corners
abused or overtrained animals, destructive	Southern Cross
abusive, strong-willed owners… for animal	Emergency Essence, Little Flannel Flower, Pink Mulla Mulla,
abusive, strong-willed owners… for owner	Dagger Hakea, Flannel Flower, Mountain Devil, Rough Bluebell
acceptance of current situation	Pink Flannel Flower
acceptance of others	Bauhinia, Freshwater Mangrove, Slender Rice Flower
acceptance, needing	Five Corners, Illawarra Flame Tree, Southern Cross
accident prone	Bush Fuchsia, Kangaroo Paw, Sundew
accident, for shock, first aid for injury, trauma	Emergency Essence, Fringed Violet
accident, head injury	Bush Fuchsia, Emergency Essence, Sundew
adapting to change	Bauhinia, Bottlebrush, Freshwater Mangrove, Slender Rice Flower, Waratah
addiction to substance, people, behaviour	Boronia + Bottlebrush, Five Corners, Monga Waratah
adhesions, scars	Slender Rice Flower + Bush Iris (applied to scar and internally)
adjusting when owner returns after absence	Crowea, Dagger Hakea, Dog Rose, Pink Mulla Mulla
adolescent animal	Adol Essence, Kangaroo Paw, Red Helmet Orchid
adopted animal	Bluebell, Boronia, Bottlebrush, Emergency Essence, Grey Spider Flower, Illawarra Flame Tree, Tall Yellow Top
adrenal disorders	Black-eyed Susan, Macrocarpa
aged animal, adapting to limitations	Bottlebrush, Bush Fuchsia, Dog Rose, Little Flannel Flower, Pink Flannel Flower
aged animal, to revitalise	Dynamis Essence, Hibbertia, Old Man Banksia, Silver Princess, Wild Potato Bush
aggressive behaviour	Bluebell, Flannel Flower, Grey Spider Flower, Kangaroo Paw, Mountain Devil, Rough Bluebell
aggressive show dogs	Black-eyed Susan, Gymea Lily, Mountain Devil, Slender Rice Flower
agitated energy of others, taking on	Dog Rose of the Wild Forces
agitation, excessive	Black-eyed Susan, Emergency Essence, Jacaranda, Kangaroo Paw
agoraphobia	Boab + Flannel Flower, Dog Rose, Grey Spider Flower, Emergency Essence
alertness, restores	Bush Fuchsia, Cognis Essence, Sundew
allergies generally	Dagger Hakea + Fringed Violet + Bush Iris
allergies reaction, to decrease	Emergency Essence, Fringed Violet
allergies, caused by stress, trauma	Black-eyed Susan, Calm & Clear, Emergency Essence
allergies, due to dietary, environmental change	Bauhinia, Bottlebrush, Crowea, Paw Paw
allopathic medication, support of	Bush Iris + Illawarra Flame Tree, Emergency Essence
aloof, hands off type animals	Bluebell, Dog Rose, Flannel Flower, Pink Mulla Mulla, Yellow Cowslip Orchid
ambush, swipe, bite, scratch	Calm & Clear, Emergency Essence
amputation of limb, phantom pain	Bush Fuchsia, Fringed Violet, Spinifex

anaemia	Bluebell, Green Essence, Kapok Bush, Little Flannel Flower
anaesthesia, after effects of	Angelsword + Fringed Violet + Macrocarpa + Sundew
anaesthesia, before	Emergency Essence for two days
anaesthesia, crisis during, cardiac arrest	Emergency Essence
anal disorders	Black-eyed Susan, Bottlebrush, Mountain Devil
anal gland infection	Billy Goat Plum, Bottlebrush, Emergency Essence Cream
anger, aggression	Dagger Hakea, Mountain Devil
anguish, extreme mental	Waratah
animals attacked by other animals	Emergency Essence, Five Corners, Southern Cross
annoyance, irritation	Bauhinia, Black-eyed Susan, Dagger Hakea, Freshwater Mangrove
antibiotics, steroids, after taking	Bush Iris + Illawarra Flame Tree, Emergency Essence
antisocial behaviour	Kangaroo Paw, Mountain Devil, Pink Mulla Mulla, Rough Bluebell, Tall Mulla Mulla
anxiety	Calm & Clear Essence, Crowea, Black-eyed Susan, Dog Rose, Dog Rose of the Wild Forces, Pink Flannel Flower, Sturt Desert Rose
anxiety for companions after fire, other trauma	Emergency Essence, Mulla Mulla
anxiety, fear, overprotectiveness	Confid Essence, Dog Rose, Five Corners
anxiety, separation	Emergency Essence + Dog Rose
anxious to please, over apologetic	Five Corners, Sturt Desert Rose, Tall Mulla Mulla
apathy, resignation	Kapok Bush, Old Man Banksia
apologetic behaviour	Confid Essence, Sturt Desert Rose
appetite, poor	Banksia Robur, Crowea, Paw Paw, Philotheca
appetite, ravenous	Bluebell, Crowea, Dog Rose, Peach-flowered Tea-tree, Yellow Cowslip Orchid
approval seekers	Gymea Lily, Red Grevillea, Tall Mulla Mulla
Arabian horses, extreme withdrawal	Dog Rose, Flannel Flower, Pink Mulla Mulla, Tall Yellow Top, Yellow Cowslip Orchid
arrogant	Gymea Lily, Hibbertia, Rough Bluebell, Slender Rice Flower
arthritic conditions	Bauhinia, Emergency Essence Cream, Little Flannel Flower, Mountain Devil, Purifying Essence
assertiveness	Dog Rose, Five Corners, Tall Mulla Mulla
assimilation of nutrients	Crowea, Dog Rose, Paw Paw, Peach-flowered Tea-tree
asthma	Bush Iris + Dagger Hakea + Fringed Violet, Tall Mulla Mulla, Sturt Desert Pea
asthma, acute attack	Emergency Essence
astral travelling, upset after	Crowea, Emergency Essence
attacking out of fear	Dog Rose, Emergency Essence Mist, Grey Spider Flower
attention deficit when being handled	Dog Rose, Jacaranda, Sundew
attention seeking	Five Corners, Gymea Lily, Illawarra Flame Tree, Isopogon
attention seeking, noisy	Kangaroo Paw
attention span low	Boronia, Bush Fuchsia, Cognis Essence, Red Lily, Sundew
aura	Angelsword, Fringed Violet
authority of owner, acceptance of	Red Helmet Orchid
autism	Bluebell, Bush Fuchsia, Dog Rose, Green Spider Orchid, Grey Spider Flower, Sundew
avoidance	Crowea, Dog Rose, Kapok Bush, Tall Mulla Mulla
awareness	Angelsword, Bush Fuchsia, Green Spider Flower, Meditation Essence, Red Lily

B

baby animal, exposure, shock after birth	Emergency Essence
baby animal, failure to thrive	Bush Fuchsia, Emergency Essence + Sundew, Fringed Violet, Sundew
baby, new, intolerance of	Bauhinia, Freshwater Mangrove, Slender Rice Flower, Sydney Rose
back problems, general	Crowea, Emergency Essence Cream applied externally, Gymea Lily
bacterial, viral infection	Black-eyed-Susan, Bush Iris, Illawarra Flame Tree, Mountain Devil, Sturt Desert Pea
bad behaviour	Kangaroo Paw
bad breath	Black-eyed Susan, Crowea, Mountain Devil, Paw Paw, Peach-flowered Tea-tree, Rough Bluebell
bad habits, breaking	Bauhinia, Boab, Boronia, Bottlebrush
bad-tempered	Black-eyed Susan, Dagger Hakea, Mountain Devil, Sydney Rose
balance major organs	Crowea, one off dose will balance 14 major organs and nervous system
balance, loss of physical, vertigo	Bush Fuchsia, Crowea, Hibbertia, Jacaranda, Yellow Cowslip Orchid
balance, physical and emotional	Black-eyed Susan, Bush Fuchsia, Crowea, Peach-flowered Tea-tree, Red Lily, She Oak
baring teeth at owner to protect young	Bauhinia, Bottlebrush, Calm & Clear, Dog Rose, Emergency Essence, Kangaroo Paw
barking, howling, yapping, excessively	Gymea Lily, Illawarra Flame Tree
barometric pressure, changes in	Bush Fuchsia, Dog Rose, Grey Spider Flower
bees stressed by human intervention	Emergency Essence
behaviour pattern, inherited	Boab
behavioural problem after punishment	Isopogon, Southern Cross, Sundew
behavioural problems generally	Dog Rose, Five Corners, Illawarra Flame Tree, Red Helmet Orchid
behavioural problems involving dominance	Gymea Lily, Red Helmet Orchid, Yellow Cowslip Orchid
belonging, sense of not	Five Corners, Illawarra Flame Tree, Tall Yellow Top
bird exhausted after bad weather	Dynamis Essence, Macrocarpa
bird shocked, injured after flying into windows	Emergency Essence
bird, stressed easily	Black-eyed Susan, Calm & Clear Essence, Emergency Essence
birth trauma	Emergency Essence, Fringed Violet
birth, revive weak animals	Emergency Essence, Fringed Violet, Macrocarpa, Sundew, Tall Mulla Mulla
birthing difficulties	Bauhinia, Black-eyed Susan, Dog Rose, Emergency Essence, Macrocarpa, She Oak
birthing, caesarian both young and mother	Emergency Essence, Fringed Violet, Macrocarpa, Sundew
birthing, regularising contractions	Bush Fuchsia, Yellow Cowslip Orchid
birthing, restlessness during	Black-eyed Susan, Boronia, Pink Flannel Flower, Sundew
births, multiple, for mother	Emergency Essence, Hibbertia, Macrocarpa
bit, refusing to take	Bauhinia, Dog Rose, Freshwater Mangrove, Isopogon, Rough Bluebell, Southern Cross
bitches whose puppies are culled	Bottlebrush, Emergency Essence, Fringed Violet, Red Suva Frangipani
bite, insect	Emergency Essence Mist, Cream or drops, Mountain Devil, Spinifex
biting and kicking, resistance to handling	Flannel Flower, Mountain Devil, Pink Mulla Mulla

biting, attacking	Dog Rose, Grey Spider Flower, Mountain Devil
biting, nipping to gain attention	Gymea Lily, Kangaroo Paw, Sydney Rose
bizarre behaviour	Dog Rose of the Wild Forces, Green Spider Orchid, Grey Spider Flower, Kangaroo Paw
bladder infection	Dagger Hakea, Dog Rose, Mountain Devil
bladder stones	Dagger Hakea, Dog Rose, Hibbertia
blame	Southern Cross
bleeding	Bluebell, Emergency Essence, Kapok Bush
blisters	Fringed Violet, Mulla Mulla, Spinifex
bloat, colic	Bauhinia, Bottlebrush, Crowea, Green Essence, Paw Paw, Peach-flowered Tea-tree
blood disorders	Bluebell, Dog Rose, Green Essence, Little Flannel Flower, Pink Mulla Mulla
blood pressure, high	Black-eyed Susan, Bluebell, Crowea, Emergency Essence, Tall Mulla Mulla
blood pressure, low	Five Corners, Kapok Bush, Southern Cross, Tall Mulla Mulla
blood vessels	Bauhinia, Bluebell, Hibbertia, Little Flannel Flower, Tall Mulla Mulla, Waratah
body clock	Bush Iris
bonding	Bluebell, Bottlebrush, Bush Gardenia, Red Helmet Orchid, Relationship Essence, Wedding Bush
bone marrow	Five Corners
bone splinters in bowel	Bottlebrush, Emergency Essence, Purifying Essence
bone, broken	Emergency Essence, Fringed Violet, Gymea Lily, Red Helmet Orchid, Sturt Desert Rose
bored animals	Dynamis Essence, Illawarra Flame Tree, Kapok Bush, Little Flannel Flower, Peach-flowered Tea-tree, Pink Flannel Flower
bored, alone animals, self destructive	Five Corners, Kangaroo Paw, Kapok Bush, Tall Yellow Top
boundaries, establishing healthy	Dog Rose of the Wild Forces, Flannel Flower, Fringed Violet, Old Man Banksia, Sturt Desert Pea
bowel	Bauhinia, Bottlebrush, Kapok Bush
bowel obstructions	Bauhinia, Bottlebrush, Red Grevillea
brain damage	Bush Fuchsia, Emergency Essence, Isopogon, Rough Bluebell, Slender Rice Flower, Sundew, Tall Mulla Mulla
brave face, putting on	Flannel Flower, Illawarra Flame Tree, Philotheca, Pink Mulla Mulla
breaking in, horses	Dog Rose, Cognis Essence, Emergency Essence, Red Helmet Orchid, Southern Cross
breathing difficulties short nosed animals	Boab, Dagger Hakea, Tall Mulla Mulla
breathing problems generally	Sturt Desert Pea, Tall Mulla Mulla + Sundew
breeding – females	Dog Rose, She Oak, Woman Essence, Yellow Cowslip Orchid
breeding – males	Dog Rose, Five Corners, Flannel Flower
bridges, crossing, fear of	Emergency Essence, Grey Spider Flower, Pink Mulla Mulla
bronchitis	Bush Iris, Dagger Hakea, Mountain Devil, Red Suva Frangipani, Sturt Desert Pea
bruises, contusions	Bluebell, Emergency Essence Cream, Five Corners, Flannel Flower, Spinifex
bucking, kicking, bolting, rearing, biting	Emergency Essence, Grey Spider Flower, Kangaroo Paw, Pink Mulla Mulla
bullying, dominance, territorial behaviour	Bush Gardenia, Dagger Hakea, Mountain Devil, Rough Bluebell, Slender Rice Flower, Sydney Rose

bullying, subjects of	Dog Rose, Five Corners, Emergency Essence, Sunshine Wattle
burn out	Alpine Mint Bush, Black-eyed Susan, Dynamis Essence, Macrocarpa
burns	Mulla Mulla, Solaris Essence
butterflies, after emerging from cocoon, if weak	Confid Essence, Dynamis Essence, Emergency Essence

C

caesarian section, to combat effects in young	Emergency Essence, Fringed Violet
caged animals	Emergency Essence, Pink Flannel Flower, Tall Yellow Top, Wild Potato Bush
caged animals, confined with own excrement	Billy Goat Plum
cages, fear of	Dog Rose, Emergency Essence
calcification in the body	Dagger Hakea, Hibbertia, Little Flannel Flower, Sturt Desert Pea
calcium, imbalance in body	Dog Rose, Hibbertia, Old Man Banksia, Paw Paw, Yellow Cowslip Orchid
calf, separated from mother when young	Bauhinia, Bottlebrush, Emergency Essence, Illawarra Flame Tree, Kapok Bush
calm	Black-eyed Susan, Calm & Clear, Crowea, Pink Flannel Flower
calm, restores	Emergency Essence Drops or Mist, Space Clearing Essence Mist
cancer, chemotherapy, remove toxins from body	Purifying Essence
cancer, day to day treatment for	Bush Iris, Illawarra Flame Tree, Macrocarpa, Mountain Devil, Philotheca, Pink Flannel Flower, Sunshine Wattle
cancer, side effects of radiation treatment	Electro Essence, Mulla Mulla + Fringed Violet
captivity, enforced	Emergency Essence + Dog Rose + Wild Potato Bush, Pink Flannel Flower
car chasing, even after being hit	Bottlebrush, Isopogon, Kangaroo Paw, Southern Cross
car sickness	Bush Fuchsia + Crowea + Paw Paw, Dog Rose, Travel Essence
car, fear of travelling in	Dog Rose, Emergency Essence, Grey Spider Flower
cardiac arrest	Emergency Essence while getting to vet, Waratah + Bluebell
carer burnout	Alpine Mint Bush
carer relationship with animal	Angelsword, Bottlebrush, Confid Essence, Five Corners, Flannel Flower, Green Spider Orchid, Macrocarpa, Red Helmet Orchid, Relationship Essence
caring for others	Alpine Mint Bush, Old Man Banksia, Philotheca, Red Grevillea, Sunshine Wattle
cataracts	Mountain Devil (to cleanse liver), Red Suva Frangipani, Sunshine Wattle, Waratah
central nervous system	Bush Fuchsia, Crowea
cerebral palsy	Bush Fuchsia + Crowea + Fringed Violet + Spinifex
chakra – base	Bush Iris, Red Lily, Waratah
chakra – brow	Boronia, Bush Iris, Green Spider Orchid
chakra – crown	Angelsword, Bush Iris, Red Lily, Waratah
chakra – heart	Bluebell, Illawarra Flame Tree, Pink Flannel Flower, Rough Bluebell, Sydney Rose, Waratah
chakra – higher chakras above crown	Green Spider Orchid, Kapok Bush, Red Lily
chakra – second or pelvic	Billy Goat Plum, Flannel Flower, She Oak, Turkey Bush
chakra – solar plexus	Crowea, Five Corners, Macrocarpa, Peach-flowered Tea-tree, Waratah
chakra – throat	Bush Fuchsia, Flannel Flower, Mint Bush, Old Man Banksia
change in circumstance, confusion with	Bottlebrush, Emergency Essence, Illawarra Flame Tree, Paw Paw, Red Suva Frangipani, Sturt Desert Pea

change in environment	Bauhinia, Bottlebrush, Emergency Essence, Freshwater Mangrove
change in routine	Bauhinia, Bottlebrush
change, break links with past	Boab, Bottlebrush, Pink Mulla Mulla
character traits, to change negative	Boab
chewing furniture, etc, when left alone	Dagger Hakea, Illawarra Flame Tree, Kangaroo Paw, Peach-flowered Tea-tree, Rough Bluebell
chewing skin, paws	Billy Goat Plum, Boronia + Bottlebrush, Dagger Hakea, Five Corners, Kangaroo Paw
chickens, poor layers	Bush Fuchsia, Bush Iris, She Oak, Yellow Cowslip Orchid
children fearful of animals	Dog Rose, Emergency Essence, Five Corners, Green Spider Orchid, Grey Spider Flower, Sydney Rose
children, animal wary of	Bluebell, Dog Rose, Flannel Flower, Green Spider Orchid, Pink Mulla Mulla
chlamydia	Mountain Devil, Peach-flowered Tea-tree, Spinifex
choking	Emergency Essence applied externally + Bottlebrush, Grey Spider Flower
choking caused by spasm of larynx	Emergency Essence + Bush Fuchsia + Black-eyed Susan + Bottlebrush externally
chronic debilitating conditions	Five Corners, Kapok Bush, Old Man Banksia
chronic, terminal conditions	Emergency Essence, Transition Essence, Waratah
circulatory problems	Bluebell, Flannel Flower, Pink Mulla Mulla, Tall Mulla Mulla
claws, problems with	Fringed Violet, Green Essence, Peach-flowered Tea-tree, Spinifex
climatic intolerance	Bottlebrush, Bush Fuchsia, Mulla Mulla
climbing curtains	Dagger Hakea, Kangaroo Paw, Peach-flowered Tea-tree, Rough Bluebell
clinging behaviour	Bottlebrush, Dog Rose, Five Corners, Southern Cross
clumsiness	Bush Fuchsia, Jacaranda, Kangaroo Paw, Sundew
coat, dull	Paw Paw, Purifying Essence, Spinifex, Tall Mulla Mulla
co-dependent relationship with owner	Angelsword, Dog Rose, Five Corners, Kangaroo Paw, Philotheca, Pink Mulla Mulla
cold, feels to touch, because of terror or shock	Emergency Essence, Grey Spider Flower
colic, bloat	Bauhinia, Bottlebrush, Crowea, Paw Paw, Emergency Essence, Green Essence, Peach-flowered Tea-tree
colitis	Bottlebrush, Crowea, Dog Rose, Kapok Bush, Red Suva Frangipani
collapse through exhaustion	Emergency Essence, Macrocarpa, Mulla Mulla, Solaris Essence, Sundew
colon spasm	Bottlebrush + Crowea, Grey Spider Flower
coma	Emergency Essence, Red Lily, Sundew
commands, won't listen, respond	Bush Fuchsia, Cognis Essence, Jacaranda, Sundew
commitment of owner to training etc	Jacaranda, Kapok Bush, Peach-flowered Tea-tree, Wedding Bush
communication	Bush Fuchsia, Bush Gardenia, Cognis Essence, Flannel Flower, Green Spider Flower
companion animals always 'in your face'	Flannel Flower, Isopogon, Kangaroo Paw, Rough Bluebell, Sturt Desert Rose
companion pet, for owner when pet dying	Bush Iris, Emergency Essence, Pink Flannel Flower, Red Suva Frangipani, Transition Essence
companion, lack of	Pink Flannel Flower, Tall Yellow Top
competence, efficiency	Black-eyed Susan, Boronia, Bush Fuchsia, Jacaranda, Paw Paw, Sundew

competition animals who lose confidence	Confid Essence, Emergency Essence, Five Corners
competition dogs after long shows	Macrocarpa, Silver Princess
competition, all animals	Black-eyed Susan, Five Corners, Gymea Lily, Mountain Devil
competitive animal, overworked	Dynamis Essence, Macrocarpa
competitive event animals	Bush Fuchsia, Jacaranda, Kapok Bush, Macrocarpa
compulsive behaviour	Boronia, Bottlebrush, Dog Rose
concealing pain	Dog Rose, Flannel Flower, Illawarra Flame Tree, Philotheca, Pink Mulla Mulla
concentration	Boronia, Cognis Essence, Jacaranda, Red Lily, Sundew
concern for young or human family, too much	Alpine Mint Bush, Crowea, Old Man Banksia, Philotheca
concussion	Emergency Essence, Sundew
confidence and trust	Confid Essence, Five Corners
confidence loss of, hesitancy, fear of failure	Dog Rose, Five Corners, Pink Mulla Mulla
confinement after previous freedom	Bottlebrush, Emergency Essence, Wild Potato Bush
confinement for long periods	Pink Flannel Flower, Tall Yellow Top, Wild Potato Bush
confrontation	Dog Rose, Five Corners, Pink Mulla Mulla, Tall Mulla Mulla, Waratah
confusion after death of owner, other change	Bottlebrush, Emergency Essence, Kapok Bush, Red Suva Frangipani, Sturt Desert Pea
congestive heart failure	Bluebell, Emergency Essence, Pink Flannel Flower, Waratah
conjunctivitis	Mountain Devil, Sunshine Wattle
consciousness, losing	Emergency Essence, Sundew, Tall Mulla Mulla
constipation	Bauhinia, Bottlebrush
controlling behaviour	Isopogon, Kangaroo Paw, Rough Bluebell, Southern Cross
convalescence	Alpine Mint Bush, Banksia Robur, Dynamis Essence, Kapok Bush, Philotheca, Red Grevillea
convulsions	Bush Fuchsia, Emergency Essence, Mulla Mulla, Sundew
cooperation, encourages	Bush Gardenia, Green Spider Orchid, Slender Rice Flower
coordination, physical	Bush Fuchsia, Kangaroo Paw, Sundew
coping difficulties	Emergency Essence, Five Corners, Kapok Bush, Red Grevillea, Sunshine Wattle
coprophagia, eating dung	Billy Goat Plum, Kangaroo Paw, Paw Paw
copy cat, has same disorders as owner	Alpine Mint Bush, Crowea, Paw Paw, Philotheca, Sturt Desert Rose
cords, cutting energetic cords	Angelsword
cough	Dagger Hakea, Emergency Essence rubbed at base of throat, Illawarra Flame Tree, Red Helmet Orchid
courage	Dog Rose, Emergency Essence, Grey Spider Flower, Waratah
coursing animals	Crowea, Dynamis Essence, Gymea Lily, Jacaranda, Macrocarpa, Sundew
cow won't let anyone near calf	Bottlebrush, Dog Rose, Pink Mulla Mulla
cowering	Dog Rose, Grey Spider Flower, Pink Mulla Mulla
cracked skin on feet	Bottlebrush + Kapok Bush, Spinifex added to base cream and rubbed in
cramp, muscular	Bottlebrush + Black-eyed Susan + Grey Spider Flower + Tall Mulla Mulla, Purifying Essence
crazy behaviour	Calm & Clear Essence, Crowea, Dog Rose of the Wild Forces, Kangaroo Paw
crisis	Emergency Essence

cruciate ligament, management after damage	Bauhinia, Crowea, Gymea Lily, Isopogon, Pink Flannel Flower, Wild Potato Bush
cruelty, to help recover from	Dagger Hakea, Five Corners, Emergency Essence, Flannel Flower, Sturt Desert Pea, Sunshine Wattle
cystitis	Bottlebrush, Dagger Hakea, Dog Rose, Mountain Devil, Mulla Mulla
cysts	Bush Iris, Dagger Hakea, Mountain Devil, Slender Rice Flower, Sturt Desert Pea

D

dandruff	Black-eyed Susan, Crowea, Spinifex, Tall Mulla Mulla
dangerous, because of terror	Dog Rose of the Wild Forces, Emergency Essence, Grey Spider Flower, Pink Mulla Mulla
deafness	Black-eyed Susan, Bush Fuchsia, Green Spider Orchid, Illawarra Flame Tree, Isopogon
death of owner, or other close animal	Emergency Essence, Red Suva Frangipani, Sturt Desert Pea
defaecation	Bottlebrush
defiance	Kangaroo Paw, Mountain Devil, Red Helmet Orchid
degenerative myopathy	Billy Goat Plum, Bush Fuchsia, Wild Potato Bush
dehydration of cells	She Oak – 2 drops in water 2-3 times daily
delinquent animals	Dagger Hakea + Gymea Lily + Mountain Devil + Rough Bluebell, Red Helmet Orchid, Rough Bluebell
demanding constant attention	Gymea Lily, Illawarra Flame Tree, Kangaroo Paw
dental treatment	Emergency Essence
dependence	Angelsword, Bottlebrush, Dog Rose, Confid Essence, Kangaroo Paw, Monga Waratah
depression with no obvious reason	Sunshine Wattle, Waratah
depression, general formula	Black-eyed Susan + Red Grevillea + Sunshine Wattle + Tall Yellow Top + Waratah
depression, illness when away from home	Boronia, Emergency Essence
dermatitis	Billy Goat Plum + Dagger Hakea + Mulla Mulla+ Rough Bluebell, Spinifex
de-sexing	Emergency Essence, Green Spider Orchid, Slender Rice Flower
despair	Waratah
despondence, hopelessness	Banksia Robur, Sunshine Wattle, Waratah
destructive behaviour, aggravated by red dyes	Dagger Hakea + Fringed Violet, Emergency Essence, Kangaroo Paw, Purifying Essence
destructive of owner's property	Dagger Hakea, Mountain Devil, Rough Bluebell, Southern Cross
detoxing body	Purifying Essence
diabetes, on insulin, help balance glucose levels	Peach-flowered Tea-tree
diabetic, where stress increased need for insulin	Peach-flowered Tea-tree + Black-eyed Susan
diarrhoea	Black-eyed Susan, Bottlebrush, Kapok Bush, Paw Paw
diarrhoea, incontinence, mess involved	Billy Goat Plum
dietary change	Bottlebrush, Crowea, Paw Paw
digestive disorders	Bauhinia, Bottlebrush, Crowea, Dog Rose, Paw Paw, Peach-flowered Tea-tree
digestive upsets	Bauhinia, Bottlebrush, Crowea, Paw Paw

dignity, restores	Billy Goat Plum, Dog Rose, Five Corners, Sturt Desert Rose
dilated pupils	Black-eyed Susan, Fringed Violet, Pink Mulla Mulla
direction, lack of	Jacaranda, Silver Princess, Sundew
disappointment	Banksia Robur, Bottlebrush, Freshwater Mangrove, Kapok Bush, Southern Cross
discipline	Hibbertia, Jacaranda, Peach-flowered Tea-tree, Red Helmet Orchid, Sundew, Wedding Bush
discouragement	Banksia Robur, Kapok Bush, Old Man Banksia
disgust	Billy Goat Plum
disinterest	Kapok Bush, Peach-flowered Tea-tree
dislike	Bluebell, Dagger Hakea, Mountain Devil, Sydney Rose
disoriented, confused, erratic	Angelsword, Bush Fuchsia, Emergency Essence, Mint Bush, Paw Paw, Red Lily, Sundew
distemper, for stress of condition over long time	Macrocarpa, Wild Potato Bush
distracted	Jacaranda, Sundew
distress	Emergency Essence
dizziness	Black-eyed Susan, Bush Fuchsia, Crowea, Jacaranda
domestic upheaval, despondent about	Angelsword, Emergency Essence, Flannel Flower + Sturt Desert Rose, Fringed Violet
domestication, stress of	Bauhinia, Bottlebrush, Emergency Essence, Pink Flannel Flower
dominance, bullying, territorial behaviour	Gymea Lily, Hibbertia, Isopogon, Rough Bluebell
dominating owner	Gymea Lily, Isopogon, Red Helmet Orchid, Sydney Rose, Yellow Cowslip Orchid
dominating, aggressive	Bluebell, Mountain Devil, Rough Bluebell
doors, waiting at all day for owner to return	Boronia
dosage	see Chapter 2 Page 31, Chapter 12 Page 129
dowsing	Angelsword, Five Corners, Freshwater Mangrove, Green Spider Orchid, Meditation Essence
dreams, fear after waking	Dog Rose, Green Spider Orchid, Grey Spider Flower
drinking, excessive	Dog Rose, Peach-flowered Tea-tree
drowsiness	Banksia Robur, Kapok Bush, Macrocarpa, Old Man Banksia, Sundew
dry skin	Dog Rose, Face, Hand & Body Cream, Mulla Mulla, Old Man Banksia, She Oak
dung eaters	Billy Goat Plum, Kangaroo Paw
duodenal ulcers	Crowea + Paw Paw
dying	Autumn Leaves, Bauhinia, Bottlebrush, Bush Iris, Calm & Clear Essence, Mist or Cream, Emergency Essence, Lichen, Pink Flannel Flower, Transition Essence

E

ear mites	Bush Iris, Green Essence, Mountain Devil
ear, inner, loss of balance	Crowea, Bush Fuchsia, Bush Iris, Sundew
ear, skin problems, tearing self apart	Dagger Hakea, Emergency Essence, Kangaroo Paw, Waratah
ears infection	Bush Fuchsia + Bush Iris + Spinifex, Emergency Essence, Mountain Devil
ears, tails down, fear	Dog Rose, Grey Spider Flower, Mountain Devil
eating problems, will only eat certain food	Crowea, Freshwater Mangrove, Hibbertia, Paw Paw
eating, will only eat from a particular bowl	Bauhinia, Boronia, Kangaroo Paw

edgy, uptight	Black-eyed Susan, Calm & Clear Essence, Crowea, Emergency Essence
egg bound birds	Bottlebrush, Emergency Essence, She Oak
egg laying, birds restless during	Boronia, Jacaranda, Sundew
elbow	Bauhinia, Bottlebrush
electromagnetic radiation, in environment	Electro Essence, place one bottle at each corner of building, replace after 8 months
electromagnetic radiation, remove from body	Bush Fuchsia, Electro Essence, Fringed Violet, Mulla Mulla
elimination problems, from change in lifestyle	Bottlebrush
embarrassment, in training etc	Billy Goat Plum, Dog Rose, Five Corners, Illawarra Flame Tree
emergency treatment	Emergency Essence
emotional upheaval	Calm & Clear Essence, Crowea, Dog Rose of the Wild Forces, Emergency Essence, Sundew
empowerment	Dog Rose, Five Corners, Southern Cross, Sturt Desert Rose
endocrine glands	see individual glands
endurance	Macrocarpa
endurance, lack of in normally strong animal	Banksia Robur, Macrocarpa
energetic, over, pulling on leash, reins	Black-eyed Susan
energy fields	Angelsword, Fringed Violet, Lichen, Meditation Essence
energy, lacking	Banksia Robur, Kapok Bush, Macrocarpa, Sturt Desert Pea
entangled repeatedly in electric fences, etc	Emergency Essence, Isopogon, Southern Cross
enthusiasm, lack of	Banksia Robur, Kapok Bush, Little Flannel Flower, Old Man Banksia, Peach-flowered Tea-tree
environment	Appropriate Essence Mist for particular environment
environment, planet earth	Emergency Essence applied to ground at energy vortexes; see Chapter 5 Page 58
environmental stress	Calm & Clear Essence Mists or drops, Emergency Essence Mist
epilepsy	Black-eyed Susan, Bush Fuchsia, Emergency Essence externally during seizure, Grey Spider Flower, Sundew
erratic dithery behaviour	Jacaranda, Sundew
escape behaviour, extreme	Flannel Flower + Sturt Desert Rose, Grey Spider Flower, Isopogon
euthanasia, before	Green Spider Orchid (for owner & animal), Grey Spider Flower
euthanasia, helps animals in transition	Transition Essence
euthanasia, helps owner adjust to loss	Emergency Essence + Red Suva Frangipani, Sturt Desert Rose, Transition Essence
euthanasia, indecision about	Green Spider Flower, Meditation Essence, Paw Paw
eventers, loss of form	Banksia Robur, Macrocarpa, Peach-flowered Tea-tree
excitable animals	Black-eyed Susan, Calm & Clear Essence, Cognis Essence, Emergency Essence
exercise wheels, preoccupation with	Boronia
exhausted, worn out animals	Macrocarpa, Old Man Banksia
exhaustion, after seizure	Fringed Violet + Angelsword, Macrocarpa, Philotheca, Sundew
exhaustion, complete mental and physical	Alpine Mint Bush, Macrocarpa, Waratah
exhaustion, temporary	Banksia Robur, Macrocarpa
expectation, too much from owner re animal	Dog Rose + Illawarra Flame Tree (for animal), Sydney Rose + Gymea Lily (for owner)
export animals, long journeys	Bottlebrush, Macrocarpa, Space Clearing Essence Mist sprayed in vessel before loading

extreme behavioural patterns	Boab, Grey Spider Flower, Red Helmet Orchid
exuberant, overwhelming animals	Black-eyed Susan, Calm & Clear Essence
eye problems	Bush Fuchsia, Dagger Hakea, Mountain Devil, Red Lily, Sunshine Wattle, Waratah
eyes, downcast	Dog Rose, Red Grevillea

F

factory farming, rescued from	Emergency Essence, Waratah
failure to thrive	Dynamis Essence, Emergency Essence, Fringed Violet, Kapok Bush, Sundew, Waratah
failure, fear of	Confid Essence, Dog Rose, Five Corners, Illawarra Flame Tree
false pregnancy	Dog Rose, Pink Mulla Mulla, She Oak, Yellow Cowslip Orchid
family changes, new member, loss of member	Bottlebrush, Emergency Essence, Red Suva Frangipani
family patterns, change	Boab
fatigue, complete exhaustion	Macrocarpa, Old Man Banksia
fear	Dog Rose, Dog Rose of the Wild Forces, Grey Spider Flower, Pink Mulla Mulla
fear of repeat of past hurt	Pink Mulla Mulla, Sunshine Wattle
fear of going outside	Dog Rose, Emergency Essence + Dog Rose, Grey Spider Flower + Flannel Flower
fear of interaction with others	Pink Mulla Mulla, Tall Mulla Mulla
fear of known things, shyness, timidity	Dog Rose
fear of lack of love, etc	Bluebell
fear of travel	Emergency Essence
fear of unfamiliar	Bauhinia, Dog Rose, Freshwater Mangrove, Waratah
fear related to fire and heat	Mulla Mulla
fear, anxiety, overprotectiveness	Crowea, Dog Rose, Old Man Banksia
fear, extreme	Grey Spider Flower
fear, intense, after punishment	Emergency Essence, Pink Mulla Mulla
fear, irrational	Calm & Clear Essence, Emergency Essence, Green Spider Orchid
feathers, loss of	Black-eyed Susan, Crowea, Dog Rose, She Oak, Sunshine Wattle, Tall Mulla Mulla
feeding problems	Crowea, Kangaroo Paw, Paw Paw
feet that are weak and brittle, horses	Emergency Essence Cream, Spinifex, Tall Mulla Mulla
feet problems	Bauhinia, Bottlebrush, Dog Rose, Red Grevillea, Spinifex, Tall Mulla Mulla
feet, painful , laminitis	Emergency Essence Cream, Sunshine Wattle
feline leukaemia	Kapok Bush, Bluebell + Little Flannel Flower, Macrocarpa
female animals coming into season	Bottlebrush, She Oak, Yellow Cowslip Orchid
female cats on constant heat	She Oak, Yellow Cowslip Orchid
fences, falling at	Bush Fuchsia, Confid Essence, Five Corners
feral, or semi feral animals	Emergency Essence, Green Spider Orchid
fertility, female	Flannel Flower, She Oak, Turkey Bush, Yellow Cowslip Orchid
fertility, incompatibility sperm, vaginal secretions	Flannel Flower + She Oak + Red Grevillea + Dagger Hakea + Slender Rice Flower, give to male & female
fertility, male	Flannel Flower, Flannel Flower + She Oak
fertility, scarring fallopian tubes	Spinifex + Slender Rice Flower

fever	Emergency Essence, Mountain Devil, Mulla Mulla
first aid for injury, shock	Emergency Essence
fish taken from natural environment, shock,	Emergency Essence added to water
fish, change of water, pH, temperature	Bush Fuchsia, Emergency Essence
fitness, form, lost for no obvious reason	Banksia Robur, Macrocarpa, Spinifex
fits, psychomotor seizures	Bush Fuchsia, Emergency Essence Mist sprayed on animal during seizure
flea allergy	Bluebell, Dagger Hakea, Fringed Violet, Green Essence, Purifying Essence, Spinifex
fleas	Bush Iris, Dagger Hakea, Green Essence, Mountain Devil
flexibility	Hibbertia, Little Flannel Flower
flexibility in tense animals	Black-eyed Susan, Crowea, Little Flannel Flower
flexibility, more one side than other	Bush Fuchsia
fluid retention	Bottlebrush, Bush Iris, Dog Rose, Philotheca, She Oak, Tall Mulla Mulla
focus, lack of	Cognis Essence, Jacaranda, Red Lily, Sundew
food, lack of interest	Banksia Robur, Crowea, Paw Paw
forebrain	Rough Bluebell
forgiveness	Bottlebrush, Dagger Hakea
foster home, raised in a	Dog Rose, Illawarra Flame Tree, Tall Yellow Top
fractures, managing animals with	Emergency Essence, Wild Potato Bush
frantic behaviour; freaking out	Emergency Essence + Dog Rose
frenzied state	Dog Rose of the Wild Forces, Emergency Essence
fright, reaction in panic	Emergency Essence + Dog Rose
frothing at mouth	Emergency Essence
fun	Little Flannel Flower
fungal infections, recurrent	Green Essence, Isopogon, Peach-flowered Tea-tree, Spinifex
fur balls	Boronia + Crowea (for excessive licking), Bottlebrush, Isopogon, Purifying Essence
fussiness	Bluebell, Dog Rose, Kangaroo Paw

G

gastrointestinal problems	Bauhinia, Bottlebrush, Crowea, Paw Paw
genetic, negative patterns, releasing	Boab
gentleness, restores	Flannel Flower
getting along with other pets in household	Bluebell, Bush Gardenia, Relationship Essence, Slender Rice Flower
giddiness	Bush Fuchsia, Crowea, Jacaranda
giving up	Kapok Bush, Sunshine Wattle
giving up completely	Waratah
giving up, body cold, critically ill	Emergency Essence, Kapok Bush
glands	see individual glands
glaucoma	Waratah
gloomy birds, parrots	Bottlebrush (for bonding), Sunshine Wattle
go-go-go type animals	Black-eyed Susan, Cognis Essence
golden staph infection	Red Grevillea
granulomas, proud flesh, scar tissue	Mulla Mulla (if from burns), Slender Rice Flower + Bush Iris
graveside, dogs that sit at grave of dead owner	Boronia, Bottlebrush, Emergency Essence, Red Suva Frangipani, Transition Essence

grief	Emergency Essence, Red Suva Frangipani, Sturt Desert Pea
grooming, shoeing, objecting to	Flannel Flower, Red Helmet Orchid
grounding, need for	Red Lily, Sundew
group harmony	Bush Gardenia, Relationship Essence, Slender Rice Flower, Sydney Rose
growling, raising hackles	Grey Spider Flower, Mountain Devil
guard dogs, overprotective	Bluebell, Bottlebrush, Mountain Devil
guide dog, over protection of owner by dog	Alpine Mint Bush, Bluebell, Old Man Banksia, Sturt Desert Rose + Flannel Flower
guide dog, training	Cognis Essence, Flannel Flower
guilt taken on from owner	Sturt Desert Rose + Fringed Violet
guilt, contriteness	Dagger Hakea, Sturt Desert Rose
gum, problems	Jacaranda, Kapok Bush, Mountain Devil, Peach-flowered Tea-tree

H

habits, to break bad	Boronia + Bottlebrush
hair loss, skin disorders when pining or worried	Boronia, Crowea, Pink Flannel Flower, Tall Mulla Mulla
hair problems	Dog Rose, Hibbertia, Tall Mulla Mulla+ Spinifex
handicapped, horses working with people	Alpine Mint Bush, Flannel Flower, Sundew
handlers, nervous of animals	Calm & Clear Essence, Dog Rose, Five Corners, Red Helmet Orchid
handlers, riders who lack confidence	Five Corners
handling animals for transport etc	Emergency Essence, Slender Rice Flower, Space Clearing Essence Mist
handling, feral animals	Confid Essence, Green Spider Orchid
handling, accepting touch	Flannel Flower
handling, animals that ignore commands	Confid Essence for handler, Red Helmet Orchid for animal and handler, Sundew for animal
handling, inattentive animal	Cognis Essence, Jacaranda, Sundew
harmony, animals in groups	Relationship Essence, Slender Rice Flower
harsh treatment previously	Dog Rose, Fringed Violet, Pink Mulla Mulla, Sunshine Wattle
hates, dislikes of specific person, vet, postman	Grey Spider Flower, Mountain Devil, Pink Mulla Mulla
healing, to help wounds heal faster	Bush Iris, Emergency Essence, Illawarra Flame Tree, Slender Rice Flower
heart attack	Emergency Essence + Bluebell till help arrives
heart disease, keep going in spite of	Old Man Banksia, Sturt Desert Rose + Flannel Flower
heart disorders	Black-eyed Susan, Bluebell, Dog Rose, Flannel Flower, Little Flannel Flower, Pink Flannel Flower, Sydney Rose
heat fluctuations in body	Old Man Banksia, Peach-flowered Tea-tree
heatstroke, exhaustion, to speed recovery	Emergency Essence, Macrocarpa, Mulla Mulla
heavy metals, remove form body	Purifying Essence, Wild Potato Bush
hepatitis	Dagger Hakea, Mountain Devil, Rough Bluebell
herd animals who won't mix with herd	Bush Gardenia, Relationship Essence, Slender Rice Flower
herd animals, easily influenced by others	Dog Rose of the Wild Forces, Red Grevillea
herding dogs, biting heels of cattle etc	Black-eyed Susan, Boab, Kangaroo Paw
hereditary conditions	Boab
hernia	Black-eyed Susan, Crowea, Dagger Hakea, Jacaranda, Mountain Devil
herpes	Spinifex + Mulla Mulla, internally or apply to lesions; also Essences for stress, immune system
hesitancy	Confid Essence, Five Corners, Jacaranda, Paw Paw

hibernation, animals coming out of	Bush Fuchsia, Macrocarpa, Yellow Cowslip Orchid
hiding from owner	Dog Rose
hiding kittens in new places constantly	Bottlebrush, Dog Rose, Pink Mulla Mulla
highly strung animals, unable to relax	Black-eyed Susan, Calm & Clear Essence
hip dysplasia, loss of bowel control associated with	Billy Goat Plum
hip problems	Bauhinia, Dog Rose, Silver Princess, Sundew, Sunshine Wattle
history, animals with unknown	Boronia, Green Spider Orchid, Sydney Rose
homeless people, companion dog of	Bottlebrush, Macrocarpa, Old Man Banksia
homesickness	Emergency Essence + Boronia
hopeless condition after long illness	Kapok Bush, Sunshine Wattle, Transition Essence, Waratah
hopelessness, extreme	Waratah
hormonal imbalance in female animals	She Oak, Yellow Cowslip Orchid
hormone imbalance	see individual endocrine glands
hospitalised for long time	Bottlebrush, Fringed Violet, Kapok Bush, Sunshine Wattle, Wild Potato Bush
hot spot, in dogs	Mulla Mulla
house training problems	Dog Rose, Cognis Essence, Crowea, Isopogon, Sundew
hunting or racing animals, at end of long season	Banksia Robur, Dynamis Essence, Macrocarpa, Peach-flowered Tea-tree
hunting animal, keep going indefinitely	Black-eyed Susan, Flannel Flower + Sturt Desert Rose, Macrocarpa, Red Grevillea
hunting dogs needing to show initiative	Black-eyed Susan, Bush Fuchsia, Five Corners, Gymea Lily, Yellow Cowslip Orchid
hunting, eventing horses, reliant on one rider	Bottlebrush, Confid Essence, Dog Rose, Monga Waratah
huskies, dingos domesticated late in life	Bauhinia, Bottlebrush, Green Spider Orchid, Grey Spider Flower
hyperactivity	Black-eyed Susan, Cognis Essence, Emergency Essence, Jacaranda, Sundew
hypersensitivity	Angelsword, Dog Rose of the Wild Forces, Fringed Violet, Red Grevillea, Red Suva Frangipani
hyperthyroidism	Old Man Banksia, Yellow Cowslip Orchid
hypochondriacal behaviour	Peach-flowered Tea-tree, Rough Bluebell, Southern Cross
hypothalamus	Bush Fuchsia
hysterectomy, setback after	Banksia Robur, Dynamis Essence, Emergency Essence, Kapok Bush, Philotheca
hysterical, berserk behaviour	Dog Rose of the Wild Forces, Emergency Essence + Dog Rose

I

identity, sense of own	Angelsword, Bush Fuchsia, Bush Iris, Five Corners, Tall Yellow Top
ignoring commands	Kangaroo Paw, Paw Paw, Red Helmet Orchid, Sundew
ileocaecal valve	Bauhinia, Red Grevillea
ill animal, reinforces their own powers of healing	Calm & Clear Essence, Green Spider Orchid
illness and exhaustion	Macrocarpa, Old Man Banksia
illness, acute	Emergency Essence
illness, critically, giving up	Emergency Essence + Kapok Bush
illness, long term debilitating	Kapok Bush, Sunshine Wattle, Wild Potato Bush
illness, long, keep struggling against the odds	Black-eyed Susan, Macrocarpa, Old Man Banksia
illness, overwhelmed by	Paw Paw

mange	Billy Goat Plum, Bush Iris, Dagger Hakea, Mountain Devil, Spinifex
manipulative behaviour	Gymea Lily, Hibbertia, Isopogon, Rough Bluebell
mares, overprotective of foals	Bluebell, Bottlebrush, Dog Rose
mating problems, poor relating	Calm & Clear Essence Mist, Relationship Essence, Space Clearing Essence Mist
mating, fear of situation or other animal	Dog Rose, Emergency Essence, Pink Flannel Flower, Pink Mulla Mulla
medication, won't take when given	Bush Gardenia, Dog Rose, Freshwater Mangrove + Crowea
memory	Isopogon, Sundew
mental anguish, extreme	Waratah
meridians, balancing	Crowea, Five Corners, Slender Rice Flower
metabolism	Black-eyed Susan, Crowea, Mulla Mulla, Old Man Banksia
miasms	Boab
mistakes in training, eventing… repeating	Cognis Essence, Isopogon, Southern Cross
mistreated animals	Emergency Essence, Grey Spider Flower, Sturt Desert Pea
moods swings	Bush Fuchsia, Peach-flowered Tea-tree, She Oak
mother separated from young	Emergency Essence, Red Suva Frangipani
mother, adjusting to demands of offspring	Bottlebrush
mother, bonding	Bottlebrush
mother, delay weaning young, overprotective	Bottlebrush, Crowea, Dog Rose
mother, destroying young at birth	Bush Fuchsia, Grey Spider Flower, Kangaroo Paw, Waratah
mother, difficulty giving birth	Bauhinia, Bottlebrush, Emergency Essence, She Oak
mother, neglecting self to nurse offspring	Alpine Mint Bush, Hibbertia, Philotheca
mother, not letting anyone near young	Bottlebrush, Grey Spider Flower, Pink Mulla Mulla
mother, restless when giving birth	Jacaranda, Macrocarpa, Peach-flowered Tea-tree, Sundew
mothers who persistently move young	Bottlebrush, Dog Rose, Isopogon
mothers, that lose offspring	Emergency Essence, Red Suva Frangipani
mouth problems	Bauhinia, Isopogon, Mulla Mulla + Spinifex
moving home	Bauhinia, Bottlebrush, Crowea, Dog Rose
multi pet households	Dagger Hakea, Relationship Essence, Slender Rice Flower
muscle tension, pain	Black-eyed Susan, Calm & Clear Essence Cream, Crowea, Emergency Essence Cream
muscular cramp	Bottlebrush, Crowea, Grey Spider Flower, Tall Yellow Top
musculo-skeletal disease	Bush Fuchsia, Crowea, Dog Rose of the Wild Forces, Gymea Lily, Sturt Desert Rose

N

nature awareness, attunement	Bush Fuchsia, Bush Iris, Green Spider Orchid
neck	Black-eyed Susan, Isopogon, Tall Yellow Top
neediness	Dog Rose, Five Corners, Southern Cross, Sturt Desert Rose
negative behaviour patterns, inherited	Boab
negative energies, remove from energy fields	Angelsword + Fringed Violet + Lichen; Space Clearing Essence Mist
neglect in early life	Fringed Violet, Illawarra Flame Tree, Pink Mulla Mulla, Tall Yellow Top
neglected animals	Dog Rose, Emergency Essence, Flannel Flower, Relationship Essence, Sunshine Wattle
nephritis	Dog Rose, Grey Spider Flower, Mulla Mulla
nerve damage pain	Bush Fuchsia + Emergency Essence + Spinifex
nerves, central nervous system	Bush Fuchsia, Crowea

nervous animals	Calm & Clear Essence, Crowea, Dog Rose, Grey Spider Flower
nervous, resistant, panicky all animals	Emergency Essence + Dog Rose
neurotic animal	Calm & Clear Essence, Crowea, Dog Rose, Freshwater Mangrove, Pink Flannel Flower
neutering, after	Emergency Essence, Macrocarpa, Wild Potato Bush
new animal, will not cooperate with owner	Bottlebrush, Emergency Essence, Red Helmet Orchid, Red Suva Frangipani
new animals	Bottlebrush, Dog Rose, Emergency Essence, Flannel Flower, Red Helmet Orchid
new technology, new equipment, adjusting to	Bauhinia, Dog Rose
nightmares, bad dreams	Green Spider Orchid, Grey Spider Flower
nipping, other attention seeking behaviour	Five Corners, Gymea Lily, Illawarra Flame Tree, Kangaroo Paw
noisiness, constant	Illawarra Flame Tree, Kangaroo Paw
nose, blocked	Bush Iris, Crowea + Tall Mulla Mulla, Dagger Hakea, Fringed Violet
nose, running	Flannel Flower
numbness from extreme cold	Bluebell, Emergency Essence, Tall Mulla Mulla

O

obedience test failure, repeated	Cognis Essence, Isopogon, Southern Cross
obedience training, hyperactive, excitable	Black-eyed Susan, Calm & Clear Essence, Cognis Essence, Jacaranda
obedience, lack of, won't listen to owner	Cognis Essence, Kangaroo Paw, Red Helmet Orchid
obese animals, lethargic	Dynamis Essence, Old Man Banksia, Wedding Bush
obesity	Bluebell, Bush Iris, Dog Rose, Dynamis Essence, Old Man Banksia, Yellow Cowslip Orchid
obnoxious behaviour with visitors	Bauhinia, Dog Rose, Freshwater Mangrove, Kangaroo Paw
obsessive behaviour	Bauhinia, Boronia + Bottlebrush, Hibbertia, Monga Waratah
obsessive grooming	Boronia + Crowea
oedema	Bush Iris, Dog Rose, Old Man Banksia, She Oak, Tall Mulla Mulla
old animals, adjusting to children	Bauhinia, Bottlebrush, Hibbertia
old animals, revitalisation	Bauhinia, Dynamis Essence, Little Flannel Flower
old cats, who have trouble grooming	Billy Goat Plum, Little Flannel Flower
old hurts and pain	Pink Mulla Mulla, Sturt Desert Pea
optimism	Sunshine Wattle
ovaries	She Oak
overactive on treadmill	Black-eyed Susan + Boronia, Cognis Essence, Pink Flannel Flower
overanxious	Black-eyed Susan, Crowea, Dog Rose, Dog Rose of the Wild Forces
over-dependent on carers	Dog Rose, Monga Waratah
overprotective	Bluebell, Bottlebrush, Dog Rose, Five Corners
oversensitive to sight, sound, touch	Bush Fuchsia, Crowea, Flannel Flower, Fringed Violet, Mulla Mulla
overweight	Bluebell, Bush Iris, Dog Rose, Dynamis Essence, Old Man Banksia, Yellow Cowslip Orchid
overwhelm	Crowea, Emergency Essence, Paw Paw, Mint Bush
own species, poor relating	Bush Fuchsia, Bush Gardenia, Green Spider Orchid
owner disappointed with animal performance	Five Corners, Freshwater Mangrove, Isopogon + Southern Cross, Silver Princess, Sunshine Wattle

owner hard on themselves and animals	Hibbertia, Little Flannel Flower, Yellow Cowslip Orchid
owner leaving, animal behaving badly when	Calm & Clear Essence, Five Corners, Grey Spider Flower, Illawarra Flame Tree, Kangaroo Paw, Rough Bluebell
owner over concern, anxiety	Black-eyed Susan, Crowea, Dog Rose
owner repeated training errors with animals	Cognis Essence, Isopogon
owner who can't say 'no' to animal	Alpine Mint Bush, Five Corners, Red Helmet Orchid, Sturt Desert Rose + Flannel Flower + Philotheca
owner who doesn't take advice of professionals	Gymea Lily, Kangaroo Paw, Red Helmet Orchid
owner who feels he hasn't done enough for animal	Old Man Banksia, Sturt Desert Rose
owner who is impatient for immediate results	Black-eyed Susan, Pink Flannel Flower
owner, doubting own intuition, judgment	Bush Fuchsia, Confid Essence, Five Corners
owner, helps to give ill animals space they need	Dog Rose, Flannel Flower + Sturt Desert Rose, Old Man Banksia
owner, new, adjusting to higher demands	Bottlebrush, Crowea, Macrocarpa
owner, responds badly to vets advice to euthanise	Dog Rose, Red Suva Frangipani, Transition Essence, Waratah
owner, who compares animals unfavourably	Bluebell, Sydney Rose
owner, who is tyrannical , dominant, macho	Bluebell, Flannel Flower, Rough Bluebell
oxygenation of tissues	Dog Rose, Mulla Mulla, Tall Mulla Mulla

P

pacing and banging into wall when alone	Boronia + Tall Yellow Top, Dog Rose, Kangaroo Paw, Mountain Devil
pack animals that fight	Mountain Devil, Slender Rice Flower
pack animals who don't get along well together	Slender Rice Flower
pain	Bluebell, Bush Iris, Emergency Essence, Spinifex, Sturt Desert Rose
pain, intense, shock associated with	Emergency Essence
pain, severe	Bottlebrush + Emergency Essence
pained expression	Southern Cross
pancreas	Peach-flowered Tea-tree
panic	Emergency Essence + Dog Rose
panic when owners going out	Emergency Essence + Dog Rose + Tall Yellow Top
paralysis from disk prolapse	Boab, Bottlebrush, Bush Fuchsia, Gymea Lily, Wild Potato Bush
paralysis, adapting to	Bauhinia, Bottlebrush, Grey Spider Flower, Pink Flannel Flower, Wild Potato Bush
paralysis, treating the physical injury	Angelsword + Fringed Violet, Bush Fuchsia + Spinifex, Emergency Essence, Gymea Lily, Tall Mulla Mulla
parasites – external	Billy Goat Plum, Emergency Essence Mist, Green Essence, Peach-flowered Tea-tree, Rough Bluebell, Spinifex
parasites – internal	Green Essence, Mountain Devil, Rough Bluebell, Spinifex
parasitic infection, extreme irritation	Dagger Hakea + Green Essence + Bluebell
parathyroid glands	Hibbertia
parrots, aggressive, jealous behaviour	Bluebell, Dagger Hakea, Mountain Devil
parrots, losing feathers	Black-eyed Susan, Calm & Clear Essence, She Oak
peace, finding sense of	Black-eyed Susan, Calm & Clear Essence, Pink Flannel Flower
pecking order, low	Confid Essence, Five Corners, Illawarra Flame Tree, Pink Flannel Flower
pelvic inflammation	Mountain Devil, Spinifex, Wisteria + Fringed Violet
performance not to capacity	Banksia Robur, Five Corners, Freshwater Mangrove, Kapok Bush, Southern Cross

perseverance, endurance	Jacaranda, Macrocarpa, Peach-flowered Tea-tree, Wedding Bush
pet motels, adjusting to	Dog Rose, Emergency Essence + Bottlebrush, Illawarra Flame Tree, Red Suva Frangipani
pet motels, despondent when left in	Pink Flannel Flower, Tall Yellow Top
pet motels, pining	Emergency Essence + Boronia
pet shop animals	Emergency Essence + Illawarra Flame Tree, Pink Flannel Flower
phobias	Boronia, Dog Rose, Emergency Essence, Grey Spider Flower
physical growth	Old Man Banksia, Yellow Cowslip Orchid
pick-me-up	Banksia Robur, Crowea, Dynamis Essence
pineal gland	Bush Iris
pining for dead or former owner, companions	Boronia + Red Suva Frangipani, Sturt Desert Pea
pining, when away from home, or after a move	Boronia
pituitary gland	Yellow Cowslip Orchid
playfulness	Little Flannel Flower
please, trying too hard to	Dog Rose, Five Corners, Red Grevillea
pneumonia	Black-eyed Susan, Macrocarpa, Mountain Devil + Sturt Desert Pea, Waratah
poisoned by oil slicks, sea birds	Bottlebrush, Emergency Essence, Purifying Essence
poisoning, remove toxins from body	Purifying Essence, Wild Potato Bush
poisoning, shock and trauma from	Emergency Essence, Emergency Essence Mist – while getting help
poisoning, support damaged nerve endings	Bush Fuchsia, Spinifex
police dogs, can't work without handler	Boab, Bottlebrush + Boronia, Dog Rose
police dogs, gun shy	Fringed Violet, Grey Spider Flower, Pink Mulla Mulla, Waratah
police horses, used for crowd control	Calm & Clear Essence, Dog Rose of the Wild Forces, Fringed Violet
ponies in new home, missing former owner	Emergency Essence + Boronia, Five Corners, Red Suva Frangipani
positivity, restores	Confid Essence, Five Corners, Sunshine Wattle
possessiveness	Bluebell, Bottlebrush, Dog Rose, Mountain Devil
post traumatic stress	Angelsword, Bottlebrush, Calm & Clear Essence, Emergency Essence, Fringed Violet, Grey Spider Flower, Pink Mulla Mulla, Sturt Desert Pea
post viral fatigue	Banksia Robur, Tall Mulla Mulla
potential not reached	Five Corners, Jacaranda, Silver Princess, Sundew, Wedding Bush
poultry terrorized by fox etc	Emergency Essence
pregnancies, phantom	Bauhinia, Freshwater Mangrove, Pink Mulla Mulla, She Oak, Yellow Cowslip Orchid
pregnancy	Bottlebrush, Five Corners, Hibbertia, She Oak, Wild Potato Bush
pregnancy, adapting to	Bottlebrush, She Oak, Yellow Cowslip Orchid
preoccupation	Red Lily, Sundew
preventative treatment before surgery	Emergency Essence for 2 days
preventative treatment when danger of infection	Black-eyed Susan, Bush Iris, Illawarra Flame Tree, Macrocarpa, Pink Flannel Flower
prickly animals that react viciously	Pink Mulla Mulla + Mountain Devil
protection from negative energies	Fringed Violet, Space Clearing Essence Mist
psychic attack	Fringed Violet
psychologically disturbed animals	Angelsword, Sturt Desert Pea, Sundew, Tall Yellow Top, Waratah, (also see depression)

puppies going to new homes	Bottlebrush, Emergency Essence
puppies to build confidence	Confid Essence, Dog Rose, Five Corners
Q	
Queensland itch	Bluebell, Dagger Hakea + Fringed Violet, Emergency Essence Mist, Mountain Devil, Purifying Essence
R	
racehorses, high performance	Black-eyed Susan, Bush Fuchsia, Cognis Essence, Crowea, Gymea Lily, Macrocarpa, Sundew
racehorses, let down after hard training, racing	Macrocarpa, Old Man Banksia, Silver Princess
racehorses, retired, living as pets	Bauhinia, Bottlebrush, Pink Flannel Flower, Silver Princess, Sturt Desert Pea
racehorses, temporary exhaustion	Banksia Robur, Macrocarpa
racing animal, fear of starter gates	Dog Rose, Calm & Clear Essence, Emergency Essence (only if extreme fear)
racing animals, pre performance	Cognis Essence
racing dogs, that don't want to race	Banksia Robur, Kapok Bush, Silver Princess
racing pigeons lost or grounded in long flight	Bush Fuchsia, Emergency Essence, Green Spider Orchid
racing, coursing animals, run till they drop	Black-eyed Susan, Old Man Banksia
radiation, clear from body	Electro Essence, Fringed Violet, Mulla Mulla
rage, frenzy	Black-eyed Susan, Dog Rose of the Wild Forces, Mountain Devil, Rough Bluebell
rearing, panicking	Calm & Clear Essence, Emergency Essence + Dog Rose
rebellious behaviour	Flannel Flower, Mountain Devil, Red Helmet Orchid, Rough Bluebell
recovering from great adversity, injury	Angelsword + Fringed Violet, Dynamis Essence, Kapok Bush, Philotheca
reflexes	Bush Fuchsia, Jacaranda
refusal to eat	Crowea + Dog Rose + Paw Paw + Peach-flowered Tea-tree
refusing handling	Emergency Essence, Flannel Flower, Red Helmet Orchid
refusing to go forward	Bauhinia, Dog Rose, Sydney Rose (horse and rider to move as one)
rejection	Illawarra Flame Tree
relationships, to support	Bush Gardenia, Relationship Essence
relaxation, to support	Black-eyed Susan, Boronia, Calm & Clear Essence, Crowea, Little Flannel Flower, Meditation Essence
repetition of mistakes	Bush Fuchsia, Isopogon, Southern Cross
repetitive behaviour	Boronia, Isopogon
reproduction, prevented leaving animal unfulfilled	Bauhinia, Sturt Desert Pea
rescue animals	Emergency Essence + Tall Yellow Top
rescue shelter animals	Emergency Essence + Illawarra Flame Tree + Bottlebrush
rescue shelter animals, despondent	Little Flannel Flower, Sunshine Wattle, Waratah
rescued animals that can't adjust to new owners	Bauhinia, Boronia, Bottlebrush, Freshwater Mangrove, Pink Mulla Mulla, Sturt Desert Pea
rescued from factory farm, vivisection, etc	Boronia, Bottlebrush, Emergency Essence, Freshwater Mangrove, Pink Mulla Mulla
respiratory failure	Emergency Essence till help available, Sturt Desert Pea, Tall Mulla Mulla
restless sleepers	Calm & Clear Essence, Green Spider Orchid, Grey Spider Flower, Macrocarpa

restlessness, if not occupied	Black-eyed Susan, Cognis Essence, Peach-flowered Tea-tree, Pink Flannel Flower
retired working animals	Banksia Robur, Bauhinia, Bottlebrush, Five Corners, Illawarra Flame Tree, Little Flannel Flower, Silver Princess, Sturt Desert Pea, Tall Yellow Top
revenge, maliciousness, suspiciousness	Mountain Devil, Rough Bluebell
rider, no confidence in	Five Corners, Pink Flannel Flower
riders, nervous of horses	Dog Rose, Five Corners, Sydney Rose
rigidity	Bauhinia, Boronia, Dog Rose, Little Flannel Flower, Hibbertia
rigidity, one sided, dressage	Bush Fuchsia, Crowea
roaching over loin of back	Crowea, Flannel Flower, Gymea Lily
running eyes, nose	Dagger Hakea, Flannel Flower
rushing animal, can't wait to go out, off lead, etc	Black-eyed Susan, Calm & Clear Essence
ruthless, bullying, frightening, dominating	Rough Bluebell

S

sad, bored, hopeless animals	Dog Rose, Little Flannel Flower, Sunshine Wattle
saddle sores	Emergency Essence Cream, Spinifex + Mulla Mulla added to base cream applied topically
saddling, difficult to	Cognis Essence, Dog Rose, Flannel Flower, Red Helmet Orchid
saddling, goes wild	Emergency Essence, Grey Spider Flower, Pink Mulla Mulla
savaging of young by mother animal	Mountain Devil, She Oak
scabies	Mountain Devil + Spinifex
scars	Bush Iris + Slender Rice Flower (internally and topically)
scars from burns	Mulla Mulla (internally and externally)
scattered attention or energies	Jacaranda, Sundew
schizophrenic type moods swings	Bush Fuchsia, Peach-flowered Tea-tree, Waratah
scratching furniture, repeatedly	Boronia + Bottlebrush to break habit, provide scratching post
scratching, persistent, from stress	Black-eyed Susan + Bottlebrush + Boronia
seabirds, exhaustion after storms	Emergency Essence + Macrocarpa
seizures, epilepsy	Bush Fuchsia, Dog Rose of the Wild Forces, Emergency Essence (when fitting), Isopogon
seizures, psychomotor, to rebalance	Bush Fuchsia, Crowea
self centred, selfish	Bluebell, Sydney Rose
self confidence	Confid Essence, Five Corners
self denying behaviour	Southern Cross
self destructive behaviour	Billy Goat Plum, Dagger Hakea, Kapok Bush, Sunshine Wattle, Tall Yellow Top, Waratah
sensitivity to environmental substances	Dagger Hakea, Fringed Violet, Purifying Essence
sensitivity, awareness, sharpened	Angelsword, Bush Fuchsia, Bush Iris, Cognis Essence, Meditation Essence, Sundew
separation anxiety	Crowea, Black-eyed Susan, Confid Essence, Emergency Essence, Grey Spider Flower
separation mix for animals being released to wild	Bush Fuchsia + Dog Rose + Dog Rose of the Wild Forces + Fringed Violet + Slender Rice Flower + Tall Yellow Top
sexual maturity, spraying in house	Flannel Flower, Kangaroo Paw, She Oak
shaky, cold to touch, fearful	Emergency Essence, Fringed Violet, Tall Mulla Mulla
shame	Billy Goat Plum, Dog Rose, Isopogon, Red Grevillea, Sturt Desert Rose
sharing	Bluebell, Slender Rice Flower

shock, mental, emotional, physical	Emergency Essence, Fringed Violet
show animals who are also pets or work animal	Bauhinia, Bottlebrush, Cognis Essence, Paw Paw
show animals, preparing for performance	Bush Fuchsia, Christmas Bell, Cognis Essence, Creative Essence, Macrocarpa, Sundew
show dogs, nervous in ring	Calm & Clear Essence, Cognis Essence, Dog Rose, Dog Rose of the Wild Forces, Emergency Essence (if extreme), Space Clearing Essence Mist
show dogs, whose owners push them too far	Paw Paw, Pink Flannel Flower, Macrocarpa
show, race horse, break starts, rush fences	Black-eyed Susan
shyness	Confid Essence, Dog Rose
skin cancer	Mulla Mulla, Solaris Essence
skin conditions	Billy Goat Plum, Dagger Hakea, Face Hand & Body Cream, Green Essence, Purifying Essence, Spinifex
skin conditions, acute	Emergency Essence Cream
skin irritations, itching, eczema	Bluebell, Dagger Hakea, Emergency Essence Mist, Fringed Violet, Mulla Mulla, Spinifex
skin, cracked	Bottlebrush + Kapok Bush, Spinifex added to base cream and applied topically, Tall Mulla Mulla, Woman Essence Cream
sled dog impatient with others not keeping up	Black-eyed Susan, Relationship Essence, Slender Rice Flower
sleep, animals who sleep too much	Dynamis Essence, Kapok Bush, Sundew
snakebite	Emergency Essence till help available
snakebite ongoing treatment	Bush Fuchsia, Purifying Essence
social skills, poor	Confid Essence, Kangaroo Paw
socialisation, extremely poor	Bush Gardenia, Dog Rose, Flannel Flower, Green Spider Orchid, Kangaroo Paw
solo puppies, who grow into demanding adults	Bluebell, Gymea Lily, Kangaroo Paw, Rough Bluebell, Sydney Rose
sore joints and muscles	Emergency Essence Cream, Mountain Devil, Purifying Essence
spacey, dazed animals	Red Lily, Sundew
spinal arthritis	Gymea Lily, Hibbertia, Little Flannel Flower, Mountain Devil
spinal disc prolapse	Boab (if problem genetic), Crowea, Emergency Essence, Gymea Lily, Tall Yellow Top (if in neck)
spirituality	Angelsword, Bush Iris, Fringed Violet, Green Spider Orchid, Meditation Essence, Mint Bush
spiteful animals, challenging territory or status	Flannel Flower, Rough Bluebell, Sturt Desert Rose
spleen	Boronia, Dog Rose, Pink Mulla Mulla
spooked	Emergency Essence, Space Clearing Essence Mist sprayed in area
sprain	Bauhinia, Black-eyed Susan, Crowea, Gymea Lily
spraying in house	Confid Essence, Five Corners, Flannel Flower, Grey Spider Flower, Kangaroo Paw
spraying to mark territory	Flannel Flower, Isopogon, Kangaroo Paw, Rough Bluebell, Slender Rice Flower, Sturt Desert Rose
spraying, scratching, biting because of change	Bauhinia, Bottlebrush, Kangaroo Paw
stable mates, too attached	Angelsword, Bottlebrush + Boronia, Flannel Flower + Sturt Desert Rose, Monga Waratah
stabling, resistance to	Dog Rose, Pink Mulla Mulla, Red Helmet Orchid, Space Clearing Essence Mist
stamina, strength, endurance	Dynamis Essence, Macrocarpa
steroids or other strong medication, use with	Bush Iris, Illawarra Flame Tree, Purifying Essence
stiffness	Calm & Clear Essence Cream, Grey Spider Flower, Hibbertia, Little Flannel Flower, Yellow Cowslip Orchid

sting, insect	Emergency Essence, Emergency Essence Mist applied to site, Mountain Devil, Spinifex
stoicism, never giving up even when exhausted	Old Man Banksia, Southern Cross
stomach problems	Bauhinia, Bottlebrush, Crowea, Dog Rose, Paw Paw, Peach-flowered Tea-tree
stray animals, exhausted, frightened	Emergency Essence + Macrocarpa
strength, stamina	Macrocarpa
stress	Black-eyed Susan, Calm & Clear Essence, Crowea, Dog Rose, Emergency Essence, Mint Bush, Red Suva Frangipani
stress allergies	Black-eyed Susan + Dagger Hakea + Fringed Violet
stress from training	Black-eyed Susan, Macrocarpa
stress resulting from changed of routine	Emergency Essence + Bottlebrush
stressful conditions like distemper, over a long time	Alpine Mint Bush, Dog Rose, Kapok Bush, Sunshine Wattle, Wild Potato Bush
stroke	Bush Fuchsia, Emergency Essence, Isopogon, Red Lily + Sundew, Slender Rice Flower, Tall Mulla Mulla
struggling to perform when physically incapable	Old Man Banksia
stubborn behaviour	Bauhinia, Freshwater Mangrove, Isopogon, Rough Bluebell
stud dog, needs owner approval to mate	Billy Goat Plum, Five Corners, Hibbertia, Illawarra Flame Tree, Monga Waratah
stud tail, male cats	Billy Goat Plum, Flannel Flower
submission to other animals, always	Dog Rose, Five Corners, Confid Essence, Grey Spider Flower, Sturt Desert Rose, Tall Mulla Mulla
suffering, long history of mental, physical	Emergency Essence, Sturt Desert Pea, Sunshine Wattle
sulkiness	Dagger Hakea, Kapok Bush, Rough Bluebell, Southern Cross
sulking, when can't get own way	Rough Bluebell
sun damage to skin	Face, Hand & Body Cream, Mulla Mulla + Spinifex applied topically, She Oak
sunstroke, heatstroke	Mulla Mulla
surgery, after to help waking	Emergency Essence, Macrocarpa, Sundew
surgery, post operative shock	Emergency Essence, Fringed Violet + Angelsword
surgery, recovery from	Banksia Robur, Kapok Bush, Philotheca, Slender Rice Flower
survival skills	Bush Fuchsia, Waratah
suspiciousness, maliciousness, revenge	Grey Spider Flower, Mountain Devil, Rough Bluebell

T

tail biting brought on by boredom, aloneness	Boronia + Bottlebrush, Tall Yellow Top, Waratah
taking on energy of others	Dog Rose of the Wild Forces, Fringed Violet, Space Clearing Essence Mist
team animals, won't cooperate with others	Black-eyed Susan, Bush Gardenia, Relationship Essence, Slender Rice Flower
teeth	Jacaranda, Paw Paw, Red Grevillea, Sundew
telepathy	Bush Fuchsia, Five Corners, Green Spider Orchid, Meditation Essence, Sundew
temperament, bad, growling, biting, kicking	Boab (if genetic), Calm & Clear Essence, Dog Rose, Kangaroo Paw, Mountain Devil
temperamental, unpredictable behaviour	Crowea, Dog Rose of the Wild Forces, Jacaranda, Kangaroo Paw, Sundew
tendons and muscles	Crowea
tenseness	Black-eyed Susan, Calm & Clear Essence, Crowea, Dog Rose

terminal condition	Emergency Essence, Transition Essence
terminal condition of animal, good for owners	Pink Flannel Flower, Red Suva Frangipani, Transition Essence
terminally ill animal, emotional ups and downs	Bush Fuchsia, Calm & Clear Essence, Crowea, Peach-flowered Tea-tree, Pink Flannel Flower
territorial aggression	Dog Rose, Flannel Flower + Sturt Desert Rose,
terror relating to a place or space	Grey Spider Flower, Space Clearing Essence Mist
terror, extreme fear, panic	Emergency Essence + Dog Rose, Grey Spider Flower
testes	Flannel Flower
throat problems	Bush Fuchsia, Bush Iris, Flannel Flower, Mountain Devil, Old Man Banksia
thrombosis	Bluebell, Red Grevillea, Tall Mulla Mulla, Waratah
thrush	Green Essence, Peach-flowered Tea-tree, Spinifex, Sturt Desert Rose
thunder storm, fireworks	Emergency Essence + Dog Rose, Pink Mulla Mulla
thymus	Illawarra Flame Tree
thyroid gland	Old Man Banksia
thyroid problem	Old Man Banksia, Yellow Cowslip Orchid
tick poisoning (paralysis tick)	Emergency Essence, Emergency Essence Mist to bite site… while taking to vet
ticks, general treatment	Emergency Essence Mist to bite site, Mountain Devil, Purifying Essence
timidity	Confid Essence, Dog Rose, Five Corners, Grey Spider Flower, Tall Mulla Mulla, Waratah
tired, worn out	Alpine Mint Bush, Macrocarpa, Old Man Banksia
tissue rejection	Slender Rice Flower, Waratah
tolerance	Bauhinia, Black-eyed Susan, Slender Rice Flower, Yellow Cowslip Orchid
touch, enjoyment of	Dog Rose, Flannel Flower, Sensuality Essence Mist
toxic environment	Electro Essence, Emergency Essence Mist, Purifying Essence, Space Clearing Essence Mist
toxicity	Emergency Essence (if serious, get professional help), Purifying Essence
train, difficult to	Angelsword, Bauhinia, Cognis Essence, Confid Essence, Five Corners, Kangaroo Paw, Red Helmet Orchid, Sundew
training, confused and overwhelmed	Cognis Essence, Paw Paw
training, helps excitable animals	Black-eyed Susan, Calm & Clear, Cognis Essence, Jacaranda
training, setback	Cognis Essence, Isopogon, Southern Cross
training, stress from	Black-eyed Susan, Crowea
training, too much, exhausted	Black-eyed Susan, Dynamis, Macrocarpa
training, when not praised for performance	Confid Essence, Cognis Essence + Five Corners, Illawarra Flame Tree
tranquilizer, sedative… overcoming effects	Purifying Essence, Red Lily, Sundew
transition	Transition Essence
transporting all animals	Emergency Essence, Space Clearing Essence Mist sprayed in vehicle, Travel Essence
transporting for breeding	Bauhinia, Bottlebrush, Calm & Clear Essence, Dog Rose, Freshwater Mangrove
trapped in snares, locked up	Emergency Essence, Red Grevillea, Sunshine Wattle, Wild Potato Bush
trauma or abuse, after… restores confidence	Angelsword, Five Corners, Fringed Violet
trauma, accident, dental work, shock, pain	Emergency Essence

trauma, for owners dealing with animal trauma	Emergency Essence
travel	Travel Essence, Mist and Cream
travel sickness	Bush Fuchsia + Crowea + Paw Paw
travel, export animals on long voyages	Bottlebrush, Emergency Essence, Macrocarpa, Pink Flannel Flower, Space Clearing Essence Mist, Travel Essence, Wild Potato Bush
travellers, companion dog of	Alpine Mint Bush, Bottlebrush, Freshwater Mangrove
treadmill, animals over-active at night	Black-eyed Susan, Kangaroo Paw
trembling	Emergency Essence, Grey Spider Flower
trial dogs, can't work without handler	Angelsword, Dog Rose, Five Corners, Kangaroo Paw, Philotheca, Pink Mulla Mulla
trial dogs, repeated failure	Illawarra Flame Tree, Kapok Bush, Pink Flannel Flower, Sunshine Wattle
trust	Bluebell, Flannel Flower, Pink Mulla Mulla, Tall Mulla Mulla, Waratah
turmoil	Black-eyed Susan, Calm & Clear Essence, Dog Rose of the Wild Forces, Emergency Essence

U

ulcers, digestive system	Crowea, Paw Paw
ulcers, mouth	Mulla Mulla + Spinifex (internally and topically)
ulcers, skin	Billy Goat Plum, Green Essence, Slender Rice Flower, Spinifex, Tall Mulla Mulla
unacceptable behaviour	Kangaroo Paw
uncertainty, imbalance	Crowea, Paw Paw
unconscious animals	Emergency Essence Mist, Sundew (applied externally)
uncontrollable behaviour	Emergency Essence, Emergency Essence Mist, Red Lily, Sundew
urinary track infection	Dagger Hakea, Dog Rose, Mountain Devil, Mulla Mulla
urination problems after change of home, ownership	Bottlebrush, Dog Rose, Kangaroo Paw, Red Helmet Orchid
urination, inappropriate	Dog Rose of the Wild Forces, Emergency Essence, Kangaroo Paw, Red Helmet Orchid
urination, defaecation, won't do it away from home	Bottlebrush, Dog Rose, Kangaroo Paw
urination, through fear	Crowea, Dog Rose, Red Helmet Orchid
urticaria	Dagger Hakea + Fringed Violet
uterus	Crowea, She Oak , Woman Essence, Mist or Cream

V

vaccination, side effects	Boab, Bottlebrush, Bush Fuchsia, Emergency Essence, Mulla Mulla, Purifying Essence
vaccination, to support positive effects	Black-eyed Susan, Bush Iris, Emergency Essence before injection, Illawarra Flame Tree, Macrocarpa
vaginitis	Dagger Hakea, Green Essence, Mulla Mulla (applied topically for burning), Sturt Desert Rose
vealers, in crates, hobbled, in dark	Green Spider Orchid, Grey Spider Flower, Red Grevillea, Wild Potato Bush
vertigo	Bush Fuchsia, Crowea, Jacaranda, Emergency Essence + Dog Rose
vet who loses animal	Emergency Essence, Red Suva Frangipani, Sturt Desert Rose
vet, to help clarify diagnosis	Angelsword, Bush Fuchsia, Cognis Essence, Green Spider

	Orchid, Meditation Essence, Yellow Cowslip Orchid
veterinary visit	Emergency Essence
vets, overwhelmed by clients	Alpine Mint Bush, Dynamis Essence, Grey Spider Flower, Kapok Bush, Paw Paw
victim, sense of being	Confid Essence, Southern Cross
vitality, perseverance	Dynamis Essence, Macrocarpa
vitality, restores	Banksia Robur, Dynamis Essence
vomiting	Paw Paw, Crowea, Wild Potato Bush
vomiting, diarrhoea if unrelated to diet	Black-eyed Susan, Crowea, Grey Spider Flower, Waratah

W

walking, insist on at same time each day, dogs	Bauhinia, Boronia
wandering animals	Flannel Flower + Sturt Desert Rose, Kangaroo Paw, Red Lily, Sundew
wandering animals, if related to sexual activity	Flannel Flower + Wisteria (males), She Oak + Wisteria (females)
weak after illness	Banksia Robur, Kapok Bush, Macrocarpa
weakness	Macrocarpa
weaning, for mother animal	Bottlebrush, Flannel Flower, She Oak, Yellow Cowslip Orchid
weaning, young animals	Bauhinia, Bottlebrush, Emergency Essence, Illawarra Flame Tree, Monga Waratah
weariness, tiredness, not coping	Alpine Mint Bush, Banksia Robur, Crowea, Dynamis Essence
weather changes that affect animals	Bottlebrush, Dog Rose, Green Spider Orchid, Fringed Violet
weighed down, feeling of being	Alpine Mint Bush, Old Man Banksia, Paw Paw, Wild Potato Bush
wild animal trapped	Emergency Essence Mist
wild animals captured, handled	Calm & Clear Essence, Emergency Essence + Dog Rose, Waratah
wild animals suddenly put in captivity	Bottlebrush, Emergency Essence + Dog Rose, Tall Yellow Top, Wild Potato Bush
wild animals, terror when caught, handled	Emergency Essence + Dog Rose, Grey Spider Flower
wing injuries, bird or bat	Bauhinia, Bottlebrush, Bush Fuchsia, Crowea, Emergency Essence, Spinifex, Wild Potato Bush
wings clipped on birds, for lopsidedness	Bauhinia, Bottlebrush, Bush Fuchsia, Crowea
withdraw from others, animals who tend to	Dog Rose, Pink Mulla Mulla, Tall Mulla Mulla
withdrawal, extreme	Emergency Essence, Grey Spider Flower, Kapok Bush, Waratah
working dogs	Bush Fuchsia, Cognis Essence, Macrocarpa
working dogs, retired, living as pets	Bottlebrush, Illawarra Flame Tree, Little Flannel Flower, Pink Flannel Flower, Silver Princess, Sturt Desert Pea
worms, infestation	Billy Goat Plum, Green Essence, Mountain Devil
worry	Crowea

Y

young animals, fragile from birth	Emergency Essence, Kapok Bush, Sundew

Z

zoo animals, frustration with life in enclosure	Peach-flowered Tea-tree, Pink Flannel Flower, Tall Yellow Top, Wild Potato Bush
zoo animals who have no interest in life	Banksia Robur, Dynamis Essence, Kapok Bush, Little Flannel Flower
zoo animals, helps in establishing boundaries	Flannel Flower + Sturt Desert Rose
zoo animals, helps living with other animals	Bush Gardenia, Relationship Essence, Slender Rice Flower

INFORMATION ABOUT INDIVIDUAL ESSENCES AND COMBINATIONS

INDIVIDUAL ESSENCES WHICH ARE IN COMBINATION ESSENCES

It is recommended that the individual Essences suggested for particular problems are given to your animal. However, if these are not readily available when needed, many of them can be found in the Combination Essence Drops, Mists and Creams which are listed below. Even though these Essence mixes may contain some other Essences that are not specifically mentioned for your pet's problem they will not hurt. Because Flower Essences work by bringing energies into balance, if they are not needed they will just dissipate. The Combination Essences are readily available from Australian Bush Flower Essence distributors, health food stores and many natural health practitioners.

ESSENCES AND THE COMBINATION ESSENCE DROPS IN WHICH THEY CAN BE FOUND

Angelsword	Emergency, Meditation
Autumn Leaves	Transition
Banksia Robur	Dynamis, Travel
Bauhinia	Purifying, Transition
Billy Goat Plum	Adol, Sexuality, Woman
Black-eyed Susan	Calm & Clear
Bluebell	Abund, Relationship
Boab	Abund, Adol, Confid, Relationship
Boronia	Calm & Clear, Meditation

Bottlebrush	Adol, Calm & Clear, Purifying, Relationship, Transition, Travel, Woman
Bush Fuchsia,	Calm & Clear, Cognis, Creative, Electro, Meditation, Travel, Woman
Bush Gardenia	Relationship, Sexuality
Bush Iris	Meditation, Purifying, Transition, Travel
Christmas Bell	Abund
Crowea	Emergency, Calm & Clear, Creative, Dynamis, Electro, Travel, Woman
Dagger Hakea	Adol, Purifying, Relationship
Dog Rose	Confid, Purifying
Dog Rose of the Wild Forces	Emergency
Five Corners	Abund, Adol, Confid, Creative, Woman
Flannel Flower	Adol, Creative, Relationship, Sexuality
Fringed Violet	Emergency, Electro, Meditation, Sexuality, Travel
Green Spider Orchid	Meditation
Grey Spider Flower	Emergency
Illawarra Flame Tree	Dynamis
Isopogon	Cognis
Jacaranda	Calm & Clear, Cognis
Kangaroo Paw	Adol
Lichen	Transition
Little Flannel Flower	Calm & Clear, Sexuality
Macrocarpa	Dynamis, Travel
Mint Bush	Relationship, Transition
Mulla Mulla	Electro, Solaris, Travel, Woman
Old Man Banksia	Dynamis, Woman
Paw Paw	Calm & Clear, Cognis, Electro, Travel
Peach-flowered Tea-tree	Woman
Philotheca	Abund
Red Grevillea	Creative, Transition
Red Helmet Orchid	Adol, Relationship
Red Lily	Meditation, Travel
Red Suva Frangipani	Relationship
She Oak	Solaris, Travel, Woman
Silver Princess	Transition, Travel
Southern Cross	Abund, Adol, Confid
Spinifex	Solaris
Sturt Desert Rose	Confid, Sexuality
Sundew	Emergency, Cognis, Travel
Sunshine Wattle	Abund, Adol
Tall Mulla Mulla	Creative, Travel
Tall Yellow Top	Adol
Turkey Bush	Creative
Yellow Cowslip Orchid	Dynamis
Waratah	Emergency, Electro
Wedding Bush	Relationship
Wild Potato Bush	Purifying
Wisteria	Sexuality

ESSENCES AND FLOWER ESSENCE MISTS AND CREAMS IN WHICH THEY CAN BE FOUND

Angelsword	Emergency Mist & Cream, Space Clearing Mist
Banksia Robur	Travel Mist & Cream
Billy Goat Plum	Face Hand & Body Cream, Sensuality Mist, Woman Mist & Cream
Black-eyed Susan	Calm & Clear Mist & Cream
Boab	Space Clearing Mist
Boronia	Calm & Clear Mist & Cream
Bottlebrush	Calm & Clear Mist & Cream, Travel Mist & Cream, Woman Mist & Cream
Bush Fuchsia	Calm & Clear Mist & Cream, Travel Mist & Cream, Woman Mist & Cream
Bush Gardenia	Sensuality Mist
Bush Iris	Travel Mist & Cream
Crowea	Calm & Clear Mist & Cream, Emergency Cream & Mist, Travel Mist & Cream, Woman Mist & Cream
Dog Rose of the Wild Forces	Emergency Cream & Mist
Five Corners	Face Hand & Body Cream, Woman Mist & Cream
Fringed Violet	Emergency Cream & Mist, Space Clearing Mist, Travel Mist & Cream
Flannel Flower	Face Hand & Body Cream, Sensuality Mist,
Grey Spider Flower	Emergency Cream & Mist
Jacaranda	Calm & Clear Mist & Cream
Lichen	Space Clearing Mist
Little Flannel Flower	Calm & Clear Mist & Cream, Face Hand & Body Cream, Sensuality Mist
Macrocarpa	Sensuality Mist, Travel Mist & Cream
Mulla Mulla	Face Hand & Body Cream, Travel Mist & Cream, Woman Mist & Cream
Old Man Banksia	Woman Mist & Cream
Paw Paw	Calm & Clear Mist & Cream, Travel Mist & Cream
Peach-flowered Tea-tree	Woman Mist & Cream
Red Lily	Space Clearing Mist, Travel Mist & Cream
She Oak	Face Hand & Body Cream, Travel Mist & Cream, Woman Mist & Cream
Silver Princess	Travel Mist & Cream
Slender Rice Flower	Emergency Cream only
Spinifex	Emergency Cream only
Sundew	Emergency Cream & Mist, Travel Mist & Cream
Tall Mulla Mulla	Travel Mist & Cream
Waratah	Emergency Cream & Mist,
Wisteria	Face Hand & Body Cream, Sensuality Mist

INDIVIDUAL ESSENCES

1. **Alpine Mint Bush**

⊖ Mental & emotional exhaustion; lack of joy and weight of responsibility of care givers.

⊕ Revitalisation; joy; renewal.

2. **Angelsword**

⊖ Interference with true spiritual connection to Higher Self; spiritually possessed; spiritual confusion.

⊕ Spiritual discernment; accessing gifts from past lifetimes; release of negatively held psychic energies; clear spiritual communication.

3. **Banksia Robur**

⊖ Disheartened; lethargic; frustrated.

⊕ Enjoyment of life; enthusiasm; interest in life.

4. **Bauhinia**

⊖ Resistance to change; rigidity; reluctance.

⊕ Acceptance; open mindedness.

5. **Billy Goat Plum**

⊖ Shame; inability to accept the physical self; physical loathing.

⊕ Sexual pleasure and enjoyment; acceptance of self and one's physical body; openmindedness.

6. **Black-eyed Susan**

⊖ Impatience; 'on the go'; over committed; constant striving.

⊕ Ability to turn inward and be still; slowing down; inner peace.

7. **Bluebell**

⊖ Closed; fear of lack; greed; rigidity.

⊕ Opens the heart; belief in abundance; universal trust; joyful sharing; unconditional love.

8. **Boab**

⊖ Enmeshment in negative family patterns; for recipients of abuse and prejudice.

⊕ Personal freedom by releasing family patterns; clearing of other, non-family, negative Karmic connections.

9. **Boronia**

⊖ Obsessive thoughts; pining; broken hearted.

⊕ Clarity; serenity; creative visualisation.

10. Bottlebrush

● Unresolved mother issues; overwhelmed by major life changes – old age, adolescence, parenthood, pregnancy, approaching death.

➕ Serenity and calm; ability to cope and move on; mother-child bonding.

11. Bush Fuchsia

● Switched off; nervousness about public speaking; ignoring 'gut' feelings; clumsy.

➕ Courage to speak out; clarity; in touch with intuition; integration of information; integration of male and female aspects.

12. Bush Gardenia

● Stale relationships; self interest; unaware.

➕ Passion; renews interest in partner; improves communication.

13. Bush Iris

● Fear of death; materialism; atheism; physical excess; avarice.

➕ Awakening of spirituality; acceptance of death as a transition state; clearing blocks in the base chakra and trust centre.

14. Christmas Bell

● Lack of abundance; sense of lack; poor stewardship of one's possessions.

➕ Helps one to manifest their desired outcomes; assists one with mastery of the physical plane.

15. Crowea

● Continual worrying; sense of being 'not quite right'.

➕ Peace and calm; balances and centres the individual; clarity of one's feelings.

16. Dagger Hakea

● Resentment; bitterness towards close family, friends, lovers.

➕ Forgiveness; open expression of feelings.

17. Dog Rose

● Fearful; shy; insecure; apprehensive with other people; niggling fears.

➕ Confidence; belief in self; courage; ability to embrace life more fully.

18. Dog Rose of the Wild Forces

● Fear of losing control; hysteria; pain with no apparent cause.

➕ Calm and centred in times of inner and outer turmoil; emotional balance.

19. Five Corners

● Low self-esteem; dislike of self; crushed, held in personality; clothing drab and colourless.

➕ Love and acceptance of self; celebration of own beauty; joyousness.

20. Flannel Flower

● Dislike of being touched; lack of sensitivity in males; uncomfortable with intimacy.

➕ Gentleness and sensitivity in touching; trust; openness; expression of feelings; joy in physical activity.

21. Freshwater Mangrove

● Heart closed due to expectations or prejudices which have been taught, not personally experienced.

➕ Openness to new experiences, people and perceptual shifts; healthy questioning of traditional standards and beliefs.

22. Fringed Violet

● Damage to aura; distress; lack of psychic protection.

➕ Removal of effects of recent or old distressing events; heals damage to aura; psychic protection.

23. Green Spider Orchid

● Nightmares and phobias from past life experiences; intense negative reactions to the sight of blood.

➕ Telepathic communication; ability to withhold information until timing is appropriate; attunement.

24. Grey Spider Flower

● Terror; fear of supernatural and psychic attack.

➕ Faith; calm; courage.

25. Gymea Lily

● Arrogant; attention seeking; craving status and glamour; dominating and over-riding personality.

➕ Humility; allowing others to express themselves and contribute; awareness, appreciation and taking notice of others.

26. Hibbertia

● Fanatical about self improvement; driven to acquire knowledge; excessive self discipline; superiority.

➕ Content with own knowledge; acceptance; ownership and utilisation of own knowledge.

27. **Illawarra Flame Tree**

- ⊖ Overwhelming sense of rejection; fear of responsibility.

- ⊕ Confidence; commitment; self reliance; self approval.

28. **Isopogon**

- ⊖ Inability to learn from past experience; stubborn; controlling personality.

- ⊕ Ability to learn from past experience; retrieval of forgotten skills; relating without manipulating or controlling; ability to remember the past.

29. **Jacaranda**

- ⊖ Scattered; changeable; dithering; rushing.

- ⊕ Decisiveness; quick thinking; centred.

30. **Kangaroo Paw**

- ⊖ Gauche; unaware; insensitive; inept; clumsy.

- ⊕ Kindness; sensitivity; savoire faire; enjoyment of people; relaxed.

31. **Kapok Bush**

- ⊖ Apathy; resignation; discouraged; half hearted.

- ⊕ Willingness; application; 'give it a go'; persistence; perception.

32. **Little Flannel Flower**

- ⊖ Denial of the 'child' within; seriousness in children; grimness in adults.

- ⊕ Care free; playfulness; joyful.

33. **Macrocarpa**

- ⊖ Drained; jaded; worn out.

- ⊕ Enthusiasm; inner strength; endurance.

34. **Mint Bush**

- ⊖ Perturbation; confusion; spiritual emergence; initial turmoil and void of spiritual initiation.

- ⊕ Smooth spiritual initiation; clarity; calmness; ability to cope.

35. **Monga Waratah**

- ⊖ Neediness; co-dependency; inability to do things alone; disempowerment; addictive personality.

- ⊕ Strengthening of one's will; reclaiming of one's spirit; belief that one can break the dependency of any behaviour, substance or person; self empowerment.

36. **Mountain Devil**

- ⊖ Hatred; anger; holding grudges; suspiciousness.

- ⊕ Unconditional love; happiness; healthy boundaries; forgiveness.

37. **Mulla Mulla**

- ⊖ Fear of flames and hot objects; distress associated with exposure to heat and sun.

- ⊕ Reduces the effects of fire and sun; feeling comfortable with fire and heat.

38. **Old Man Banksia**

- ⊖ Weary; phlegmatic personalities; disheartened; frustrated.

- ⊕ Enjoyment of life; renews enthusiasm; interest in life.

39. **Paw Paw**

- ⊖ Overwhelm; unable to resolve problems; burdened by decision.

- ⊕ Improved access to Higher Self for problem solving; assimilation of new ideas; calmness; clarity.

40. **Peach-flowered Tea-tree**

- ⊖ Mood swings; lack of commitment to follow through projects; easily bored; hypochondriacs.

- ⊕ Ability to complete projects; personal stability; take responsibility for one's health.

41. **Philotheca**

- ⊖ Inability to accept acknowledgement; excessive generosity.

- ⊕ Ability to receive love and acknowledgement; ability to let in praise.

42. **Pink Flannel Flower**

- ⊖ Feeling of life being dull and flat; lacking joy or appreciation for the every day aspects of life.

- ⊕ Gratitude; joie de vivre; keeping one's heart chakra open; appreciation.

43. **Pink Mulla Mulla**

- ⊖ Deep ancient wound on the psyche; an outer guarded and prickly persona to prevent being hurt; keeps people at a distance.

- ⊕ Deep spiritual healing; trusting and opening up.

44. **Red Grevillea**

- ⊖ Feeling stuck; oversensitive; affected by criticism and unpleasant people; too reliant on others.

- ⊕ Boldness; strength to leave unpleasant situations; indifference to the judgement of others.

45. **Red Helmet Orchid**

- ⊖ Rebelliousness; hot-headed; unresolved father issues; selfishness.

- ⊕ Male bonding; sensitivity; respect; consideration.

46. Red Lily

⊖ Vague; disconnected; split; lack of focus; daydreaming.

⊕ Grounded; focused; living in the present; connection with life and God.

47. Red Suva Frangipani

⊖ Initial grief, sadness and upset of either a relationship at rock bottom or of the death of a loved one; emotional upheaval, turmoil and rawness.

⊕ Feeling calm and nurtured; inner peace and strength to cope.

48. Rough Bluebell

⊖ Deliberately hurtful, manipulative, exploitive or malicious.

⊕ Compassion; release of one's inherent love vibration; sensitivity.

49. She Oak

⊖ Female imbalance; inability to conceive for non-physical reasons.

⊕ Emotionally open to conceive; female balance.

50. Silver Princess

⊖ Aimless; despondent; feeling flat; lack of direction.

⊕ Motivation; direction; life purpose.

51. Slender Rice Flower

⊖ Prejudice; racism; narrow mindedness; comparison with others.

⊕ Humility; group harmony; co-operation; perception of beauty in others.

52. Southern Cross

⊖ Victim mentality; complaining; bitter; martyrs; poverty consciousness.

⊕ Personal power; taking responsibility; positiveness.

53. Spinifex

⊖ Sense of being a victim to illness.

⊕ Empowers one through emotional understanding of illness.

54. Sturt Desert Pea

⊖ Emotional pain; deep hurt; sadness.

⊕ Letting go; triggers healthy grieving; releases deep held grief and sadness.

55. Sturt Desert Rose

⊖ Guilt; regret & remorse; low self-esteem; easily led.

⊕ Courage; conviction; true to self; integrity.

56. Sundew

⊖ Vagueness; disconnectedness; split; indecisive; lack of focus; daydreaming.

⊕ Attention to detail; grounded; focused; living in the present.

57. Sunshine Wattle

⊖ Stuck in the past; expectation of a grim future; struggle.

⊕ Optimism; acceptance of the beauty and joy in the present; open to a bright future.

58. Sydney Rose

⊖ Feeling separated, deserted, unloved or morbid.

⊕ Realising we are all one; feeling safe and at peace; heartfelt compassion; sense of unity.

59. Tall Mulla Mulla

⊖ Ill at ease; sometimes fearful of circulating and mixing with others; loner; distressed by and avoids confrontation.

⊕ Feeling relaxed and secure with other people; encourages social interaction.

60. Tall Yellow Top

⊖ Alienation; loneliness; isolation.

⊕ Sense of belonging; acceptance of self and others; knowing that you are 'home'; ability to reach out.

61. Turkey Bush

⊖ Creative block; disbelief in own creative ability.

⊕ Inspired creativity; creative expression; focus; renews artistic confidence.

62. Waratah

⊖ Despair; hopelessness; inability to respond to a crisis.

⊕ Courage; tenacity; adaptability; strong faith; enhancement of survival skills.

63. Wedding Bush

⊖ Difficulty with commitment.

⊕ Commitment to relationships; commitment to goals; dedication to life purpose.

64. Wild Potato Bush

⊖ Weighed down; feeling encumbered.

⊕ Ability to move on in life; freedom; renews enthusiasm.

65. Wisteria

⊖ Feeling uncomfortable with sex; closed sexually; macho male.

⊕ Sexual enjoyment; enhanced sensuality; sexual openness; gentleness.

66. Yellow Cowslip Orchid

⊖ Critical; judgemental; bureaucratic; nit picking.

⊕ Humanitarian concern; impartiality-stepping back from emotions; constructive; a keener sense of arbitration.

COMPANION ESSENCES

97. Autumn Leaves

⊖ Difficulties in the transition of passing over from the physical plane to the spiritual world.

⊕ Letting go and moving on; increase awareness and communication with the loved ones in the spiritual world.

98. Green Essence

⊖ Emotional distress associated with intestinal and skin disorders.

⊕ Harmonises the vibration of any yeast, mould or parasite to one's own vibration; purifying.

99. Lichen

⊖ Not knowing to look for and move into the Light when passing over; earth bound in the astral plane.

⊕ Eases one's transition into the Light; assists separation between the physical and the etheric bodies; releases earth bound energies.

COMBINATIONS

Emergency Essence

⊖ Panic; distress; fear.

⊕ Ability to cope; gives comfort, reassurance and courage.

Helps ease distress, fear, panic, etc. If a person needs specialised medical help, this Essence will provide comfort until treatment is available. Administer this remedy every hour or more frequently if necessary until the person feels better. It can also be applied topically.

Bush Flower Essences: Angelsword, Crowea, Dog Rose of the Wild Forces, Fringed Violet, Grey Spider Flower, Sundew, Waratah. Moisturisers, mists and oral sprays include Slender Rice Flower and Spinifex.

✓ *Drops* ✓ *Mist* ✓ *Moisturiser* ✓ *Oral Spray*

Abund Essence

⊖ Pessimistic; closed to receiving; fear of lack; poverty consciousness.

⊕ Joyful sharing; belief in abundance; clears sabotage; universal trust.

Releases negative beliefs, family patterns, sabotage and fear of lack. In so doing it allows you to be open to fully receiving great riches on all levels, not just financial.

Bush Flower Essences: Bluebell, Boab, Christmas Bell, Five Corners, Philotheca, Pink Flannel Flower, Southern Cross, Sunshine Wattle.

✓ *Drops*

Adol Essence

⊖ Hopelessness; insensitivity; sense of not belonging; "it's not fair" attitude; rebellious; anger.

⊕ Coping with change; consideration of others; enhances communication and self esteem.

Addresses the major issues teenagers commonly experience. It enhances acceptance of self, communication, social skills, harmony in relationships, maturity, emotional stability and optimism.

Bush Flower Essences: Billy Goat Plum, Boab, Bottlebrush, Dagger Hakea, Five Corners, Flannel Flower, Kangaroo Paw, Red Helmet Orchid, Southern Cross, Sunshine Wattle, Tall Yellow Top.

✓ *Drops*

Calm & Clear Essence

- ⊖ Always over committed; no time for self; always last priority.
- ⊕ Encourages own time and space; healthy contemplation & relaxation.

Encourages the time and space for relaxation, to unwind, contemplation of one's self, to enjoy relaxing pursuits. Helps with the inability to find time for one's self, to relax without external pressures and demands, to wind down and enjoy relaxing pursuits.

Bush Flower Essences: Black-eyed Susan, Bottlebrush, Boronia, Bush Fuchsia, Crowea, Jacaranda, Little Flannel Flower, Paw Paw.

✓ *Drops* ✓ *Mist* ✓ *Moisturiser* ✓ *Oral Spray*

Cognis Essence

- ⊖ Daydreaming; confusion; overwhelm.
- ⊕ Clarity and focus.

Gives focus and clarity when speaking, singing, reading or studying. It assists problem solving by improving access to the Higher Self, which stores all past knowledge and experiences. It balances the intuitive and cognitive processes and helps integrate ideas and information.

Bush Flower Essences: Bush Fuchsia, Isopogon, Jacaranda, Paw Paw, Sundew.

✓ *Drops*

Confid Essence

- ⊖ Low self-esteem; guilt; shyness; lack of conviction; victim mentality.
- ⊕ Confidence; integrity; taking responsibility for one's life; personal power; true to oneself.

Brings out the positive qualities of self esteem and confidence. It allows us to feel comfortable around other people and be true to ourselves. It resolves negative subconscious beliefs we may hold about ourselves as well as any guilt we may harbour from past actions.

Bush Flower Essences: Boab, Dog Rose, Five Corners, Southern Cross, Sturt Desert Rose.

✓ *Drops*

Creative Essence

- ⊖ Creative blocks and inhibitions.
- ⊕ Enhances singing; creative expression; clarity of voice; public speaking.

Frees your voice and opens your heart. Inspires creative and emotional expression in a gentle and calm way and gives courage and clarity in public speaking and singing.

Bush Flower Essences: Bush Fuchsia, Crowea, Five Corners, Flannel Flower, Red Grevillea, Tall Mulla Mulla, Turkey Bush.

✓ *Drops*

Dynamis Essence

- ⊖ Temporary loss of drive; enthusiasm and excitement.
- ⊕ Renews passion and enthusiasm for life; centres and harmonises your vital forces.

Renews enthusiasm and joy for life. It is for those who feel 'not quite right', drained, jaded, disheartened or burdened by their physical body. It also helps with feelings of physical restriction and limitation.

Bush Flower Essences: Banksia Robur, Crowea, Illawarra Flame Tree, Macrocarpa, Old Man Banksia, Yellow Cowslip Orchid.

✓ *Drops*

Electro Essence

- ⊖ Feeling drained and flat; out of balance with earth rhythms.
- ⊕ Reduces emotional effects of radiation.

Greatly relieves emotional fear and distress associated with earth, electrical and electromagnetic radiation. It helps to bring one into balance with the natural rhythms of the earth.

Bush Flower Essences: Bush Fuchsia, Crowea, Fringed Violet, Mulla Mulla, Paw Paw, Waratah.

✓ *Drops*

Body Love Essence

- ⊖ Dislike of physical self; body, skin texture & touch.
- ⊕ Acceptance of physical body; love & nurturing of self.

Encourages acceptance of physical body, love and nurturing of self, feel – touch and self massage. Helps to deal with the dislike & non acceptance of body, skin texture and touch.

Bush Flower Essences: Billy Goat Plum, Five Corners, Flannel Flower, Little Flannel Flower, Mulla Mulla, She Oak, Wisteria.

✓ *Moisturiser*

Meditation Essence

⊖ Psychic attack; damaged aura; tense and uptight; psychically drained.

⊕ Awaken spirituality; enhanced intuition; inner guidance; access Higher Self; deeper meditation.

Awakens one's spirituality and allows one to go deeper into any religious or spiritual practice. Enhances access to the Higher Self whilst providing psychic protection and healing of the aura. Highly recommended for anyone practising meditation.

Bush Flower Essences: Angelsword, Boronia, Bush Fuchsia, Bush Iris, Fringed Violet, Green Spider Orchid, Red Lily.

✓ *Drops*

Purifying Essence

⊖ Emotional waste; feeling encumbered; emotional baggage.

⊕ Sense of release and relief; spring cleaned.

To release and clear emotional waste and residual by-products, to clear built-up emotional baggage.

Bush Flower Essences: Bauhinia, Bottlebrush, Bush Iris, Dagger Hakea, Dog Rose, Wild Potato Bush.

✓ *Drops*

Relationship Essence

⊖ Confusion; resentment; emotional pain and turmoil; blocked emotions; inability to relate.

⊕ Expressing feelings; communication; forgiveness; breaks family conditioning; renews interest.

Enhances the quality of all relationships, especially intimate ones. Clears and releases resentment, blocked emotions and the confusion, emotional pain and turmoil of a rocky relationship. Helps one verbalise, express feelings and improve communication. Breaks the early family conditioning and patterns which affect us in our current adult relationships. For intimate relationships a perfect remedy to follow this combination is Sexuality Essence.

Bush Flower Essences: Bluebell, Boab, Bottlebrush, Bush Gardenia, Dagger Hakea, Flannel Flower, Mint Bush, Red Helmet Orchid, Red Suva Frangipani, Wedding Bush.

✓ *Drops*

Sensuality Essence

⊖ Fear of emotional & physical intimacy.

⊕ Encourages intimacy; passion & sensual fulfilment.

Encourages the ability to enjoy physical and emotional intimacy, passion and sensual fulfilment.

Bush Flower Essences: Bush Gardenia, Billy Goat Plum, Flannel Flower, Little Flannel Flower, Macrocarpa, Wisteria.

✓ *Mist*

Sexuality Essence

⊖ Shame, uptight about sexuality, fear of intimacy, lack of sensitivity.

⊕ Renews passion, sensuality, enjoy touch and intimacy, self acceptance, fulfilment.

It allows one to feel comfortable with and to fully accept one's body. It enables the individual to be open to sensuality and touch and to enjoy physical and emotional intimacy. It is helpful for releasing emotional shame. Sexuality Essence renews passion and interest in relationships.

Bush Flower Essences: Billy Goat Plum, Bush Gardenia, Flannel Flower, Fringed Violet, Little Flannel Flower, Sturt Desert Rose, Wisteria.

✓ *Drops*

Solaris Essence

⊖ Emotional fear and distress associated with fire.

⊕ Greatly relieves the emotional effects of heat, fire, sun.

Greatly relieves the emotional effects of heat, fire and sun. Relieves the emotional fear and distress associated with heat, fire and sun.

Bush Flower Essences: Mulla Mulla, She Oak, Spinifex.

✓ *Drops*

Space Clearing Essence

⊖ Negative mental, emotional and psychic energies.

⊕ Clears negative environments, creates safe harmonious environments.

Creates sacred, safe and harmonious environments. Purifies and releases environments of built up negative emotional, mental and psychic energies. Great for clearing tense situations and environments and restoring balance.

Bush Flower Essences: Angelsword, Boab, Fringed Violet, Lichen, Red Lily.

✓ *Mist*

Transition Essence

● Feeling stuck; lack of direction; fear of death; fear of the unknown; non acceptance.

● Acceptance of change; serenity; eases fear of death; passing over in peace.

This combination helps one to cope and move through any major life change. It brings about an awareness of one's life direction especially for people who are at a crossroad. Alternatively those who know what they want but do not know how to achieve it will benefit from this combination. It also eases the fear of death as well as helping one come to terms with it. This remedy, consequently, allows one to easily and gently pass over with calmness, dignity and serenity.

Bush Flower Essences: Autumn Leaves, Bauhinia, Bottlebrush, Bush Iris, Lichen, Mint Bush, Red Grevillea, Silver Princess.

✓ *Drops*

Travel Essence

● Personally depleted and drained; disorientation.

● Centres; refreshes; maintains sense of personal space.

Beneficial for distress associated with all forms of travel, although it particularly addresses the problems encountered with jet travel. It enables a person to arrive at their destination feeling balanced and ready to go.

Bush Flower Essences: Banksia Robur, Bottlebrush, Bush Fuchsia, Bush Iris, Crowea, Fringed Violet, Macrocarpa, Mulla Mulla, Paw Paw, Red Lily, She Oak, Silver Princess, Sundew, Tall Mulla Mulla.

✓ *Drops* ✓ *Mist* ✓ *Moisturiser*

Woman Essence

● Mood swings; weary; physical dislike.

● Female life cycle balance; calm and stable; coping with change.

To encourage a woman's own innate strength and beauty through life's emotional cycles and seasons of change. Remaining calm & stable, discovering & feeling good about self, beauty and body whilst coping with change. Harmonises any emotional imbalances through puberty, menstruation, pregnancy and menopause.

Bush Flower Essences: Billy Goat Plum, Bottlebrush, Bush Fuchsia, Crowea, Five Corners, Mulla Mulla, Old Man Banksia, Peach-flowered Tea-tree, Pink Flannel Flower, She Oak.

✓ *Drops* ✓ *Mist* ✓ *Moisturiser* ✓ *Oral Spray*

BIBLIOGRAPHY

Alexander, Prof R McNeill. *The Collins Encyclopedia of Animal Biology.* William Collins Sons & Co Ltd. Sydney, Australia, 1986.

Benyus, Janine M. *The Secret Language and Remarkable Behavior of Animals.* Black Dog & Leventhal Publishers Inc., New York, USA, 1998.

Bönisch, Susanne. *Natural Healing for Dogs.* Sterling Publishing Co, New York, USA, 1996.

Bray, Michael Frances. *Angels are Real.* Rainbow Spirit, Rockdale, NSW, Australia, 1995.

Brown, Steve & Taylor, Beth. *See Spot Live Longer.* Creekobear Press, USA, 2004.

Campbell Jenny, compiled by. *Smarter than Jack.* Avocado Press Limited, PO Box 170, Ferntree Gully, Victoria, Australia, 2003.

Churchill, Jennie BVSc. *Pet Sense.* Collins/Angus & Robertson Publishers, North Ryde, Australia, 1990.

Devi, Lila. *Flower Essences for Animals.* Beyond Words Publishing Inc, Hillsboro, Oregon, USA, 2000.

Downer, John. *Supersense – Perception in the Animal World.* BBC Books, London UK, 1988.

Edey, Maitland, edited by. *Animal Behaviour.* Life Nature Library, Silver Burdett Co, Morristown, New Jersey, USA 1965, 1971.

Flint, Dr Elsa. *Understanding Your Dog.* New Holland Publishes, Frenchs Forest, Australia, 2003.

Fogle, Dr Bruce. *The Encyclopedia of Dog.* Harper Collins, London UK, 1995.

Fogle, Dr Bruce. *Natural Cat Care.* Dorling Kinders Limited, London UK, 1999.

Fossey, Dian. *Gorillas in the Mist.* Penguin Books AustraliaLtd,Ringwood,Victoria,Australia,1983,1988.

Gaita, Raimond. *The Philosopher's Dog.* The Text Publishing Company, Melbourne, Australia, 2002.

Gerber, Richard. *Vibrational Medicine: New Choices for Healing Ourselves.* Bear & Co, Sante Fe, NM, USA, 1988.

Gerber, Richard. *Vibrational Medicine, The Handbook of Subtle-Energy Therapies.* Bear & Co, VT, USA, 2001.

Gurudas. *Flower Essences.* Brotherhood of Life Inc., NM, USA, 1983

Healey, Janet. *Encyclopaedia of Australian Wildlife.* Reader's Digest (Australia) Pty Ltd, Sydney, 1997.

Herriot, James. *Dog Stories.* Pan Books Ltd, London, UK, 1987.

Herriot James. *All Creatures Great and Small.* Pan Books Ltd, London, UK, 1983.

Isaacs, Jennifer. *Australian Dreaming.* Lansdowne Press, Sydney, Australia, 1988.

Jung, Carl G et al. *Man and His Symbols.* Aldus Books 1964, republished Dell, USA, 1968.

Keyes, Ken Jr. *The Hundredth Monkey.* Vision Books, Oregon, USA, 1982.

Kohut, John J & Sweet, Roland. *Strange Tails.* Michael O'Mara Books Ltd., London, UK, 2000.

Mike Lingenfelter & David Frei. *The Angel at my Side.* Hay House Inc, Carlsbad, CA, USA, 2002.

Meredith, Annie. *Australian Bush Flower Essences Correspondence Course.* Bush Biotherapies Pty Ltd, Terrey Hills, NSW, Australia, 2002.

McBride, Glen & Berrill, NJ, major contributors. *Animal Families.* Reader's Digest Association Pty Ltd, Surry Hills, NSW, Australia, 1973.

McKenna, Martin. *The Dogman – An Expert Explains Dog Sense.* ABC Books, for Australian Broadcasting Corporation, Sydney, NSW Australia, 2001.

MacLaine, Shirley. *Out on a Leash.* Atria Books, New York, USA, 2003.

Miller, Robert M. *Most of My Patients Are Animals.* W H Allen & Co. Pic, London, UK, 1987.

Murray, Eva. *Living with Wildlife.* Reed Books Pty Ltd, Frenchs Forest, NSW, Australia, 1989.

Myss, Caroline. *Sacred Contracts.* Harmony Books, New York, USA, 2001.

Neidjie, Bill. *Story About Feeling.* Magabala Books, Broome, Western Australia, 1989.

Newton, Michael. PhD. *Journey of Souls.* Llewellyn Publications, Minnesota, USA, 1988.

Parelli, Pat. *Natural Horse-Man-Ship.* Western Horseman Inc. Colorado Springs, USA, 1993.

Roberts, Monty. *The Man who Listens to Horses.* Arrow Books Ltd, London, UK, 1997.

Rogers, Lesley J. & Kaplan, Gisela. *Not Only Roars & Rituals – Communication in Animals.* Allen & Unwin, St Leonards, NSW, Australia, 1998.

Sams, Jamie & Carson, David. *Medicine Cards – The Discovery of Power Through The Ways of Animals.* Bear & Co, Santa Fe, NM USA, 1988.

Sheldrake, Rupert. *Dogs That Know When Their Owners Are Coming Home and Other Unexplained Powers of Animals.* Arrow Books, London, UK, 1999.

Shuker, Dr. Karl PN. *The Hidden Powers of Animals.* Universal International Pty Ltd, Gordon, NSW 2072, Australia, 2001.

Stein, Diane. *Natural Healing for Dogs and Cats*. Crossing Press, CA, USA, 1993.

Taylor, David. *Small Pet Handbook*. HarperCollins Publishers, London, UK, 1996.

Thear, Katie & Dr Fraser, Alistair, editors. *The Australia & New Zealand Complete Book of Raising Livestock and Poultry*. Australian & New Zealand Book Co Pty Ltd, Sydney, Australia, 1980.

Tinbergen, Niko & editors. *Animal Behavior*. Time-Life Books, New York, 1965, 1971.

Tucker, Michael. *Dog Training Made Easy*. Rigby Publishers Ltd, Sydney, Australia, 1980.

Ullman, Hans-J. *The New Dog Handbook*. Barron's Educational Series Inc, New York, USA, 1985.

Verny, Thomas. *The Secret Life of the Unborn Child*. Dell, USA, 1981.

Von Bingen, Hildegard. *Hildegard von Bingen's: Physica*. Translated and published, Herder Spektrum, Freiburg, Germany, 1992

Weiss, Brian L MD. *Many Lives, Many Masters*. Simon & Schuster, New York, USA, 1988.

White, Ian. *Australian Bush Flower Essences*. Findhorn Press, Forres, UK, 1993.

White Ian. *Australian Bush Flower Healing*. Transworld Publishers (Aust) Pty Ltd, Moorebank, NSW Australia, 1999.

Woodhouse, Barbara. *The Dog – the Breeds, the Care and the Training*. Orbis Publishing Ltd, London, 1976, 1982.

Wrigley, John W. & Fagg, Murray. *Australian Native Plants*. Reed New Holland, French's Forest, Australia, 1996, 2001.

Yarden, C. Miriam. *Hey Pup Let's Talk*. Barron's Educational Series Inc, New York, USA, 2000.

REFERENCES FROM WORLD WIDE WEB

Animal Communication and Healing, article author unknown, accessed 18 April 2004.
www.healinghandsoflight.homestead.com

Breeding in zoos and overweight animals, accessed 22 February 2006. www.bronxzoo.com

Buffalo, the Life and Spirit of the American Indians, extract by Thomas E Mails 1996, accessed 24 April 2006. www.ilhawaii.net/~stony/buffalo.html

Cadigal Wangal Country and Culture, dated 2004, accessed 24 April 2006. www.cadigalwangal.com.au/

Carol's Baby Book, blog research by Donald Shelter of Rochester University 1989, accessed 20 February 2006. www.parentingdecisions.com/baby/book.htm

Colour Therapy Healing for Animals, article by Valerie Logan-Clarke, June 2005, accessed 3 June 2006. www.colourtherapyhealing.com/articles/

Contribution of the Pet Care Industry to the Australian Economy, report by BIS Shrapnel 1995, accessed 27 May 2006. www.petnet.com.au/power/

Cultural Impressions of the Wolf, with specific reference to the man-eating wolf in England, thesis by Paul Williams University of Sheffield 2003, accessed 20 February 2006. www.feralchildren.com

Dolphin Dreams, article by Anupama Bhattacharya, February 2000, accessed 24 April 2006. www.lifepositive.com/spirit/entities/dolphins/

Dr Edward Bach, Edward Bach Centre web site, accessed 23 April 2006. www.bachcentre.com/centre/drbach.htm

Dolphins' Complex Communication extract from book *The Mind of the Dolphin* by Dr John Lilly, accessed 20 January 2006. www.johnclilly.com

Equine Emergency! When to Call the Vet, article by Jayne Pedigo, dated 2006, accessed 6 February 2006. www.equisearch.com/horses

Greyfriars Bobby, from Wikipedia, the Free Encyclopedia, accessed 20 February 2006. en.wikipedia.org/wiki/Greyfriars_Bobby

Heart Connections and the Healing Power of Horses, article by Bonnie Treece, dated December 2005, accessed 2 April 2006. www.equusspirit.com/article13.htm

Inexpensive Medication Stimulates Early Ovulation in Mares, report by Patrick W. Concannon. November 1997, accessed 14 February 2006. www.vet.cornell.edu/

Information on emotional patterning, Miriam Seward, accessed 6 February 2006. www.kinergetics.com.au

Interview Rupert Sheldrake, via e-mail by Barbara Petura, dated 2 November 2000, accessed 21 April 2004. www.workingdogweb.com

Lascaux Cave Paintings and Location from The Alpha and the Omega, extract by Jim A Cornwell 1995, accessed 14 May 2006.
www.mazzaroth.com/ChapterOne/LascauxCave.htm

Man and Dog: The Psychology of a Relationship, article by Bergler, 1986, accessed 27 May 2006.
www.anthrozoology.org/database/bergler.htm

Managing Grief Responses, article by Kenneth Marcella DVM, Oct 2004, accessed 3 April 2006. dvm.adv100.com/dvm/

Mark of Domestication: Animal Burials, from K Kris Hirst, accessed 19 April 2006. www.archaeology.about.com/

Mother's Enriched Environment Alters Brains of Unborn Rats, Brain/Mind Bulletin 12, no. 7, research paper by Marion Diamond 1987, accessed 3 April 2006.

www.mothering.com/articles/pregnancy_birth/birth_preparation/womb.html

Paracelsus and the Medical Revolution of the Renaissance, article by Allen G Debus, 1998, accessed 23 April 2006. www.nlm.nih.gov/exhibition/paracelsus/

Peter Singer's Animal Liberation (Part 2), by James Parker, 4 August 2000, accessed 21 April 2004. www.PeterSingerLinks.com

Pets and people: The psychology of pet ownership, article B. Gunter 1999, accessed 25 May 2006. www.anthrozoology.org/database/gunter.htm

Psychically Communicate with Your Pet – the When, Why, and How to, article by Sandra Helton, accessed 18 April 2004 www.apparitionarts.com/animalspirituality.html

Religion and Ethics: Animal Ethics, accessed 20 February 2006. www.bbc.co.uk/religion/ethics/

Report at America Zoological Association Conference, by von Muggenthaler et al. September 2001, accessed 29 January 2006. www.pbs.org/wnet/nature/tallblondes/infrosound.html

Report on research, by Dr Ellen Gehrke, dated March 2006, accessed 2 April 2006. www.heartmath.org

Saint Hildegard of Bingen, article, dated 1998–2006, accessed 17 July 2006. www.americancatholic.org/Features/Saints

Spirituality: Dreaming Stories, article by Bilyana Blomely 1996, accessed 24 April 2006. www.dreamtime.net.au/indigenous/spirituality.cfm

Taming and Training Your Reptile, by Valerie Haecky, accessed 24 April 2006. www.petstation.com/reptame.html

Telling It Like It Is, Richard Farinato 2000, accessed 22 February 2006. www.satyamag.com/jul00/farinato.html

The Cave of Lascaux, Metropolitan Museum of Art 2000–06, accessed 27 May 2006. www.metmuseum.org/toah/hd/lasc/hd_lasc.htm

The Celts, article by Megan Balanck, accessed 20 February 2006. www.ancientspiral.com/Celt.htm

The Chakra System of Animals, article by Calidad, dated December 2005, accessed 3 June 2006. www.circle-of-light.com/Calidad/chakras.html

The Felid Purr: A bio-mechanical healing mechanism, by Dr Gordon Robinson, Clinton Rubin and others 2001, accessed 29 January 2006. www.animalvoice.com

The Hippo and the Tortoise who became friends, news report, Reuters 28 June 2005, accessed 6 June 2006. www.truthorfiction.com/rumors/h/hippo-tort.htm

The Magic of Listening, article by Billie Dean, dated 2003, accessed 27 June 2004. www.billiedean.com

The Religion of the Ancient Celts, by JA MacCullock, originally published 1911, accessed 14 February 2006. www.sacred-texts.com

Tourist information, published 2006, accessed 20 February 2006. www.abbotsbromley.com/horndance

Unexplained Powers of Animals, series of articles 2005, accessed 22 February 2006. www.sheldrake.org/papers/Animals/

War Dogs, by Jeffrey P Bennett, accessed 20 February 2006. www.war-dogs.com/main.htm

When Cats Grieve, article by Sarah Hartwell 2004, accessed 14 February 2006. www.messybeast.com/catarchive.htm

Why Do Cats Purr, by Leslie A Lyons Jan 2003, accessed 22 February 2006. www.sciam.com

Wolves and Early Saints, by Ivy Stanmore 2004, accessed 20 February 2006. www.wolfsongalaska.org

OTHER REFERENCES

An Elegant Solution, TV documentary series screened SBS (Australia) 7.30pm Mondays, December 2004.

Animal Communications, a talk presented by Sandy Lee at 'Pet Health and Wellbeing Day', Sydney, 21 November 2004.

Aussie Animal Rescue, TV documentary series screened 6.30pm ABC (Australia) each weekday night, December 2004.

Dolphins, Deep Thinkers? TV documentary ABC (Australia) screened 8 May 2004.

Life in the Undergrowth, TV documentary shown ABC (Australia) March 2006.

Primal Instincts – Aggression, TV documentary screened ABC (Australia) 25 February 2004.

Richard Morecroft Goes Wild, 'Technowolf' TV documentary screened ABC (Australia) 26 June 2004.

Richard Morecroft Goes Wild, 'Parrot Passion' TV Documentary screened ABC (Australia) 16 May 2004.

Quote in Chapter Two from Paracelsus from: www.brainyquote.com/

Quote heading Chapter Six by Kahlil Gibran from: *A Guide for the Advanced Soul*, by Susan Hayward. In-Tune Books, Avalon, NSW, Australia, 1985.

Quote heading Chapter Ten by T S Elliot from: *The Naming of Cats*, from *Old Possum's Book of Practical Cats*, Faber & Faber, London, UK, 1939.

Quotations for other chapter headings from: www.quotations.home.worldnet.att.net www.quotegarden.com/animals.html www.animalliberationfront.com

INDEX

A

Aborigines
See Australian Aboriginal Dreamtime;
Australian Aboriginal people and animals
Adol Essence, 39, 74
adolescents, 73–74
ageing animals, 101–103
behaviour change, 102–103
body temperature, 102
death, 105–108
diet, 102
euthanasia, 106
health, 102
retirement, 104–105
aggressive behaviour, 74–77
ailments
See physical ailments
alpha animal, 19
Alpine Mint Bush, 65, 67, 122
American Indian spirituality, 110
Angelsword, 52, 58, 62, 64, 77, 90, 116, 122, 137, 145
animal numbers, 14
anxiety, 61, 66
See also stress
Australian Aboriginal Dreamtime, 14, 110
Australian Aboriginal people and animals, 13–14
Australian Bush Flower Essence Insight Cards, 29
awareness, 113–114

B

Bach, Dr Edward (1886-1936), 24
Banksia Robur, 104
Bauhinia, 38, 41, 43, 55, 61, 66, 77, 78, 79, 83, 94, 95, 97, 104, 106, 125, 132
behaviour
and individuality, 15–17
birds, 20–21
cats, 20
dogs, 19
horses, 20
in captivity, 118–121
natural, 68, 69
behaviour problems
adolescent period, 73–74
ageing, 102–103
aggressive, 74–77
boredom, 77
defending territory, 78–79
obsessive, 78
stubbornness, 79
behaviour problems, causes of
bonding, 69–70
breeders, 69–70
cruelty, 77–78
diet, 72
domestication, 68–69
orphaned, 69
pet shops, 70–71
poor handling/training, 72

rejection, 71–72
treatment as humans, 79–80
Billy Goat Plum, 143
birds, 20–21, 61
birth, 92–94
bitch, 89
Black-eyed Susan, 51, 61, 62, 65, 66, 94, 103, 121, 124, 125, 136, 142
Bluebell, 39, 42, 71, 72, 78, 85, 87, 97, 117, 129, 133
Boab, 40, 50, 52, 55, 61, 72, 77, 90, 142, 145
body temperature, 102, 123
bonding, 18–19, 69–70, 122–123
boredom, 77
Boronia, 39, 52, 55, 61, 62, 78, 85, 105, 121
Bottlebrush, 38, 39, 43, 52, 55, 61, 62, 66, 78, 85, 92, 93, 94, 95, 97, 98, 99, 103, 105, 121, 122, 123, 125, 126, 127, 132, 144, 145
breeding
and hormones, 89–90
effect of light, 89–90
health, 89
making the experience positive, 90
planning, 89
role of breeder, 69–70, 88–89
self esteem, 71
Bush Fuchsia, 47, 49, 52, 67, 70, 83, 90, 95, 116, 121, 122, 123, 125, 126, 127, 130, 131, 142, 147
Bush Gardenia, 38, 52, 67, 120, 125, 129
Bush Iris, 62, 78, 90, 94, 96, 117, 125, 131, 136, 142

C

Calm & Clear Essence, 32, 42, 61, 62, 72, 74, 91, 92, 103, 108, 124, 127, 130, 133
captivity
See zoo animals
case histories, 143–148
cats
and defending territory, 78–79
and humans, 20
characteristics, 20, 124
stress, 61, 66
survival strategies, 124
training, 50
wild, 20
chakra, 27–28, 136
See also energy fields
children, 43
Christmas Bell, 71
Cognis Essence, 49, 52, 61, 128, 133
communication, 44
animal to animal, 45–46
de-sexing, 99
intuition, 45–46
methods, 45, 46–47, 48
non-verbal, 47
companions, 105–108
compassion, 113
Confid Essence, 38, 39, 40, 47, 52, 54, 55, 61, 62, 72, 74, 79, 90, 98, 122, 126, 128, 133
creams and mists, 31–32

Creative Essence, 128
Crowea, 36, 41, 55, 61, 63, 67, 69, 85, 94, 97, 99, 100, 103, 117, 125, 126, 127, 137, 145, 146, 147
cruelty, 77–78

D

Dagger Hakea, 36, 41, 42, 43, 55, 57, 65, 73, 85, 87, 96, 103, 105, 131, 138, 143, 144, 145, 148
de-sexing, 99–100
death, 105–108
    See also ageing; grieving
depression, 65–66
diet, 72, 79, 102, 125
Doctrine of Signatures, 23–24
Dog Rose, 39, 43, 51, 55, 57, 61, 63, 77, 87, 92, 99, 103, 108, 121, 123, 125, 126, 128, 136, 144, 146, 147
Dog Rose of the Wild Forces, 50, 54, 56, 63, 72, 85, 125, 128, 137
dogs
    and humans, 19
    pack instinct, 19, 49
    stress, 61
    training, 49
domestication
    and behaviour, 68
    and emotions, 19
    and instinctive behaviour, 35
    and life expectancy, 19
    See also birds; cats; dogs; horses
dominant animal
    See alpha animal
dosage, 31, 33, 129
Dose Strength, 26
dowsing tool, 29
Dreamtime, 110
dying, 105–108
Dynamis Essence, 62, 66, 77, 80, 90, 94, 97, 99, 120, 121, 122, 128, 130, 133

E

Earth energy, 58
Electro Essence, 62, 126
Emergency Essence, 32, 33, 38, 39, 40, 43, 48, 52, 54, 56, 57, 58, 59, 61, 62, 64, 66, 70, 72, 74, 76, 77, 85, 90, 93, 94, 95, 97, 98, 99, 102, 103, 106, 108, 112, 121, 123-124, 125, 126, 127, 128, 129, 130, 131, 132, 133, 137-9, 142, 144, 147, 148
Emergency Essence Cream, 32, 94, 137, 139
Emergency Essence Mist, 32, 124, 127, 130, 137, 138
emotional imbalance, 28
emotions, 17–18, 19, 23–24, 28, 86–87
energy, 26–28, 57–58, 62, 127
energy centres, 27
energy fields, 26–27, 28
environment, 126–127
essences and combinations, 31, 175–185
euthanasia, 106

F

Face, Hand & Body Essence Cream, 32, 94
failure to thrive, 94–97
family treatment, 66–67
farm animals, 128

dosing large numbers of, 129
farmer and animal relationship, 129
grieving, 82–83
handling groups of, 130–131
laying eggs, 131
market, 129–130
opposition to farming, 132–134
surgery, 131
travel, 132
fear
    causes of, 54–55
    of places or situations, 57–58
    recognising, 38
    survival mechanism, 53–54
    See also frightened; timid
Five Corners, 38, 39, 42, 47, 49, 52, 55, 72, 74, 79, 87, 90, 92, 98, 105, 122, 126
Flannel Flower, 38, 39, 41, 42, 43, 48, 51, 52, 56, 57, 65, 67, 70, 72, 76, 77, 79, 80, 87, 90, 91, 92, 94, 96, 98, 99,120, 121, 122, 123, 126, 130
Freshwater Mangrove, 38, 43, 47, 57, 62, 77, 78, 79, 117, 133
frightened, 54–56, 58–59
    See also fear; timid
Fringed Violet, 36, 56, 57, 58, 62, 63, 64, 67, 73, 77, 86, 92, 94, 96, 97, 100, 117, 123, 125, 137, 144, 145, 147

G

Green Essence, 144, 148
Green Spider Orchid, 37, 39, 46, 52, 56, 67, 73, 83, 92, 117, 122, 130, 133
Grey Spider Flower, 40, 42, 43, 56, 57, 59, 62, 64, 77, 121, 125, 128, 136, 137, 146, 147
grieving, 81
    cheering up a household, 86
    death of an owner, 82, 84–85
    death of family member, 82
    farm animals, 82–83
    human, 107–108
    separation anxiety, 85–86
    supporting the animal, 83–84
    variations due to personality and situation, 83
    wild animals, 82
Gymea Lily, 50, 71, 76, 123, 133, 145

H

healing powers of plants
    See history of flower essences
health
    and age, 102
    and breeding, 89
    and children, 43
    and pregnancy, 91
    and stress, 60–61
    benefits of animals, 18–19
    failure to thrive, 94–97
    of family members, 66–67
health checks, 139
Hibbertia, 83, 92
Hildegard von Bingen, Abbess (12th century), 23–24
history of animal/human interaction, 13–14
history of animals and emotions, 17–18
history of flower essences, 23–25

hormones, 28, 60, 66, 89–90
horse whispering, 51
horses
    and grief, 84
    and humans, 20
    and separation anxiety, 85–86
    and stress, 61
    characteristics, 20
    training, 50–51
humans
    and animal interaction, 13–14, 19
    and birds, 21
    and cats, 20
    and dogs, 19
    and grief, 107–108
    and horses, 20
    and zoo animals, 122–123
connection with animals, 114–115
health benefits of animals, 18–19
living with animals, 13–14
treatment of animals, 79–80

I
Illawarra Flame Tree, 40, 41, 48, 56, 62, 65, 71, 77,
    94, 96, 97, 98, 99, 105, 125, 128, 133, 136, 142
imprinting, 37
individuality in animals, 15–17
ingredients, 31
insight cards
    See Australian Bush Flower Essence Insight Cards
instinct, 14–16, 19, 35, 49
intelligence, 16, 44–45
intuition, 45–46, 113–114
Isopogon, 49, 76, 79, 95, 103

J
Jacaranda, 37, 49, 100, 147

K
Kangaroo Paw, 52, 70, 73, 77, 79, 121
Kapok Bush, 47, 56, 65, 77, 97, 105, 125, 145

L
labour, 92–93
life expectancy, 19
light and breeding, 89–90
Little Flannel Flower, 39, 40, 56, 65, 77, 78, 85, 100,
    103, 105, 120
living in present time, 17
loss
    See grieving
love, 86–87, 117, 133–134

M
Macrocarpa, 57, 61, 62, 66, 94, 99, 103, 122, 123, 124,
    125, 126, 130, 131, 136, 142, 144, 146, 147
market, 129–130
mating
    See breeding
Meditation Essence, 37, 62, 92, 116, 117
Mint Bush, 65, 117
mists and creams, 31–32
Monga Waratah, 78, 87, 99, 123, 126

Mother Tincture, 26
Mountain Devil, 40, 42, 57, 59, 65, 71, 73, 74, 76, 87,
    94, 95, 98, 103, 105, 117, 120, 131, 145
Mulla Mulla, 57, 62–63, 96, 102, 103, 123, 126, 131,
    142, 145, 148
muscle testing, 30

N
negative energy, 57–58, 62
new animal, 34–35
nurturing, 96–98

O
obsessive behaviour, 78, 104
Old Man Banksia, 67, 123, 147
orphans, 69, 96

P
pain, 17
panic, 57
Paracelsus (16th century), 24
Paw Paw, 37, 49, 58, 86, 97, 125, 131, 143, 147
Peach-flowered Tea-tree, 39, 77, 121, 125, 133, 144
pendulum, 29
people
    See humans
performance animals, 104–105, 127–128
pet shops, 70–71
pets
    adopting, 39–41
    arrival, 37–39
    caring for, 36
    children and, 43
    costs of, 35–36
    instinct of, 35
    multiple pet households, 41–43
    selection of, 35–37
physical ailments
    and emotions, 136
    history taking, 135
    protection from infectious disease, 140
    vaccination choices, 140–142
    when to visit a vet, 142–143
Pink Flannel Flower, 43, 63, 65, 66, 77, 87, 90, 91, 105,
    108, 117, 120, 125, 128, 130, 133, 136, 142
Pink Mulla Mulla, 40, 42, 56, 57, 63, 73, 77, 78, 83, 90, 95
post traumatic stress, 62–64
pregnancy, 91–92
present time living, 17
Purifying Essence, 63, 90, 106, 123, 126, 139, 142, 147

R
race animals, 104–105, 127–128
Red Grevillea, 144
Red Helmet Orchid, 38, 40, 49, 52, 59, 73, 74, 86, 99,
    122, 129
Red Lily, 63
Red Suva Frangipani, 39, 78, 85, 98, 100, 106, 108, 146
rejection, 71–72
relationship
    basis for a good, 48
    between animals and humans, 18–21
    treating animals as humans, 79–80

with an orphaned animal, 69–70
  with captive animals, 122–123
Relationship Essence, 40, 42, 52, 56, 67, 90, 92, 120,
  122, 125, 129
releasing wild animals, 125–126
repertory of symptoms, 149–174
retirement, 104–105
Rough Bluebell, 50, 70, 73, 76, 79, 87, 117

S
sacred contracts, 115–116, 128
selection of an essence, 29–31
self esteem, 71
sensing danger, 115
Sensuality Essence Mist, 32, 91
separation anxiety, 85–86
She Oak Essence, 32, 90-91, 92, 99, 103, 121, 131, 147
shock, 93–94, 123–124
show animals, 127–128
Shuker, Dr Karl, 26, 27
shy
    See timid
Silver Princess, 51, 105
Slender Rice Flower, 42, 43, 63, 67, 69, 79, 99, 120,
  125, 130, 131, 138, 145
socialisation, 37, 54
Solaris Essence, 126
souls, 111
Southern Cross, 56, 117, 147
Space Clearing Essence Mist, 32, 58, 73, 91, 117, 120,
  127, 128, 132
Spinifex, 131, 143, 144, 145, 146, 147, 148
spiritual agreements, 115–116, 128
spirituality, 109–112, 113, 115–117
Stock Strength, 26
storage, 33
stress
    and birds, 61
    and dogs, 61
    and health, 60–61
    and horses, 61
    cats, 61, 66
    circumstances, 61
    hormones, 60, 66
    post traumatic stress, 62–64 (See also trauma)
    support, 65
    symptoms of, 61
stubbornness, 79
Sturt Desert Pea, 40, 41, 63, 65, 73, 85, 106, 108, 123, 145
Sturt Desert Rose, 39, 42, 67, 79, 80, 85, 96, 120, 123,
  126, 130, 133
Sundew, 37, 49, 63, 94, 95, 97, 137
sunlight and breeding, 89–90
Sunshine Wattle, 40, 57, 65, 78, 143, 147
surgery, 131, 137
survival strategies, 124–125
Sydney Rose, 78, 86, 87, 92, 117, 130, 133
symbolism, 111
symptoms and essences, 150–177

T
Tall Mulla Mulla, 56, 57, 71, 77, 123, 146
Tall Yellow Top, 40, 41, 42, 56, 57, 59, 65, 66, 77, 85,
  97, 99, 105, 125, 143, 146

territory markings, 78–79
therapeutic qualities of plants, 26
timid, 54, 55, 56–57
    See also fear; frightened
toxic environments, 126–127
training, 48
    cats, 50
    dogs, 49
    horses, 50–51
    human factor, 48
Transition Essence, 106–107, 108, 130
trauma, 63–65
    See also post traumatic stress
travel, 132
Travel Essence, 132
Travel Essence Cream, 32, 128, 132
Travel Essence Mist, 32, 128, 132
treatment, 31, 33
treatment length, 31
trust, 70–71

U
unconditional love, 86–87

V
vaccination, 89, 140–142
vet, 142–143
vibrational medicine, 17, 21, 23–25

W
Waratah, 56, 65, 78, 85, 97, 99, 103, 125, 137, 147
weaning, 98–99
Wedding Bush, 39, 51, 62
White, Ian, 25
wild animals, 34, 123–126
    and shock, 123–124, 125
    cats, 20
    diet, 125
    grieving, 82
    horses, 20
    instinct, 15–16
    releasing, 125–126
    survival strategies, 124–125
Wild Potato Bush, 66, 92, 100, 120, 123, 130, 132, 145,
  146, 147
Wisteria, 76, 91, 121
Woman Essence Mist & Cream, 32
working animals, 104–105

Y
Yellow Cowslip Orchid, 67
young, 88–89, 96–98, 122

Z
zoo animals
    behaviour, 118–121
    caring for, 122–123
    design of enclosure, 119
    instinct, 14–15
    relationship with carers, 122–123
    sedation, 123
    sex drive, 121